COLLECTED WHEEL PUBLICATIONS

VOLUME 22

NUMBERS 329 – 344

BPE

BPS Pariyatti Editions

BPS Pariyatti Editions
An imprint of Pariyatti Publishing
www.pariyatti.org

Copies of this book for sale in the Americas only. Although this is an American edition, we have left any British spelling of words unchanged.

First BPS Pariyatti Edition, 2025
ISBN: 978-1-68172-208-5 (Print)
ISBN: 978-1-68172-209-2 (PDF)
ISBN: 978-1-68172-210-8 (ePub)
ISBN: 978-1-68172-211-5 (Mobi)
LCCN: 2018940050

Contents

WH 329 & 330 The Therapeutic Action of Vipassana
Dr. Paul R. Fleischman 1

WH 331 to 333 The Buddhist Philosophy of Relations
Ledi Sayādaw Mahāthera 39

WH 334 Anāthapiṇḍika
Hellmuth Hecker 107

WH 335 & 336 Buddhist Stories (From the Dhammapada Commentary, Part III)
Eugene Watson Burlingame/Bhikkhu Khantipālo 139

WH 337 & 338 One Foot in the World
Lily de Silva 183

WH 339 to 341 The Tragic, the Comic and the Personal
Sāmaṇera Bodhesako 229

WH 342 to 344 Gemstones of the Good Dhamma
Ven. S. Dhammika 297

Key to Abbreviations

A	Aṅguttara Nikāya	Paṭis	Paṭisambhidāmagga
Ap	Apadāna	Peṭ	Peṭakopadesa
Bv	Buddhavaṃsa	S	Saṃyutta Nikāya
Cp	Cariyāpiṭaka	Sn	Suttanipāta
D	Dīgha Nikāya	Th	Theragāthā
Dhp	Dhammapada	Thī	Therigāthā
Dhs	Dhammasaṅgaṇī	Ud	Udāna
It	Itivuttaka	Vibh	Vibhaṅga
Ja	Jātaka verses and commentary	Vin	Vinayapiṭaka
Khp	Khuddakapāṭha	Vism	Visuddhimagga
M	Majjhima Nikāya	Vism-mhṭ	Visuddhimagga Sub-commentary
Mil	Milindapañha	Vv	Vimānavatthu
Nett	Nettipakaraṇa	Nidd	Niddesa

The above is the abbreviation scheme of the Pali Text Society (PTS) as given in the *A Dictionary of Pāli* by Margaret Cone.

The commentaries, *aṭṭhakathā*, are abbreviated by using a hyphen and an "a" ("-a") following the abbreviation of the text, e.g., *Dīgha Nikāya Aṭṭhakathā* = D-a. Likewise the sub-commentaries are abbreviated by a "ṭ" ("-ṭ") following the abbreviation of the text.

The sutta reference abbreviation system for the four Nikāyas, as is used in Bhikkhu Bodhi's translations is:

AN	Aṅguttara Nikāya	DN	Dīgha Nikāya
MN	Majjhima Nikāya	Sn	Saṃyutta Nikāya
J	Jātaka story	Mv	Mahāvagga (Vinaya Piṭaka)
Cv	Cullavagga (Vinaya Piṭaka)	SVibh	Suttavibhaṅga (Vinaya Piṭaka)

The Therapeutic Action of Vipassana

Why I Sit

by

Dr. Paul R. Fleischman

WHEEL PUBLICATION NO. 329/330

Preface

In the summer of 1982, at the end of a meditation course, and during the time when a number of old students were discussing the creation of a meditation center in North America to facilitate the teachings of this pure tradition, Goenkaji suggested to me that I write an article about meditation. "Since you are a psychiatrist, people will believe you." The result was "The Therapeutic Action of Vipassana." The thrust of this article is to explain how a scientifically trained physician could understand, validate, and practise Vipassana meditation, as taught by S. N. Goenka, and to show what is universally practical, efficacious, and therapeutic about it, while at the same time clarifying the divergency between psychotherapy and the Dhamma: the art of living taught by the Buddha.

That summer, the Vipassana Meditation Center was born, in Shelburne Falls, Massachusetts.

I found, however, only half my work was done. Friends, colleagues, fellow meditation students, sometimes ask my opinion: "What *is* meditation ... does it *really* work ... *how* does it work ... how does it compare to psychiatry?" Now I could just hand over a copy of "The Therapeutic Action... !" But people also ask a more difficult question: "Why?" To answer this question, I had to seek inward. Inside, revealed to me through the practice itself, was a mixture of holy and unholy motives—some true to the mark and others wide of the entire target. I wrote "Why I Sit" to explain to people of my time and place—psychiatrists, postdoctoral fellows in my Psychiatry and Religion seminar, fellow parents, carpenters at work on my beams—the real human heart of the matter, in case the question was asked from the heart. An unplayed guitar, in a room where another is being played, will vibrate to it.

Koshi Ichida, a Soto Zen priest and a dear friend, unveiled many aspects of Buddhism to me in hundreds of hours of conversation. Jim Phillips, life-long colleague with wide-angle vision and sharp focus, compelled critical re-writing—as did my wife, Susan, who also lives the whole thing with me.

Paul R. Fleischman

The Therapeutic Action of Vipassana

Vipassana meditation, as taught by S. N. Goenka of Igatpuri, India, and of Shelburne Falls, Massachusetts, is alleged to be the meditation practice expounded by the historical Buddha as the direct way to complete liberation from human suffering. Long before that goal is reached, however, the committed ordinary student may gain profound therapeutic benefits from Vipassana. Having practised this technique religiously for many years, and being a practising psychiatrist as well, I thought I would describe these therapeutic actions in contemporary psychological language, for the benefit of new and prospective students. All these benefits are potential in the technique; which ones, and how much, accrue to any individual's practice, varies with who one is, where one is coming from, and one's adherence to the technique day after day for a lifetime. I will not attempt to describe the actual practice itself, since that requires the lived experience of a ten-day training course.

I

According to traditional descriptions of the mind as seen through the media of Vipassana, a great part of human mental activity consists of wishes for the future and fears about the future, and desires from the past and fears from the past. The freer the mind is from memories and yearnings, and from desires and hatreds, the more it rests in the present, and the more mental contents come to reflect clear, immediate reality as it is. The technique of meditation allows the controlled release of mental contents, while simultaneously anchoring the student in concrete contemporary reality. This reality-based, equanimous position enables craving and aversion, past and future, to rise to the surface of the mind and to pass away without provoking a reaction. In this way the mind is deconditioned, and one's life becomes characterized by increased awareness, reality-orientation, non-delusion, self-control, and peace.

Self-Knowledge

This lucid and logical psychology hardly expresses the animated human drama that in fact unfolds whenever anyone undertakes training in Vipassana. No matter who we are, our inner lives are less like a box with separate compartments than like a flood-tide on a river. When we sit down to be still, a seemingly endless stream of memories, wishes, thoughts, conversations, scenes, desires, dreads, lusts, and emotionally driven pictures of every kind wells up in us, thousands upon thousands. The clearest, most immediate and inescapable effect of meditation is to increase one's self-knowledge. This may be curious, exciting, and interesting but it also could be devastating. Taking this into account, therefore, the technique enables one's vision of one's true inner life to expand in the structured, protected, controlled, holding and nurturant environment essential to a safe launching on high seas.

The qualities of the appropriate environment have been studied, codified, and transmitted for millennia from teacher to teacher. Like the map to a traveller, they constitute the framework of the correctly taught course and define the qualities of the teacher. A precise adherence to the details of the technique, and the embracing, generous human love of the teacher, enable any ordinary person to open the doors of his or her own heart and mind. Nothing in the human condition will remain unknown or strange to one who has sat, hour after hour, thus safely stationed and continuously aware.

Basic Trust

As a corollary to the expansion of knowledge of one's inner life, then, there is the activation of that basic trust, which contemporary psychology posits as deriving from the earliest trust a child extends to the parent who nurtures, warms, and feeds it and which forms the substrate for later intimate human relationships. In the context of Vipassana, this trust operates as the informed adult faith that permits full engagement with the technique without wishful thinking about what magical results it may bring. Such faith must be rooted in thoughtful understanding, reasonable confidence, and the commitment to proceed as directed. Willfulness has to be surrendered, for the platform of knowing is participation.

Integration of the Past

The millions of vignettes, scenes, and anecdotes that flood up from one's personal past, arise to pass away; paradoxically, before they do, one sees who one has been, one knows where one has come from. Even while walking towards the common centre, everyone starts from a particular position on the periphery. That position is beyond one's control, because everyone has been conditioned by his past experiences, by the thousands, and many of these are not what we would have wished for ourselves. So the present can be grasped, but the past is both elusive yet inescapable. Sitting with it hour after hour necessitates that one come to terms with it. There is no running away, no distraction. Coming to terms with the past, acceptance of what has been, the personal integration of all of oneself without rejection or denial—these are also therapeutic effects of meditation.

Future and Will

Similarly, in spite of any effort to the contrary, the meditation student will find himself thinking, preparing, planning and anticipating. Even as this often fanciful activity declines, it enables the meditator to see his real volition emerge. When, as usually happens in life, volition is rapidly followed by action, we find the action more memorable and gripping. Thus retrospectively, we construe life as a series of actions causally linked. We explain ourselves to ourselves based upon what has happened to us and what we did, thus covertly coming to believe ourselves to be dependent products of events, reactors rather than agents.

But the command to ourselves to remain seated, alert, aware, and unmoving, breaks the automaticity of that sequence. The choices and decisions—the motive will in our lives—are pulled out from the shadows to stand on an unobstructed stage. What occurred in fleet milliseconds, to be rapidly followed by loud sequences of actions, now occurs ... and that is all. With the conviction of experience we see how we move, shape, push, and bend with our hearts and minds moment after moment to build the next platform for action. Our future may take us less by surprise, and may ironically require less planning, when we increase our awareness of how our wills mould it. Another therapeutic effect of meditation is to decrease our need to plan, control, and organize the future, because it activates our determination right now to observe, identify, and consciously participate in the thousands of decisions that determine us each day.

Responsibility

Helplessness is one of the most threatening feelings. To be out of control, to be a victim of fate, is universally dreaded. The rites and rituals of organized religion—one of the most widespread phenomena of human culture—are intended to restore a sense of potency, control, and order over events. The wisdom teachings of diverse cultures, on the other hand, eschew reliance on external powers that must be cajoled, coerced, or implored, and teach instead ownership of one's own feelings and actions.

For example, Freud stressed that mental life was not capricious and incomprehensible, but lawful and orderly. Similarly, the Book of Job teaches that apparently arbitrary events can be seen to be caused and meaningful if one maintains the correct attitude; and Jesus's ethics focused on the role of intention and wish in the ultimate destiny of the soul. Existentialism stresses that the individual alone is the maker of his own essence. Viktor Frankl, the existentialist philosopher and psychiatrist, writing from personal experience, claims that even in Auschwitz the individual in essence determined his own fate and had no one else to beseech or blame.

For the meditation student, neither faith nor philosophy, but systematic observation of mind clarifies that every mental event is meaningful, caused, one's own responsibility. Even in fixed conditions, we determine our own attitudes and our responses to those conditions. One mind moment conditions the next: the more experientially convinced of this we become, the more fully we shoulder responsibility for our own lives. A greater sense of control and responsibility directly follows activation of determination through clarification of will.

Right Concentration and Ethics

But merely "observing the mind" or "watching memories and expectations" is impossible. We cannot simply objectify the very mind that seeks to objectify. There is a technique of meditation that enables us to see the stream of mind-moments rather than be swept along by it. One aspect of the technique is concentration, right concentration. Right concentration is achieved, not by willfully blotting out, repressing, or trampling distraction, but by eliminating distraction's root. So concentration, the treasure of human integrative capacities, which gives coherence and direction to life, cannot be built with a sledgehammer, but requires a feather. When we cease to be distracted in our heart, so too our mind.

Right concentration depends upon ethical living. Ethics creates inner harmony, the unity of the multiple parts of our being, so that the complexity of a human being attains a point of focus only when the actions of daily life are lined up in the same direction. For right concentration, then, a soft, subtle stimulus is necessary, because the concentration that results from loud demands merely obscures the inner patchwork. Attempting to concentrate upon the difficult-to-concentrate-on produces unavoidable awareness of exactly what is distracting one. So the meditation leads not only to self-awareness, committed participation, integration with and acceptance of one's past, clarity about one's causal role in the future, and a sense of responsibility for one's life, but also to direct experiential knowledge of the basis of ethics. To have peace, we must be at peace.

Distractions from concentration, when neither followed nor suppressed, but *seen,* are generally desire and fear concerning the past or the future. To concentrate on the subtle, we must dwell in the present and relinquish the multitude of self-enhancing or self-protecting manoeuvres that constitute the incessant psychological pressure to fantasy. Then the natural qualities of a mind facing reality become evident.

Self-Control

Concentration—built on harmony, built on ethics, built on an integration with rather than a struggle against reality—occurs not only at the moment-to-moment level but also at the level of life-structure. Order, self-control, and discipline are part of the life of meditation. There is no concentration without them, and they in turn express a focused life. The technique of meditation interlocks with the technique of living; some regulation of sleep, food, sex and physical motion expresses and enhances awareness and equanimity. But a disciplined life is not a cold or rigid one. As the waves of sentiment wash up on the shore and then—unresponded to—wash away again, we find not flatness of feeling, but depth of emotion, the ocean that underlies the waves.

The frequent misconception that peacefulness is dullness, that detachment is heartlessness, that calm is lethargy, comes from a mind that equates agitation, excitement, and passion with pleasure. But beyond pleasure and displeasure, personal preference, titillation and taste, are the deep pools of live participation and energy. Rather than static compartmentalization, the disciplines of meditation allow full emotional access, spontaneous and generous flows of compassionate, empathetic feeling.

Conflict Resolution

From the ancient religious masters like the Buddha, Jesus, St. Paul, Krishna, and Rumi to modern theologians like Tillich, Buber, and Eliade, human wholeness has been considered the goal and meaning of religion. Freud claimed that conflict or disunity was the cause of neurosis, and post-Freudian psychology has intensely studied integrative aspects of the personality, such as identity. Meditation is a direct method of decreasing psychological conflict through its prescriptive ethical codes, its integration of past and future, its elucidation of self-responsibility, concentration, and will. Conflict resolution could be said to be the main thrust of the practice.

Yet life is dynamic. There is no final static formula that can encase the fluid ocean of reality that we experience as commitments, goals, meanings, and concerns. So meditation often heightens awareness of existential conflicts as it decreases the level of division, fragmentation, or disunity. There is no automatic drive pedal in Vipassana, no end to renewed right effort and real challenge.

History and Community

Vipassana meditation comes from people of the past, and is part of contemporary lives. It passes from person to person—not from books or lectures or mass media. The depth of feeling created by the practice is not an abstraction, a religious ideal. Friendship, companionship, actual human warmth are part of the technique. This is not chattering sociability, but the mutual respect and support of those who see the pre-dawn stars side-by-side.

Just as the practice is shared now, it has been shared across time. A sense of heritage, lineage, history is an inevitable experience of the Vipassana student. Awareness of one's personal history increases one's sense of personal integrity, and experience of the meaning of human history is a critical element of all deep psychological healing. Like our language, our meditation places us in a transtemporal human community. Membership in generative continuity is a sweet antidote to self-aggrandizement. The finest plant has to be modest in the presence of the soil. Philosophical meaning is an idle abstraction to those whose hands actually reach across generations.

Time and Change

Location within the transmission of generations is only one way that Vipassana opens the student's eyes to the reality of time and change. Improving the student's capacity to look directly at the reality of impermanence, flux, emptiness, and death is at the core of the practice. The technique involves seeing reality fully, but only after appropriate preparation. Confrontation with pain and dissolution, however, is a universal human experience; Vipassana enables that meeting to occur with equanimity. So the technique contains an irony: the starker our confrontation with reality, the deeper our equanimity; the deeper our equanimity, the more superficial desires and fears peel off like onion skins and the closer we come to the core anxieties of human existence.

Physical immobility is a core human fear (*everyone* has had the dream of paralysis, being unable to run, unable to speak); Vipassana prepares us to face it. Physical pain is a core human fear (some psychiatrists consider it the bedrock of all fear); Vipassana leads us into it, and out of it. Loneliness is a core human fear; Vipassana leads us to trust, community, faith, but also to profound solitude in silence, and we can learn to turn that ice into a cool drink for a hot mind. Ancient and modern theories of the human heart frequently point to death as the node, the point where character forms, where knowledge is tested, and where the deepest anxieties take their root. Socrates, of course, considered philosophy the art of dying; a large body of contemporary psychiatric theory echoes that, as does the technique of Vipassana meditation.

One reason the mind is always in flight, daydreaming, thinking, planning, remembering, is that concentration on immediate physical reality will inevitably clarify the feared truth: the body is decaying right now, every moment, irreversibly. One of the paradoxes of the Vipassana technique is that the deep physical concentration and relaxation, the exquisite luminescent peace, will lead to the core of dread ... which in turn can be experienced as a simple sweet truth like night followed by dawn, hunger followed by food, tiredness followed by sleep, rest followed by morning stars. A mind that returns to the body knows both the limitations of that body, and the vibrating universal energy flowing from form to form.

Bodily Integration

Vipassana is not a mental activity. It happens in a body, and is more analogous to learning to ride a bicycle than to learning to read. Awareness of all of our body all of the time is one of the keys to the practice. Thoughts and emotions inevitably have counterparts in bodily events. So systematic awareness of ourselves requires awareness of how we sit, eat, sleep, think, and feel directly through the body itself. Emotions that were formerly placeless ghosts in the halls of ourselves can be experienced as producing specifically located sensations in the skin, heart, eyes, scalp. Desires and fears that drove us half-consciously to a ceaseless flurry of comfort-seeking can be found to affect the bodily process at deep and subtle levels. Even the past and future, to which we previously did obeisance as awesome external powers, will be found in us, in our vibrating physical selves, as excitation, hunger, and lethargy.

Since all bodies decay, dissolve, and pass away, physical pain and illness are inevitable universal human experiences; and Vipassana can quickly disperse a student's covert belief in his own invulnerability. But another fraction of suffering stems from ignorance: reactions blindly stored in muscle spasms, engorged overconsumptions, chronic constrictions of self-chastisement, recoiling and clamping down, in blood vessels or intestines. Deepened bodily awareness is the best method of observing the living organic root of thought and emotion, and may also reorder bodily habits, occasionally effecting cures of psychosomatic headaches, gastrointestinal spasms, and the like.

Relationship

The experience of ceaseless, continuous change in every molecule of the body in every moment casts life in a different perspective. Meanings and purposes organized around oneself alone are clearly pointless. In every millisecond life rises out of the whole and returns to it again, rearising fresh, new, different. We exist in the whole, like flecks of spray thrown up momentarily out of the ocean. What is the point of those self-aggrandizing efforts we were so recently, so strenuously pursuing?

Contemporary psychiatry has expressed a renewed interest in the way a person organizes a sense of self in relation to other selves; in Vipassana we experience directly the arsenal of attitudes, postures, lectures, and reactions we all elaborate to create and sustain the image of our own impregnable, eternal, inviolate existence—and how doomed a defense that is. The psychology of the self is a study of building castles of granite on quicksand. That static self that we yearn for, demand, and forever insist upon is a plastic sticker pasted over flow, process, interaction, relation. Without preaching or ideation, the direct experience available through meditation washes away our entitlement, grandiosity, self-preoccupation, and incorporative greed. This cleansing is particularly refreshing to people from modern Western cultures, which have been called cultures of self-absorption.

Truth

Truth is not a content, but a process. It means an attitude of expectation and freshness, a willingness to mentally restructure again and again. Vipassana meditation could be described as the technique of living by the truth. The truth in this sense is not a school, an idea, a doctrine. It doesn't imply an "us" and a "them." It doesn't imply a possession. It doesn't mean that people living in other ways don't have the truth. The practice simply points to one technique whereby a person's life can stake itself out to the process of exploration every day, day after day, up to death itself, which hopefully can be greeted with the same query: objectively, what is the nature of the reality of my mind and body at this moment? Science, philosophy, or any open-minded living share in this truth. Meditation is one well-tried and proven technique, and it contains the paradox of an objective approach to the subjective, an inquiry into the nature of ourselves. Truth is not just the "highfalutin," and the living attempt to express oneself truthfully in fleeting conventional moments is one of the finest tools to pry loose the door of the over-defended self.

Human Love

What *does* the experience of meditation reveal in the human heart? Underneath the self-protective shields of anger, aggression, possession, and control lies the well of clear, simple, loving, energetic, vital life. Generosity, compassion, and human love are not virtues, but attributes. Everybody yearns to feel love, engagement, and the light of truth. But fear and caution encourage us to continually take detours. We imagine that one more wall, one more lock will keep us safe. Practising Vipassana means practising the direct action of human love. It crystallizes the yearning in us, the call, so that we feel ourselves in possession of the jewel for which we'd been searching.

II

There are a few questions I am frequently asked when people find out that a psychiatrist has chosen to root his life in meditation.

Do I teach patients to meditate? Definitely not. As a secular professional, I don't impose practices or world views (beyond the broadly sanctioned general ethics of the dominant culture) on patients who come to me. No one is value-free, but a psychiatrist must be ready to listen to and nurture many ways of being a human being. Central to the profession is the capacity to follow another person's need and lead. People who are called to the practice of meditation will come to it, so I neither hide it nor flaunt it. A number of patients who have seen me have come to know about my way of life; most haven't, knowing that as a professional I offer not a person to emulate or admire, but a treatment that enables them to be more fully and deeply themselves.

In my own mind I imagine that the truth has many facets but one essence. I respect the facets. In any case, a psychiatrist frequently is the interface for the exercise of a bitter cynicism, not to mention the panorama of perversions, rages, paralyzing confusions, and so many other phenomena of hurt lives. People start in different places and require various modes of help—in this light psychiatry, too, is also very limited.

Then do I use meditation at all in my work? Yes—it *is* my work, heart and core. For in all those variations of human pain, I see myself as I have seen myself as I sit. There is little in the phenomenology of my patients' lives that is not in mine also. Meditation has greatly enriched my empathy, and my vision of what it is to be a human being: the fear and anxiety and dependency and exhaustion and desperation and defeat and revival and acceptance and vision and work and delight and struggle and doggedness and creativity and appreciation and gratitude. By having experienced my own deeper, truer nature I know more; by experiencing those vibrations in every hour of my daily work with people, I have been able to open more fully, to receive and hold, to drop defenses of my own, to really listen, to really understand.

Interestingly, Freud described a similar process; he said that the psychoanalyst has to turn off his conscious thinking, but to open his own being like a receiver to the transmitting antennae of the patient. I can hold more, and it is clear to me that I've been given more to hold. But practising psychiatry is more than being nice, and I've also learned from meditation how long, difficult, demanding, and very painful it is to face reality, to break old molds.

Is meditation really effective? I think so, but only with devoted practice. While I have seen many lives, my own included, send down taproots into the simple, common, human decency that transcends theology, philosophy, and psychology, I have also known many people who have meditated for periods of time and then just tumbled on. Meditation cannot be practised casually alone in the bedroom; there must be real training. But there is also an essential requirement for disciplined regularity in daily life. According to the Buddha, the ultimate source of human suffering is ignorance, which includes within itself a resistance to knowing the truth that can set us free. The moment we turn away is when the bird glides into its nest. When we skip, miss, forget, can't make it—that's when the unconscious controls us. Systematic choiceless routine is essential for opening the mind to observation, for in one small lapse the large source of that lapse is obscured. If you draw a water bucket steadily up from a well for five minutes, and then let go for one split second ... the result is clear.

Although the practice of Vipassana is not a religion in the sense of buying into or swallowing dogma, ritual, or blind faith, I think it is critical to practise "religiously": that is, with devoted centrality of commitment. Meditation as a desultory practice, an amusement, an occasional hobby in a cluttered life, has little effect, and may stir up more confusion than it relieves. Unfortunately I have seen intermittent, self-directed meditation used to hide from reality, to devalue painful dilemmas, and, in one instance, to aggrandize the self to the point of madness and suicide.

Vipassana references itself to universal human wisdom rather than to particular culture forms. It is nonsectarian in thought. Its framework is mirrored whenever people ponder the art of living. For example, Thoreau wrote, in Massachusetts, in the nineteenth century: "Renew thyself completely each day; do it again, and again, forever again ... To affect the quality of the day, that is the highest art ... no method or discipline can supersede the necessity of being forever on the alert ..."

The potential therapeutic actions of Vipassana include increased self-knowledge, deepened human trust and participation, integration with and acceptance of one's past, deepened activation of one's will, increased sense of responsibility for one's own fate; greater concentration, deepened ethical commitments, firm yet flexible life structures and disciplines, fluid access to deeper streams of feeling and imagery, expanded historical and contemporary community; prepared confrontation with core realities such as time, change, death, loss, pain, leading to an eventual diminution of dread, anxiety, and delusion; fuller body-mind integration, decreased narcissism, and a fuller panorama of character strengths such as generosity, compassion, and human love. Each student starts at a different place, and progresses individually; there is no magic and no guarantees.

III

To consider meditation from the standpoint of its therapeutic actions is only one way of describing this technique of living. Seen from another direction, meditation transcends the merely therapeutic, the way that the water of the planet exceeds its mere thirst-quenching property, the way the sun exceeds its life and warmth-giving qualities, the way a timeless poem exceeds the personal pleasure that we may individually extract from it. We are part of a reality that is more than a cure for our personalities. The point is not towards ourselves, but towards everything else.

The entire description of Vipassana meditation via its therapeutic actions clarifies some points, but obscures a very central one. While meditation is therapeutic—enhancing many other human qualities—it has intrinsic value as an activity in itself. Art may help us to appreciate life; it also expresses human nature's artful heart, eye and hand. Meditation is most therapeutic when it is not looked upon for therapeutic effect, but is put into practice as an end in itself, an expression of an aspect of human nature. That aspect is not a single attribute, like one slice of a pie, but a sustaining, synthesizing, creative force in all other aspects, like the heat that baked the pie. It is more like the bony skeleton than like one limb. So meditation expresses something about the integrated process of a person, rather than being merely a means to ends in other spheres of life.

Meditation expresses that aspect of us which can receive: the non-selective embracing receptor. We can know ourselves as member cells of an integrated whole. Occasionally a person will feel this way during special hours of special days: watching a sunset from the rimrocks of a sandstone canyon in a wilderness of pinyon pine and ancient ruins. These moments are inspirational, serendipitous interludes. Meditation entails the systematic cultivation of this formative human potential as a life-long centering enterprise. While some activation of this receptive, interpenetrative, non-judgemental mode is the foundation of any art or science, any significant engagement of the world, it has been most exquisitely expressed by certain writers, like Tagore, Whitman, Thoreau, the Socratic dialogues, Chinese and Japanese Zen poets, and the nameless authors of many classical Pali and Sanskrit texts from ancient India.

This equanimous, aware, unfiltered, receptivity is the *sine qua non* of religious experience (as opposed to mere religious membership or affiliation). Opening it up makes us feel whole and alive just as eating does. There is no need to rationalize supper as being therapeutic; it is an essential expression of life itself. Similarly, to open up and know with our being is not health-giving, but life-giving. I have come to believe that meditation activates the process underlying all religious life when looked at for what lies inside the specific cultural or religious formulas, that it contains the essential ingredient of all the pleomorphic panorama of religion—based on studying the great students of the psychology of religion: William James, Carl Jung, Paul Tillich, Erik Erikson, Jerome Frank, Mircea Eliade, et al.

But when we open to receive the whole, a great darkness floods in too. Our previously selective, circumscribed flashlight cannot illumine it alone. We can no longer exclude the devouring mouths of time, the Hitlerian epochs cauterizing living limbs of whole centuries, civilizations, peoples; our fears for ourselves and all we love seem like ephemeral flecks of spray foaming up and vanishing endlessly on a boundless endless ocean. Human culture itself, with its religious and artistic and scientific geniuses, has provided candles, torches, even suns for us, that reveal miraculously the dry land between the seas. Vipassana is one of these. It is a technique that enables us to hear the wisdom of life itself, contained in our organism just like the wisdom of hunger, revealing the deepening shaft of vision, determination, more indomitable skill and gentleness in service of the life in which we live. Inside us and around us is the maker for whom we care. Vipassana meditation is one way to activate an enduring, sustaining love in the web of all contacts.

Students who undertake training in this discipline will find themselves walking into a large, dark hall at 4:00 AM. Around them will be one hundred silent, seated, erect friends along the way, men and women, professors and unemployed travellers, lawyers and mothers, who have been there, morning after morning, day after day, for ten days. Darkness will fade, there will be fewer stars, the crescent moon will glow alone, birds will unroll a curtain of life before the new day, and then depart. The hall will be light, yet still, motionless, silent; a chant will begin, whose twenty-five hundred year-old words simply point us towards the best in us; and even slightly bleary and dry, the students may motionlessly reach up and pluck an invisible jewel of immeasurable worth.

Why I Sit

This morning the first thing I did was to sit for an hour. I have done that religiously for nine years, and have spent many evenings, days and weeks doing the same. The English word "meditate" until recently had a vague meaning, referring to any one of a set of activities like extended deep thought, or prayer, or religious contemplation. Recently, "meditation" gained a pseudo-specificity: "T.M.," deep relaxation, or alpha-wave conditioning, with connotations of Hinduized cult phenomena like mantras, gurus, and altered states of consciousness. To "sit" is a basic word, with connotations ranging from chicken coops to boredom and sagacity, so it forms a neutral starting point for an explanation of why I have spent thousands upon thousands of hours "sitting," and why I have made this activity the center of my life.

I

I would like to know myself. It is remarkable that while ordinarily we spend most of our lives studying, contemplating, observing, and manipulating the world around us, the structured gaze of the thoughtful mind is so rarely turned inwards. This avoidance must measure some anxiety, reluctance, or fear. That makes me still more curious. Most of our lives are spent in externally oriented function, that distract from self-observation. This relentless, obsessive drive persists independently of survival needs such as food and warmth, and even of pleasure. Second for second, we couple ourselves to sights, tastes, words, motions, or electric stimuli, until we fall dead. It is striking how many ordinary activities, from smoking a pipe to watching sunsets, veer towards, but ultimately avoid, sustained attention to the reality of our own life.

So it is not an intellectual intrigue with the platonic dictum that leads me to sit, but an experience of myself and my fellow humans as stimulus-bound, fundamentally out of control, alive only in reaction. I want to know, to simply observe, this living person as he is, not just as he appears while careening from event to event. Of course, this will undoubtedly be helpful to me as a psychiatrist, but my motives are more fundamental, personal, and existential.

I am interested in my mind, and in my body. Previous to my having cultivated the habit of sitting, I had thought about myself, and had used my body as a tool in the world, to grip a pen or to chop firewood, but I had never systematically, rigorously, observed my body—what it feels like, not just with a shy, fleeting glance, but moment after moment for hours and days at a time; nor had I committed myself to observe the reciprocal influence of mind and body in states of exhaustion and rest, hunger, pain, relaxation, arousal, lethargy, or concentration. My quest for knowing is not merely objective and scientific. This mind-and-body is the vessel of my life. I want to drink its nectar, and if necessary, its sludge, but I want to know it with the same organic immersion that sets a snow goose flying ten thousand miles every winter and spring.

It seems to me that the forces of creation, the laws of nature, out of which this mind and body arose, must be operative in me, now, continuously, and whenever I make an effort to observe them. The activity of creation must be the original and continuing cause of my life. I would like to know these laws, these forces, my maker, and observe, even participate, in the ongoing creation.

Newton founded modern science with his assumption that there is one continuous world, one unbroken order, one set of laws governing both earth and sky; so along with this great tradition, and along with the ancient religions of India as well, I assume that the physics of the stars is the physics of my body also. The laws of chemistry and biology, predicated on the laws of physics, are also uniform throughout nature. Since these laws operate continuously, without reserve or sanctuary, but uniformly and pervasively, I deduce that eternal, unbroken laws operate in me, created me, and create me, that my life is an expression of them continuously linked by cause and effect to all that antedated, all that follows, and all that is co-existent; and that, to the extent that I am conscious and capable of learning, a systematic study and awareness of creation's ways is available to me if I live with attention to this field.

Even if I am frequently incapable of actually observing the most basic levels of reality, at least the mental and physical phenomena that bombard me are predicated on nature's laws, and must be my laboratory to study them. I want to sing like a bird, like a human. I want to grow and rot like a tree, like a man. I want to sit with my mind and body as they cast up and swirl before me and inside me the human stuff which is made of and ordered by the matter and laws governing galaxies and wrens.

Because the harmony in me is at once so awesome and sweet and overwhelming that I love its taste yet can barely compel myself to glimpse it, I want to sit with the great determination that I need to brush aside the fuzz of distraction, the lint of petty concerns. To sit is to know myself as an unfolding manifestation of the universals of life. A gripping, unending project. Hopefully one I can pursue even when I look into death's funnel. For me, this knowing is a great force, and a great pleasure.

II

I sit because of, for, and with, an appreciation of daily life. The great poets sing of the omnipresent ordinary pregnant with revelation—but I know how easily and recurrently my own life yields to distraction, irritation, tunnel vision. I do not want to miss my life the way I once missed a plane at La Guardia. It may be ironic that simply to wriggle free of daydreams and worries I need a technique, a practice, a discipline, but I do; and I bow to that irony by doing what I *must* do to pry my mind off ephemeral worries, to wake to more dawns, to *see* my child unravel through his eddying transformations.

It may be contrary that I must work so hard to be at peace with myself, but I do; and I have become increasingly convinced, learning as I sit and live and sit and live, that "being at peace" is not a state of mind, but a state of mind and body. At the core of my life is a receptive drinking in. The simple beauty of things keeps flooding in to me. I live for this draught, and build my life around it. Yet it slips away. I can try to crash back through by taking dramatic journeys—to India, or to lakes at tree line in the Rocky Mountains—but this kind of breathtaking beauty is only an interlude, a punctuation mark. It reminds me of what I intended to emphasize in my life, but like an exclamation point, it has limited use.

The clear direct sentence—the death sentence, the sentence of love—ends with a mere period. This declarative beauty is more like looking up over the slums of Montreal to see the moon wearing a pendant of Venus in 4:00 AM darkness. Not what is sought or built, but what I discover when the walls fall away. I walk alone in the autumn forest, up and down gneiss and schist hills and ridges of Vermont, and I become confused whether that intense pulsatile drumming is the "booming" of grouse wings, or my own heart, strained by the last climb. Not what excites, moves, or informs me, but the beat of recognition. The tuning fork of my life humming in response to the living world.

This receipt—like a parent accepting back a soggy, half-eaten cracker—requires, for me, a framework, a matrix in my body, that, simple as it should be, I do not simply have. This knowing requires a bodily preparation. I sit to open my pores, skin and mind both, to the life that surrounds me, inside and outside, at least more often if not all the time, as it arrives at my doorstep. I sit to exercise the appreciative, receptive, peaceful mode of being filled up by the ordinary and inevitable. For example, the sagging floorboards in the crooked bedroom where I am a husband. Or my two-year-old son, tugging one splinter at a time, to help me stack firewood in new January snow.

III

I feel a need for a rudder, a keel, a technique, a method, a way to continue on course. I need ceaselessly increasing amounts of self-control (though not constriction, deadening, or inhibition). It seems to me that the best of human life is lived on a narrow ledge, like a bridge over a stream in Nepal, or like a trail in the Grand Canyon, between two chasms. On the one side is desire, on the other side is fear. Possibly it is because of my work as a psychiatrist, often with essentially normal people, who are none the less pushed and pulled about by their inner forces like tops, that I feel so sensitized to these faults that can send seismic shudders through apparently solid lives. But my own life has ground enough for these observations.

Sitting is, among other things, the practice of self-control. While sitting one does not get up, or move, or make that dollar, or pass that test, or receive reassurance from that phone call. But military training, or violin lessons, or medical school, are also routes to self-control in this ordering and restrictive sense. Sitting is self-control around specific values. Observation replaces all action. What is the point of committing one's life to this practice, only to spend the time with erotic daydreams, or anxious yearnings for promotion and recognition? Of course, those will happen anyway. They are part of the human make-up. Cultures would not have proliferated the ubiquitous moral codes, the Ten Commandments, it we were not so replete with ten million urges.

But moral invective, preaching, always seemed feeble to me—possibly just a measure of my wild horses and snails. I need a constantly usable, constantly renewable lens to see through my yearnings into my loves, to see through my anxieties into my faith. What is a bedrock feeling, the core of my identity, and what is a titillation that will ultimately be discarded? What characters walk in front of the mirror of my soul day after day, year after year, and who are the clowns that steal the stage for a scene?

An hour of sitting is one thing; longer periods another. Once a year, under the guidance of a teacher, I sit for ten days, all day. That kind of practice induces pain. To face pain has become a regular inescapable part of my life. It is for most people—laborers, poor, infirm, cold, infected, hungry people throughout the world. But I have not elected sentimental, identificatory masochism. I am looking at another side of myself. While I spontaneously seek to avoid pain, a higher wisdom than knee-jerk reaction tells me that, in Socrates' words: "... pain and pleasure are never present to a man at the same instant, and yet he who pursues either is compelled to take the other; their bodies are two, but they are joined by a single head" (Phaedo).

Just how serious am I about being who I said I was? How integrated do I want to be with this screaming body that has to be fed, slept, positioned just right, or it howls unbearably? I sit because I know I need a self-control that does not lecture or stomp on my tendencies, but reorganizes desire into love, and pain and fear into faith.

IV

As I understand it, love is not an emotion, but an organization of emotions. It is not a room, but a dwelling; not a bird, but a migratory flyway. It is a structure of emotions, a meta-emotion. This is in contrast to love understood as a sentimental gush of attachment or as romantic sexuality. Sitting has helped me to find love, to live by love, or at least, to live more by love. It has helped me come alive as a husband, father, psychiatrist, and citizen, within the bounds of my character and capabilities. It pried me open beyond either my previous sentimental position or my rational moral knowledge and has given me a tool, a practice, an activity expressive of love. For me it is both crowbar and glue.

As Erik Erikson has written, it is only "ambivalence that makes love meaningful—or possible." In other words, it is only because we are both separate, and united, that love exists. If we had no individual existence, no personal drives, there would be merely the homogeneous glob of the world, devoid of emotion, unknowing, like a finger on an arm. Yet if we were irreconcilably separate there would only be self-maintaining cold stars co-existing in dead space. I understand love to mean the organization of human emotions into those complex states where separation and merging, individuality and immersion, self and selflessness paradoxically co-exist. Only an individual can love; and only one who has ceased to be one can love. Sitting has helped me develop both these poles. It breaks me open where I get stuck; and where I fall off as a chip, it sticks me back on to the main piece.

Sitting pushes me to the limit of my self-directed effort; it mobilizes my willed, committed direction, yet it also shatters my self-protective, self-defining maneuvers and my simple self-definition. It both builds and dismantles "me." Every memory, every hope, every yearning, every fear floods in. I no longer can pretend to be one selected set of my memories or traits.

If observed, but not reacted upon, all these psychic contents become acceptable, obviously part of myself (for there they are in my own mind, right in front of me): yet also impersonal, causally—linked, objective phenomena-in-the-world, that move ceaselessly, relentlessly, across the screen of my existence, without my effort, without my control, without *me*. I can see more, tolerate more, in my inner life, at the same time that I am less driven by these forces. Like storms and doves, they are the personae of nature, crossing one inner sky. Psychic complexity swirls up from the dust of cosmetic self-definition. At the same time, the determination and endurance I have to muster to just observe, grow like muscles with exercise. Naturally the repetition of this mixture of tolerance and firmness extrapolates beyond its source in sitting, out to relationships.

There is little I have heard from others—and it is my daily business to hear—that I have not seen in myself as I sit. But I also know the necessity of work, training, and restraint. Dependence, loneliness, sensuality, exhaustion, hunger, petulance, perversion, miserliness, yearning, inflation are my old friends. I can greet them openly and warmly in people close to me, both because I know them from the inside and therefore cannot condemn them without condemning myself; and also because I have been learning to harness and ride their energy. To love, I try to hold the complex reality of myself at the same time that I try to catch the complex reality of another.

I have known my wife for twelve years. We have dated and swam, married and fought, travelled, built cabins, bought houses, delivered and diapered together; in short, we have attained the ordinary and ubiquitous. In a world of three billion people, this achievement ranks with literacy, and would have no bearing on why I sit, except that it does. Even the inevitable is fragile. I, we, am, and are, buffered by unshy thanks. We are sharpened by life with an edge.

I sit and life moves through me, my married life too. This sphere also takes its turn before my solitary, impeachable witness to my own existence and its eternal entanglements. As a married man, I sit as if in a harbour from my selfish pettiness, where the winds of my annoyance or anger have time to pass; I sit as a recipient of a generous outpouring of warmth that I have time to savour; I sit as a squash or pumpkin with his own slightly fibrous and only moderately sweet but nonetheless ample life to lay on someone else's table; I sit as one oxen in a team pulling a cart filled with rocking horses, cars, and porches that need paint; I sit knowing myself as a sick old man of the future awaiting the one person who can really attend, or as the future one whose voice alone can wave death back behind someone else's hospital curtain for another hour; I sit as a common man of common desire, and as a dreamer who with the bricks of shared fate is building a common dream; and I sit alone in my own life anyway.

How fortunate to have this cave, this sanctuary, this frying pan, this rock, and this mirror of sitting, in which to forge, drop, haul, touch, release my love, and not get lost. To sit is the compass by which I navigate the seas of married love. It is also the string by which I trip up the fox on his way to the chicken coop. To love is a deep yearning and hard work. It cannot be done alone! There are many ways to receive help, and many ways to give it. Martin Buber says that men and women cannot love without a third point to form a stable triangle: a god, task, calling, or meaning beyond their dyadic individuality. What about two who just know the pole star?

There is a joke in "Peanuts": "I love mankind. It's just people that I hate." I think love is concrete and abstract. If it is only an amorphous generalized feeling, it remains a platitude, a wish, a defense against real entanglement. This is what sounds hollow in the pious, sanctimonious "love" of some churches and martyrs. But if love is only concrete, immediate, personal, it remains in the realm of possession, privatism, materialism, narcissism. This is the paternalistic love a person has for his house, cars, family. My understanding is that actual love expands outward in both spheres. Riding the wings of the ideal, it sweeps up and carries along those who are encountered.

I sit to better love my wife, and those friends and companions with whom I share even a day's journey on my flight from the unknown to the unknown. It is difficult to love the one with whom my fate is most closely entangled during those moments when I would like to batter down the corridors of that fate. But it is easy to love her when we sweeten each other's tea. It is easy to feel affection for friends I encounter on weekends devoted to family life and outdoor play; it is difficult to let our lives, our health and finances, entangle. Such an embrace threatens private safety. And it is more difficult still to try to place this way of being, first among all others, and risk myself over and over again.

Shall I keep all my money, or risk it on a charitable principle? Shall I study the text sanctioned by the authorities, or sing out from my heart? When I sit, money does me little good; approval evaporates; but the tone of the strings of my heart, for better or worse, is inescapable. I sit to tie myself to the mast, to hear more of the song of elusive and unavoidable love.

V

A baby looks fragile, but if you neglect his meal or hold him the wrong way, your eardrums will have to reckon with an awesome wrath! Anger springs from and participates in the primary survival instinct of the organism. Yet how much trouble it causes us in daily life, not to mention large-scale social relations! Probably the height of inanity would be to sit, angry. What is the point of such impotent stewing?

I sit to grow up, to be a better person, to see trivial angers rise up and pass away, arguments on which I put great weight on Thursday morning fade by Thursday noon; and to be compelled to re-order, re-structure, re-think my life, so that, living well, my petty anger is orchestrated ahead of time into flexibility, co-operation, or the capacity to see other viewpoints. Sitting helps me to transcend the irritable, petulant infant in me.

But that only solves the periphery of the problem. I am no longer angry about my diapers. I am angry that my votes and taxes have been turned to oppressing other nations; I am angry that I will be judged for the rest of my life by multiple choice exams; I am angry that research is ignored and dogma is used to coerce one religion's point of view: I am angry that mountains are scoured for energy to manufacture throwaway soda cans. I sit also, then, to express my anger, and the form of expression is determination. I sit with force, will, and, when the pain mounts, something that feels fierce. Sitting helps me harness authentic anger.

I have been sitting at least fifteen hours a week for nine years, and when, as often happens, I am asked how I find the time, I know that part of the certainty in my aim is an anger that will not allow the rolling woodlands and hilltop pastures of my psyche to be bulldozed by T.V., non-nutritional food, fabricated news, tweed socialization, pedantic file cabinets of knowledge, or loyalty rallies to leaders, states, gods, and licensures. The voices of the herd will not so easily drive me from my forest cabin of deeply considered autonomy and honest talk, because I have had practice in this sort of firmness. A child's anger is the kindling of adult will. I can stay true to myself yet mature, be willed but not willful, by sitting in the spirit of Woody Guthrie's song: "Don't you push me, push me, push me, don't you push me down!"

VI

As I understand it, the lifelong disciplined practice of sitting is not exactly religion, but is not not a religion either. For myself, I am not bound to scriptures, dogma, hierarchies; I have taken no proscriptions on my intelligence, or on my political autonomy; nor have I hidden from unpleasant realities by concretizing myth. But I have become increasingly aware of the inextricable role of faith in my practice.

The faith I have been discovering in myself is not blind, irrational, unsubstantiated, or wishful ideas. Following the definitive clarification of these English terms by Paul Tillich, I would call those former "beliefs." I hope sitting has helped me to free myself from my beliefs even further than my scientific education did. Nor does faith mean what I live for—goals, personal preferences, commitments, and loves. These are ideals, visions, tastes—very important—but not faith. Faith is what I *live by*, what empowers my life. The battery, the heart-pump, of my being. It is not the other shore, but the boat. It is not what I know, but how I know. It is present, rather than past or future, and is my most authentic, total reaction, a gut reaction deeper than my guts. Tillich defined faith as a person's ultimate concern—the bedrock of what we in fact take seriously. I would like to describe faith, as I have found it, to be the hunger of my existence.

Hunger springs up from my body. It antedates my mental and psychological life, and can even run havoc over them. I do not eat because of what I believe or hope or wish for, or because of what an authority prescribes or what I read. I eat because I am hungry. My body is a dynamic, metabolizing system, an energy exchanger, constantly incorporating, re-working, re-moulding—this is the vitality intrinsic to the life of any oak, deer, or human. This being I am consumes, reworks, then creates more emotional, spiritual life. Not what I digest, but the ordered process in me that gives coherence and direction to this continuous organism, constitutes faith.

Faith is not something I have (e.g., "I believe!"); it is something that I realize has already been given to me, on which the sense of "me" is predicated. I find it or receive it, not once, but intermittently and continuously. It is not a set of thoughts, and it provides no concrete, reducible answers. Who am I? What is this life? Where does it come from? Where is it headed? I don't know. On these important questions, I have no beliefs. Yet no day has shaken this strange bird from his perch!

I sit with impassioned neutrality. Why? This activity is not *in order to get* answers with which to live my life. It *is* my life. Bones are not in order to hang skin and muscle on. (In scientific thought, too, teleology—goal-directed thinking—leads nowhere. Who knows the goal of the universe? Then what is the goal of any part of it?) I eat, I read, I work, I play, I sit. If I have no big intellectual belief by which I can justify my day, myself, my life, my suppertime, I eat anyway! Usually with pleasure.

I am neither an existentialist, a Marxist, nor an anorectic. Hunger is a spontaneous action of life in me. The hunger of my existence also demands sustenance daily. The nourishment I take becomes my body; the sustenance I take becomes my being. To be alive, to be alert, to be observant, to be at peace with myself and all others—vibrating in ceaseless change—unmoving: I find this is my sustaining passage through the incandescent world doing the same.

As a scientific fact, I know I am alive only inside the body of life. Physically, I am aware of myself as a product of other lives—parents, ancestors. I breathe the oxygen created by plants, so that, as I breathe in and out, I am a tube connected to the whole life of the biosphere, a tiny, dependent digit. Through digestion and metabolism I biotransform the organic molecules created by plants and animals, which I call food, into other biochemicals with which I mould this form called my body, which is constantly, continuously being re-moulded, re-formed, like a cloud. And this form will eventually cease its re-generation and vanish, as it arose, from causes, forces in nature.

It is easy for me to comprehend this description of physical reality, which is so obvious and scientific. But my person, my psychological reality, is also a product of causes: things I have been taught, experiences I have had, cultural beliefs, social forces. This uninterrupted web of causality—physical, biological, psychological, cultural—connecting from past to future, and out across contemporaneousness, is the ocean in which the bubble of my life briefly floats. Death must be inevitable for such an ephemeral bubble. Yet while it is here, I can feel how vital is this breathing, pulsating being, alive, resonant in exchange with past and future, people and things—creator, transducer, knower, taut node in the web, message in the synaptic mind of creation.

The faith that underlies my practice is not in my mind, but is the psychological correlate of animation. I experience faith not as a thought, but as the overwhelming mood which drives this thrust upward of emerging. By sitting I can know, assume, become, this direct hum of energy. Retrospectively, verbally, I call this "faith." When I am bored, pained, lazy, distracted, worried, I find myself sitting anyway, not because I believe it is good, or will get me into heaven, nor because I have particular will power. My life is expressing its trajectory. All mass is energy, Einstein showed. My life is glowing, and I sit in the light.

VII

Sitting enabled me to see, and compelled me to acknowledge, the role that death had already played, and still continues to play, in my life. Every living creature knows that the sum total of its pulsations is limited. As a child I wondered: Where was I before I was born? Where will I be after I die? How long is forever and when does it end? The high school student of history knew that every hero died; I saw the colours of empires wash back and forth over the maps in the books like tides. (Not me!) Where can I turn that impermanence is not the law? I try to hide from this as well as I can, behind my youth (already wrinkling, first around the eyes, and greying), and health insurance: but no hideout works.

Every day ends with darkness; things must get done today or they will not happen at all. And, funny, rather than sapping my appetite, producing "nausea" (which may be due to rich French sauces rather than real philosophy), the pressure of nightfall helps me to treasure life. Isn't this the most universal human observation and counsel? I aim each swing of the maul more accurately at the cracks in the oak cordwood I am splitting. I choose each book I read with precision and reason. I hear the call to care for and love my child and the forest trails that I maintain as a pure ringing note of mandate. I sit at the dawn of day and day passes. Another dawn, but the series is limited, so I swear in my inner chamber I will not miss a day.

Sitting rivets me on the psychological fact that death is life's door. No power can save me. Because I am aware of death, and afraid. I lean my shoulder into living not automatically and reactively, like an animal, nor passively and pleadingly, like a child pretending he has a father watching over him, but with conscious choice and decision of what will constitute each fleeting moment of my life. I know that my petals cup a volatile radiance.

But to keep this in mind in turn requires that an ordinary escapist constantly re-encounters the limit, the metronome of appreciation, death.

I sit because knowing I will die enriches, and excoriates my life, so I have to go out of my way to seek discipline and the stability that is necessary for me to really face it. To embrace life I must shake hands with death. For this, I need practice. Each act of sitting is a dying to outward activity, a relinquishment of distraction, a cessation of anticipatory gratification. It is life now, as it is. Some day this austere focus will come in very, very handy. It already has.

VIII

I sit to be myself, independent of my own or others' judgements. Many years of my life were spent being rated, primarily in school, but, as an extension of that, among friends and in social life. As much as I tried to fight off this form of addiction, I got hooked anyway. As often happens, out of their concern for me, my parents combed and brushed me with the rules of comparison: I was good at this, or not good, or as good, or better, or worse, or the best, or no good at all.

Today I find that sitting reveals the absurdity of comparative achievement. My life consists of what I actually live, not the evaluations that float above it. Sitting enables me to slip beyond that second, commenting, editor's mind, and to burrow in deep towards immediate reality. I have made progress in becoming a mole, an empty knapsack, a boy on a day when school is cancelled. What is there to gain or lose as I sit? Who can I beat, who can I scramble after? Just this one concrete day, all this, and only this, comes to me on the tray of morning, flashes out now.

I am relieved to be more at home in myself, with myself. I complain less. I can lose discussions, hopes, or self-expectations, more easily and much less often, because the talking, hoping, and doing is victory enough already. Without props or toys or comfort, without control of the environment, I have sat and observed who I am when there was no one and nothing to give me clues. It has happened that I have sat, asked for nothing, needed nothing, and felt full. Now my spine and hands have a different turgor. When I am thrown off balance, I can fall somewhat more like a cat than like a two-by-four. When I sit, no one—beloved or enemy—can give me what I lack, or take away what I am.

So as I live all day, I can orient myself into becoming the person I will have to live with when I next sit. No one else's commentary of praise or blame can mediate my own confrontation with the observed facts of who I am. I'm not as bad as I thought I was—and worse. But I'm definitely sprouting and real. It's a pleasure to relinquish yearning and fighting back, and to permit ripples. And I sit to share companionship with other spring bulbs. I feel like one leaf in a deciduous forest: specific, small, fragile, all alone with my fate, yet shaking in a vast and murmuring company.

IX

Sitting is a response to, and an expression of, my social and historical conditions. Although I practise an ancient way that has been passed on from person to person for two and a half millennia and must be useful and meaningful wider a variety of conditions, I sought and learned this practice for reasons particular to myself.

One of the most powerful forces that pushed my life into the form it has taken was World War II, which ended, almost to the day, when I was born. It was a backdrop, very present in my parents' sense of the world, and in other adults around me, that left little scope for hope. Fear seemed the only rational state of mind, self-defense the only rational posture. Cultured, civilized men had just engaged in an extended, calculated, concerted sadism the scope of which is incomprehensible. Victory by goodness had brought reactive evil: nuclear weapons. The world-view I was taught and absorbed was to study hard, save my money, and build my own self-protective world, using the liberal, rational, scientific cultures as stepping-stones to an anxious fiefdom of private family life. It was only in that private space that the sweet kernel of affection and idealistic aspiration could be unveiled. I did that well, and to some extent it worked.

Yet at the same time, I had been guided to, and later chose to, spend my summers in the woods, learning about white-tailed deer, mosquitoes, freedom, and canoes, surrounded, it seemed, by a primal monistic goodness that I located in nature and those who lived close to it. I read Thoreau the way many people read the Bible. The world of cold streams running under shady hemlocks, and its ecstatic prophets, seemed an antidote to the haunted, dull, convention-bound, anxious lives of my immediate environment. Moving between these two worlds, I learned a dialogue of terror and ecstasy, survivorship and care, that filled me with an urgency to find the middle way.

This motivated a search that led through intense intellectual exploration in college, medical school, and psychiatric training, and finally to the art of "sitting," as taught by S. N. Goenka, a Vipassana meditation teacher from whom my wife and I first took a course near New Delhi in 1974. Those ten days of nothing but focusing on the moment by moment reality of body and mind, with awareness and equanimity, gave me the opportunity iron-ically both to be more absolutely alone and isolated than I had ever been before, and at the same time to cast my lot with a tradition, a way, as upheld, manifested, explained, and transmitted by a living person. I am continuously grateful to Goenka for the receipt of this technique.

Vipassana meditation was preserved in Asia for two thousand five hundred years since its discovery by Gotama, the historical Buddha. His technique of living was labelled, by western scholars, "Buddhism," but it is not an "ism," a system of thought. It is a practice, a method, a tool of living persons. It does not end its practitioner's search. For me, it provides a compass, a spy glass, a map for further journeys. With daily practice, and intensive retreats mixed into the years, I find the marriage of autonomy and heritage, membership and lonely continuity.

Vipassana is the binoculars—now I can search for the elusive bird.

Before I received instructions in how to sit, my journey through life was predominantly intellectual. I had found lectures and books to be inspiring, suggestive, artful, but evasive. One could advise, one could talk, one could write. But sitting is a way for me to stand for something, to sit as something, not just with words, but with my mind, body, and life. Here is a way to descend by stages, protected by teacher, teaching, technique, and practice, into the light and darkness in me, the Hitler and Buddha in me, the frightened child of a holocaust world riding a slow bus in winter through dark city streets, and the striding, backpacking youth wandering through sunlight cathedrals of Douglas fir, who, shouting or whimpering, spans the vocabulary of human potentials from sadism to love.

I now can see that I carry the whip and boots of the torturer, I suffer with the naked, I drink from mountain streams with poets and explorers. All these lives live *in* me. And I find ways, often covert and symbolic, to express these psychological potentials in me as overt actions in my daily life. Everything I am springs from the universally human. I cause myself, I express myself, as the conditions of the world roll through me. I see this fact, as I sit, as clearly as I see the impact of history and the inspiration of vision. I sit in clear confrontation with everything that has impinged on me and caused me to react, and in reacting, I mould myself.

Life begins in a welter of conditions; mere reactions to these conditions forge limitations; awareness of and conscious response to conditions produces freedom. This clarity regarding my choices enables me to return from sitting to action as a more focused, concentrated vector of knowing, empathic life.

Sitting itself transforms my motives for sitting. I started in my own historical circumstances, but I was given a technique that has been useful in millions of circumstances over thousands of years. I started with personal issues, and I have been given timeless perspectives to broaden my viewpoint. My search is particular, but not unique. The transmission of this tool has made my work possible. Because others have launched the quest for a fully human life, because others will follow, my own frailty, or villainy, can become meaningful, because these are the soil which I must use to grow. And my own efforts, however great they feel to me, are in the shadow of the much greater efforts of others.

I can flower as one shrub in a limitless forest of unending cycles of life. To flower, for a human being, is to work on the science of honest observation that enables a true picture of humanity to be born. Even coming from my conditioning of nihilism and dread, without the comfort of simple beliefs, aware of awesome human evil and hatred, of wars that kill decamillions, I can be, I will be, an expression of contentless faith. I cannot be much but I can root deep into what is true, how to see it, and how to pass it on.

In response to the overwhelming sense of evil, fear, meaninglessness, and paranoid privatism of my times, and in response to the hope, idealism, and pregnant sense of eternity of my youth, I learned to sit, to better stand for what I found most true. This helps me live out what had before been an unconscious faith. It helps me express something healing, useful (in both my personal and professional life), and meaningful to me despite apparently absurd conditions, because it is a link to the universal. It puts me in touch with the fundamentally human that is present in every gesture of mine, and every action of other people, in each immediacy. This in turn has enabled me to join with the generative dance of nature. I practice knowing myself, and make that the workshop of the day. I refrain from measuring events by my own inchworm life. I frequently forget time, and so join history.

X

I sit in solitude to lose my isolation. What is least noble in me rises up to the surface of my mind, and this drives me on to be more than I was. When I am most shut into my dark self I find the real source of my belonging.

Freud claimed that the bedrock of human fear is castration anxiety. This, he felt, is more feared than death itself. I understand castration anxiety to mean physical pain, bodily mutilation, and social isolation, ostracism, loss of membership, generativity, continuity in the cycle of generations. The two greatest difficulties I have, in fact, faced while sitting for extended hours or days are physical pain, and the loss of the social position that I had previously seemed headed for and entitled to in the community of men. Pain that starts in the knees or back can flood the whole body and burn on and on. The self-protection of calculated membership, and its comfortable rewards, are lost to me in those aching, endless hours.

I imagine my other options: a better house, winter vacations in the tropics, the respect of colleagues listening to me speak as I climb the career ladder. I imagine the financial crises I am less prepared to withstand. I imagine the humiliating rejection that crushes the refugee from poverty or racism or any form of powerlessness, all of which are in my heritage and possibly in my future (and in anyone's heritage or future if you look far enough). Why do I sit there? A thrush hops onto a low limb at the edge of a wooded clearing and shatters the Vermont evening with triumphant song. Knowing yet staying, I am an inheritor and transmitter, flooded with gifts from those who loved and left their trace; and this still, glowing, posture is the song of my species.

Sitting helps me overcome my deepest fears. I become freer to live from my heart, and to face the consequences, but also to reap the rewards of this authenticity. Much of what I called pain was really loneliness and fear. It passes, dissolves, with that observation. The vibrations of my body are humming the song that can be heard only when dawn and dusk are simultaneous, instantaneous, continuous. I feel a burst of stern effort is a small price to pay to hear this inner music—fertile music from the heart of life itself.

It has been my fortune along the way to find and follow an older brother who, like a long unobserved mushroom, no longer can be shaken from the stump because his roots have reached the heartwood. From him I have caught a glimmer of two lights: devotion and integrity. And it has been an extra pleasure—and sometimes I think a necessity—to be able to sit beside my wife. Even the stars move in constellations.

XI

I sit to find mental freedom. I was lucky to be able to think rationally, logically, scientifically, in a culture where focused, aggressive thought is the sword of survival. But even Reason's greatest apologist, Socrates, balanced himself with equal reverence for mythopoetic knowing. In fact, many Socratic dialogues point towards the limits of logic and the essential role of myth. As I sit, a million thoughts cross my mind, but, in keeping with the traditions passed on from ancient India's great teachers, I attempt to let all of them go, to let them pass like clouds, like water, like time. Needless to say, I often get caught and find myself spinning around one point like a kite trapped by the uppermost twig. But eventually boredom, exhaustion, will-power, or insight—the wind—spins me free and I'm off again.

Sitting gives me a way back to fluctuant, pre-formed mind, the pregnant atmosphere in which metaphor, intuition, and reason are sparks. Surrounded by a culture of intellectual conquest, I have a preserve of wholeness, a sanctuary in which the wild deer of poetry and song can slip in and out among the trunks of medical cases and conferences. In this sense, sitting is also a nag, tattletale, a wagging finger, reminding me, as well as enabling me. I've got to return to the potential, because any one tack is just a shifting situational response to the origin—less wind.

XII

I sit to anchor my life in certain moods, organize my life around my heart and mind, and to radiate out to others what I find. Though I shake in strong winds, I return to this basic way of living. I can't throw away my boy's ideals and my old man's smile. The easy, soothing comfort and deep relaxation that accompany intense awareness in stillness, peel my life like an onion to deeper layers of truth, which in turn are scoured and soothed until the next layer opens. I sit to discipline my life by what is clear, simple, self-fulfilling, and universal in my heart. There is no end to this job. I have failed to really live many days of my life, but I dive again and again into the plain guidance of self-containment and loving receipt. I sit to find and express simple human love and common decency.

The Buddhist Philosophy of Relations

Paṭṭhānuddesa Dīpanī

by

Ledi Sayādaw Mahāthera

Translated by

Sayādaw U Nyāna

WHEEL PUBLICATION NO. 331/332/333

Foreword

The author of the present treatise, the Venerable Ledi Sayādaw, was one of the most eminent Burmese Buddhist scholar-monks of recent times. Born in the Shwebo District of Burma in 1846, by the time he passed away in 1923 he had written over seventy manuals on different aspects of Theravada Buddhism and established centres throughout Burma for the study of Abhidhamma and the practise of insight meditation. His profound erudition, original thinking and lucid writings have won him the esteem of the entire Buddhist world.

The *Paṭṭhānuddesa Dīpanī* is Ledi Sayādaw's treatment of one of the most difficult and complex subjects of Theravada Buddhist thought—the philosophy of conditional relations. The *Paṭṭhāna,* the seventh and last book of the Abhidhamma Piṭaka, works out the system of relations in six large volumes. In the present slim volume the Venerable Ledi Sayādaw has extracted the essential principles underlying this vast system and explained them concisely but comprehensively, with lucid illustrations for the Paṭṭhāna's twenty-four conditional relations.

An English translation of the *Paṭṭhānuddesa Dīpanī* by the Sayādaw U Nyāna, a direct disciple of the author, was published in Rangoon in 1935. This translation, with a few minor changes, appeared serialized in the Burmese Buddhist journal *The Light of the Dhamma,* and later was included in a collection of Ledi Sayādaw's works, *The Manuals of Buddhism* (Rangoon: Union Buddha Sāsana Council, 1965). A Thai reprint of the latter work (Bangkok: Mahāmakut, 1978) was used as the basis for the present edition, which reproduces the original with a few minor alterations of style and choice of renderings.

In including the *Paṭṭhānuddesa Dīpanī* in *The Wheel* series, the publishers recognise that the treatise will not be easy reading even for those seriously involved in Abhidhamma study. However, since copies of the earlier editions are now almost impossible to obtain, it was felt that the value and importance of this work for understanding the Buddhist philosophy of conditionality justify its being reissued. As the treatise presupposes prior familiarity with the Abhidhamma gained elsewhere, footnotes have been kept minimal; if footnotes had been added to elucidate every difficult point, the annotations would have become unmanageable. The original translator had chosen to retain much of the Pali terminology in the exposition, and this edition follows suit. Since the author's own explanations make the meanings of the Pali terms very clear, the reader who is keen on study should not find this a serious obstacle, and moreover will be able to deal with them more precisely in the original than in makeshift English renderings.

Readers who wish to extend their knowledge of the Abhidhamma in connection with the present work would do best to turn to the classical summary of Abhidhamma thought, the *Abhidhammatthasaṅgaha.* This has been published by the BPS in an English translation by the Venerable Nārada Thera as *A Manual of Abhidhamma.* The first two volumes of the *Paṭṭhāna* itself have been published by the Pali Text Society under the title *Conditional Relations,* translated by the Paṭṭhāna Sayādaw, U Nārada.

Nyanaponika Thera,
The Editor, BPS

Translator's Preface to the First Edition

Buddhism views the world, with the exception of Nibbāna and *paññatti*,[1] as impermanent, liable to suffering, and without soul-essence. So Buddhist philosophy, to elaborate the impermanency as applied to the Law of Perpetual Change, has from the outset dissolved all things, all phenomena both mental and physical, into a continuous succession of happenings of states of mind and matter, under the Fivefold Law of Cosmic Order (*niyāma*). The happenings are determined and determining, both as to their constituent states and as to other happenings, in a variety of ways, which Buddhist philosophy expresses by the term *paccaya* or "relations." One complex happening of mental and material states, with its three phases of time—genesis or birth, cessation or death and a static interval between—is followed by another happening, wherein there is always a causal series of relations. Nothing is casual and fortuitous. When one happening by its arising, persisting, cessation, priority, and posteriority, is determined by and determining another happening by means of producing (*janaka*), supporting (*upatthambhaka*), and maintaining (*anupālana*), the former is called the relating thing (*paccaya-dhamma*), the latter the related thing (*paccayuppanna-dhamma*), and the determination or the influence or the specific function is called the correlativity (*paccayatā*). As the various kinds of influence are apparently known, the relations are classified into the following twenty-four kinds:

1. *hetu*—condition or root
2. *ārammaṇa*—object
3. *adhipati*—dominance
4. *anantara*—contiguity
5. *samanantara*—immediate contiguity
6. *sahajāta*—coexistence

1. *Paññatti* means concept or idea. The venerable author's and the translator's view that concepts are not subject to impermanence is not supported by the canonical texts nor by the ancient commentaries. (Editor)

7. *aññamañña*—reciprocity
8. *nissaya*—dependence
9. *upanissaya*—suffering condition
10. *purejāta*—pre-existence
11. *pacchājāta*—post-existence
12. *āsevana*—habitual recurrence
13. *kamma*—*kamma* or action
14. *vipāka*—effect
15. *āhāra*—food
16. *indriya*—control
17. *jhāna*—absorption
18. *magga*—path
19. *sampayutta*—association
20. *vippayutta*—dissociation
21. *atthi*—presence
22. *natthi*—absence
23. *vigata*—abeyance
24. *avigata*—continuance.

These twenty-four relations are extensively and fully expounded in the seventh and last of the analytical works in the Abhidhamma Piṭaka of the Buddhist Canon, called the *Paṭṭhāna* ("The Eminence") or the *Mahāpakararaṇa* ("The Great Treatise").

The well-known Ledi Sayādaw Mahāthera, D. Litt., Aggamahāpaṇḍita, has written in Pali a concise exposition of these relations known as *Paṭṭhānuddesa Dīpanī*, in order to help those who wish to study the Buddhist philosophy of relations expounded in the *Paṭṭhāna*. In introducing these relations to the student of philosophical research before he takes the opportunity of making himself acquainted with the methodological elaboration of correlations in the *Paṭṭhāna*, the Mahāthera deals with the subject under three heads:

1. The *Paccayattha-dīpanī* or the analytical Exposition of Relations with their denotations and connotations.
2. The *Paccayā-sabhāga* or the Synthesis of Relations.
3. The *Paccayā-ghaṭanānaya* or the Synchrony of Relations.

The following translation has been undertaken with the hope of rendering Ledi Sayādaw's work intelligible to the English student. If the present translation makes any contribution to the advancement of learning and knowledge in the matter of apprehending the general scheme of causal laws in terms of "relations" in the field of Buddhist philosophy, the translator will deem himself well rewarded for his labour. It may, however, be necessary to mention here that the original form, sense, and meaning of the Venerable Author are, as far as possible, cautiously preserved; hence the literal character of the translation—if it appears so—in some places. Nevertheless, the translator ventures to hope that any discrepancy that may have crept in, will be accordingly overlooked.

In conclusion, it is with great pleasure that I express my indebtedness to U Aung Hla, M.A. (Cantab.), Barrister-at-Law, who has very kindly, amidst his own many duties, taken the trouble of revising the manuscript and has also helped me in getting it through the press and in the correction of the proofs. My thanks are also due to Sayā U Ba, M.A., A.T.M., for his valuable assistance, and to the printers for their courtesy and cooperation.

Last, but not least, I must gratefully acknowledge the timely help from U Ba Than and Daw Tin Tin, of Rangoon, who have voluntarily and so generously undertaken to meet the cost of publication of one thousand copies of the book, which but for their kind suggestion, would not have materialised in this form.

Sayādaw U Nyāna
Masoyein Monastery,
Mandalay West, Burma
February, 1935

The Buddhist Philosophy of Relations

The Exposition of Relations (*Paccayattha Dīpanī*)

1. *Hetu-paccaya*: The Relation by Way of Root

What is the *hetu*-relation? It is greed (*lobha*), hate (*dosa*), delusion (*moha*), and their respective opposites: non-greed or dispassionateness (*alobha*), non-hate or amity (*adosa*) and non-delusion or intelligence (*amoha*). All are *hetu*-relations.

What are the things that are related by these *hetu*-relations? Those classes of mind and of mental qualities that are in co-existence along with greed, hate, delusion, dispassionateness, amity and intelligence, as well as the groups of material qualities which co-exist with the same—these are the things that are so related. All these are called *hetu-paccayuppanna-dhamma,* since they arise or come into existence by virtue of the *hetu*-relation.

In the above exposition, by "the groups of material qualities which co-exist with the same" are meant the material qualities produced by *kamma* at the initial moment of the *hetu*-conditioned conception of a new being, as well as such material qualities as may be produced by the *hetu*-conditioned mind during the lifetime. Here by "the moment of conception" is meant the nascent instant of the rebirth-conception, and by "the lifetime" is meant the period starting from the static instant of the rebirth conception right on to the moment of the dying-thought.

In what sense is *hetu* to be understood? And in what sense *paccaya*? *Hetu* is to be understood in the sense of root (*mūlattha*); and *paccaya* in the sense of assisting in (*upakārattha*) the arising, or the coming to be, of the *paccayuppanna-dhamma* of these two; the first is the state of being a root pertaining to the root greed and so on, as shown in the *Mūla-yamaka*. We have illustrated this point in the *Mūlayamaka Dīpanī* by the simile of a tree. However, we shall deal with it here again.

Suppose a man is in love with a woman. Now, so long as he does not dispel the lustful thought, all his acts, words and thoughts regarding this woman will be cooperating with lust (or greed), which at the same time has also under its control the material qualities produced by the same thought. We see then that all these states of mental and material qualities have their root in lustful greed for that woman. Hence, by being a *hetu* (for it acts as a root) and by being a *paccaya* (for it assists in the arising of those states of mind and body) greed is *hetu-paccaya*. The rest may be explained and understood in the same manner—i.e. the arising of greed by way of desire for desirable things; the arising of hate by way of antipathy against hateful things; and the arising of delusion by way of lack of knowledge respecting dull things.

Take a tree as an illustration. We see that the roots of a tree, having firmly established themselves in the ground, draw up sap from the soil and water, and carry that sap right up to the crown of the tree; thus the tree develops and grows for a long time. In the same way, greed, having firmly established itself in desirable things, draws up the essence of pleasure and enjoyment from them and conveys that essence to the concomitant mental elements, till they burst into immoral acts and words. That is to say, greed brings about transgression as regards moral acts and words. The same is to be said of hate, which by way of aversion draws up the essence of displeasure and discomfort, and also of delusion, which by way of lack of knowledge nurtures the growth of the essence of vain thought on many an object.

Transporting the essence thus, the three elements—greed, hate, and delusion—operate upon the component parts, so that they become happy (so to speak) and joyful at the desirable objects, etc. The component parts also become as they are operated upon, while the co-existent material qualities share the same effect. Here, from the words "it conveys that essence to the concomitant mental elements," it is to be understood that greed transports the essence of pleasure and enjoyment to the concomitant elements.

Coming now to the bright side—suppose the man sees danger in sensual pleasure and gives up that lustful thought for the woman. In doing so, dispassionateness (*alobha*) as regards her arises in him. Before this, there took place impure acts, words and thoughts having delusion (*moha*) as their root, but for the time being these are no longer present and in their place there arise pure acts, words and thoughts having their root in dispassionateness. Moreover, renunciation, self-control, *jhāna*-exercise or higher ecstatic thoughts also come into being. Dispassionateness, therefore, is known as *hetu-paccaya;* it being *a hetu* because it acts as a root, while it is a *paccaya* because it assists in the arising of the concomitants. The same explanation applies to the remainder of dispassionateness and also to amity and intelligence, which three are the opposites of greed, hate and delusion respectively.

Here, just as the root of the tree stimulates the whole stem and its parts, so it is with non-greed. It dispels the desire for desirable things and having promoted the growth of the essence of pleasure void of greed, it nurtures the concomitant elements with that essence till they become so happy and joyful that they even reach the height of *jhānic* path, or fruition-pleasure. Similarly, amity and intelligence respectively dispel hate and delusion with regard to hateful and dull or delusive things, and promote the growth of the essence of pleasure void of hate and delusion. Thus the operation of the three elements (*alobha, adosa* and *amoha*) lasts for a long time, making their mental concomitants happy and joyful. The concomitant elements also become as they are operated upon, while the co-existent groups of material qualities are affected in the same way.

Here the word *lobha-viveka-sukha-rasa* is a compound of the words *lobha, viveka, sukha* and *rasa. Viveka* is the state of being absent. *Lobha-viveka* is that which is absent from greed, or the absence of greed. *Lobha-viveka-sukha* is the pleasure which arises from the absence of greed. Hence the whole compound is defined thus: *Lobha-viveka-sukha-rasa* is the essence of pleasure derived from the absence of greed.

What has just been expounded is the Law of Paṭṭhāna in the Abhidhamma. Turning to the Law of Suttanta, the two elements of delusion and greed, which are respectively termed nescience (*avijjā*) and craving (*taṇhā*), are the sole roots of all the three rounds of misery.[2] Hate, being the incidental consequence of

2. The three rounds of misery are: the round of defilements (*kilesa-vaṭṭa*), the round of *kamma* (*kamma-vaṭṭa*) and the round of *kamma*-result (*vipāka-vaṭṭa*), See *The Path of Purification* (*Visuddhimagga*), tr. Ñāṇamoli, Ch. XVII, para 298.

greed, is only a root of evil. The two elements of intelligence and dispassionateness, which are respectively termed wisdom and the element of renunciation, are the sole roots for the dissolution of the rounds of misery. Amity, being the incidental consequence of non-greed, is only a root of good. Thus the six roots become the causes of all the states of mind and body, which are either co-existent or non-co-existent. Now, what has been said is the Law of Suttanta.

End of the Hetu-relation.

2. *Ārammaṇa-paccaya*: The Relation of Object

What is the *ārammaṇa*-relation? All classes of consciousness, all states of mental concomitants, all kinds of material qualities, all phases of Nibbāna, all terms expressive of concepts, are *ārammaṇa*-relations. There is, in fact, not a single thing (*dhamma*) which does not become an object of mind and of the mental elements. Stated concisely, objects are of six different kinds: visible object, audible object, odorous object, taste object, tangible object and cognizable object.

Which are those things that are related by the *ārammaṇa*-relations? All classes of mind and their concomitants are the things that are related by the *ārammaṇa*-relations. There is indeed not a single class of consciousness that can exist without its having an existing (*bhūtena*) or non-existing (*abhūtena*) object (*bhūtena* and *abhūtena* may also be rendered here as "real" and "unreal," or as "present" and "non-present," respectively).

Here the present visible object is the *ārammaṇa-paccaya*, and is causally related to the two classes, good and bad, of consciousness of sight. Similarly, the present audible object is causally related to the two classes of consciousness of sound; the present odorous object to the two classes of consciousness of smell; the present taste object to the two classes of consciousness of taste; the present three classes of tangible object to the two classes of consciousness of touch; and the present five objects of sense to the three classes of consciousness known as the triple element of apprehension.[3] All

3. The triple element of apprehension is the threefold mind-element

these five objects of sense—present, past or future—and all objects of thought present, past, future or outside time are *ārammaṇa-paccaya* and are causally related, severally, to the seventy-six classes of consciousness known as mind-cognitions (or elements of comprehension).[4]

In what sense is *ārammaṇa* or "object" to be understood, and in what sense *paccaya*? *Ārammaṇa* is to be understood in the sense of *ālambitabba*, which means that which is held or hung upon, so to speak, by mind and mental elements. *Paccaya* is to be understood in the sense of *upakāraka*, which means that which assists or renders help (in the arising of *paccayuppanna-dhamma*).[5]

Concerning the word *ālambitabba*, the function of the *ālambana* of minds and their mental factors is to take hold of or to attach to the object. For instance, there is in this physical world a kind of metal which receives its name of *ayokantaka* (literally, "iron-desire"), lodestone, on account of its apparent desire for iron. When it gets near a lump of iron, it shakes itself as though desiring it. Moreover, it moves itself forward and attaches itself firmly to the iron. In other cases, it attracts the iron, and so the iron shakes itself, approaches the lodestone, and attaches itself firmly to it. Here we see the power of the lodestone, which may be taken as a striking representation of the *ālambana* of mind and the mental factors.

The mind and its concomitants not only attach themselves to objects, but at the stage of their coming into existence within a personal entity, rise and cease every moment while the objects remain present at the avenues of the six doors.[6] Thus the rising

---

(*mano-dhātu*); the consciousness which adverts to the five sense objects (*pañca-dvārāvajjana*), and the two which receive them (*sampaṭicchana*) by way of wholesome-result or unwholesome-result.

4. *Mano-viññāṇa-dhātu*: this includes all classes of consciousness dealt with in the Abhidhamma except the ten kinds of sense-consciousness and the threefold mind-element.

5. In this relation, *paccaya* is generally known as *ārammaṇa* = "hanger" (as a pot-hook) = "object"; and *paccayuppannā* is known as *ārammaṇika* = "hanger-on" = "subject." (Translator.)

6. The six doors of the senses—mind, in Buddhist philosophy, being the sixth sense.

and ceasing is just like that of the sound of a gong, which is produced only at each moment we strike its surface, followed by immediate silence. It is also like that of the sound of a violin, which is produced only while we move the bow over its strings and then immediately ceases.

To a sleeping man, while the life continua are flowing (in the stream of thought), *kamma*, the sign of *kamma* and the sign of the destiny awaiting him in the succeeding life—which had distinctly entered the avenues of the six doors at the time of approaching death in the preceding existence—are *ārammaṇa*-relations, and are causally related to (the nineteen classes of) consciousness known as the life-continuum (*bhavaṅga*).

End of the Ārammaṇa-relation.

3. *Adhipati-paccaya*: The Relation of Dominance

The relation of dominance is of two kinds: objective dominance and co-existent dominance. Of these two, what is the relation of objective dominance? Among the objects dealt with in the section on the *ārammaṇa*-relation, some objects are most agreeable, most lovable, most pleasing and most esteemed. Such objects exhibit the relation of objective dominance. Objects may, naturally, be either agreeable or disagreeable, but only the most agreeable objects—those objects most highly esteemed by this or that person—exhibit this relation. Excepting the two classes of consciousness rooted in aversion,[7] the two classes of consciousness rooted in ignorance and the tactual consciousness accompanied by pain, together with the concomitants of all these, it may be shown, analytically, that all the remaining classes of *kāma*-consciousness, *rūpa*-consciousness, *arūpa*-consciousness and transcendental consciousness,[8] together with all their respective concomitants and all the most agreeable material qualities, exhibit the causal relation of objective dominance.

---

7. Unprepared (spontaneous—*asaṅkhārika*) and prepared (prompted—*sasaṅkhārika*).

8. Sense-sphere consciousness, fine-material consciousness, immaterial consciousness and supramundane consciousness.

Of these, sense-objects are said to exhibit the causal relation of objective dominance only when they are highly regarded, otherwise they do not. But those who reach the *jhāna* stages are never lacking in high esteem for the sublime *jhānas* they have obtained. Ariyan disciples also never fail in their great regard for the transcendental states[9] they have obtained and enjoyed.

What are the things that are related by this relation? The eight classes of consciousness rooted in greed (*lobha*), the eight classes of *kāmaloka* moral consciousness, the four classes of inoperative *kāmaloka* consciousness connected with knowledge, and the eight classes of transcendental consciousness—these are the things related by this relation. Here the six mundane objects[10] are causally related to the eight classes of consciousness rooted in greed. The seventeen classes of mundane moral consciousness are related to the four classes of moral *kāma*-consciousness disconnected from knowledge. The first three pairs of the path and fruit and Nibbāna, together with all those classes of mundane moral consciousness, are related to the four classes of moral *kāma*-consciousness connected with knowledge. The highest—the fourth stage of the path and fruit of Arahantship—together with Nibbāna are related to the four classes of inoperative *kāma*-consciousness connected with knowledge. And Nibbāna is related to the eight classes of transcendental consciousness.

In what sense is *ārammaṇa* to be understood, and in what sense *adhipati*? *Ārammaṇa* is to be understood in the sense of *ālambitabba* (see *ārammaṇa-paccaya*) and *adhipati* in the sense of dominance. Then what is dominance? Dominance is the potency of objects to control those states of mind and mental qualities by which they are highly regarded. It is to be understood that the relating things (*paccaya-dhamma*) of *ārammaṇādhipati* resemble the overlords, while the related things (*paccayuppanna-dhamma*) resemble the thralls in human society.

In the Sutasoma Jātaka, Porisāda the king, owing to his extreme delight in human flesh, abandoned his kingdom solely for

---

9. Supramundane states (*lokuttara-dhamma*) are here meant, i.e. the four pairs made up of the four stages of the path with the fruit and Nibbāna. (Translator)

10. Sights, sounds, odours, savours, contacts, ideas.

the sake of the taste of human flesh and lived a wanderer's life in the forest. Here the savour of human flesh is the *paccaya-dhamma* of *ārammaṇādhipati* and King Porisāda's consciousness rooted in greed is the *paccayuppana-dhamma.*

And again, King Sutasoma, having a very high regard for Truth[11] forsook his sovereignty, all his royal family and even his life for the sake of Truth, and went to throw himself into the hands of king Porisāda. In this case, Truth is the *paccaya-dhamma* and King Sutasoma's moral consciousness is the *paccayuppanna-dhamma.* Thus must we understand all objects of sense to which great regard is attached.

What is the relation of co-existent dominance? Intention or desire-to-do, mind[12] or will, energy or effort, and reason or investigation, which have arrived at the dominant state, belong to this relation.

What are the things related by this relation? Classes of mind and of mental qualities which are adjuncts of the dominants, and material qualities produced by dominant thoughts, are the things related by this relation.

In what sense is co-existent (*sahajāta*) to be understood, and in what sense dominance (*adhipati*)? Co-existent is to be understood in the sense of "co-producing," and dominance in the sense of "overpowering." Here, a phenomenon, when it appears, does not appear alone, but simultaneously causes its adjuncts to appear. Such a causal activity of the phenomenon is termed the co-producing. And the term "overpowering" means overcoming. For instance, King Cakkavatti, by his own power or merit, overcomes and becomes lord of the inhabitants of the whole continent, whom he can lead according to his own will. They also become according as they are led. In like manner, those four influences which have arrived at the dominant stage become lords of their adjuncts, which they lead according to their will in each of their respective functions. The adjuncts also follow according as they

11. Truth here means the sincerity of the promise he had given. (Translator)

12. Mind here refers to one of the apperceptions which are usually fifty-five in all, but in this connection we must exclude the two classes of deluded consciousness as well as aesthetic pleasure. The other three dominants are their own concomitants. (Translator)

are led. To take another example, in each of these masses—earth, water, fire and air—we see that the four elements—extension, cohesion, heat and motion—are respectively predominant, and each has supremacy over the other three components and makes them conform to its own intrinsic nature.[13] The other three members of the group of four elements also have to follow after the nature of the predominant element. In the same way, these four dominants, which have arrived at the dominant stage through their power, make the adjuncts conform to their own intrinsic nature. And their adjuncts also have to follow after the nature of the dominants. Such is the meaning of overpowering.

Here some might say: "If these things, leaving out intention, are to be called dominants on account of their overcoming the adjuncts, greed also ought to be called a dominant, for obviously it possesses a more overwhelming power over the adjuncts than intention." But to this we may reply, "Greed is indeed more powerful than intention, but only with ordinary unintelligent men. With the wise, intention is more powerful than greed in overwhelming the adjuncts. If it is assumed that greed is more powerful, then how could people, who are in the hands of greed, give up the repletion of their happy existence and wealth, carry out the methods of renunciation, and escape from the circle of misery? But because intention is more powerful than greed, those people who are in the hands of greed are able to give up the repletion of happy existence and wealth, fulfill the means of renunciation and escape from the circle of misery. Hence intention is a true dominant, and not greed." The like should be borne in mind—in the same fashion—when intention is contrasted with hate, and so forth.

Let us explain this more clearly. When there arise great and difficult manly enterprises, the accomplishment of such enterprises necessitates the arising of these four dominants. How? When ill-intentioned people encounter any such enterprise, their intention recedes. They are not willing to undertake it. They leave it having no inclination for it, and even say, "The task is not within the

13. In no mass of earth, water, fire or air do these "elements" exist in a state of absolute purity. The other "elements" are always present, but in a very subordinate proportion.

range of our ability." As to well-intentioned people, their intention becomes full of spirit at the sight of such a great enterprise. They are very willing to undertake it. They make up their minds to accomplish the task saying, "This has been set within the orbit of our ability." A person of this type is so persuaded by his intention that he is unable to give up the enterprise during the course of his undertaking, so long as it is not yet accomplished. And since this is the case the task will someday arrive at its full accomplishment even though it may be a very great one.

Now let us turn to the case of men of the indolent class. When they come face to face with such a great task they at once shrink from it. They shrink from it because they foresee that they will have to go through great hardships and also undergo bodily and mental pain if they wish to accomplish it. As to the industrious man, he becomes filled with energy at the sight of it and wishes to set himself to it. He goes on through thick and thin with the performance of the task for any length of time. He never turns back from his exertions nor does he become disappointed. What he only thinks about is that such a great task cannot be accomplished without unswerving efforts every day and every night. And this being the case, the great task will certainly reach its end one day.

Let us take the case of the feeble-minded. They also turn away when they see such a great task. They will certainly never think of it again. But it is quite different with the strong-minded person. When he sees such a task he becomes highly interested in it. He is quite unable to dispel the thought of it. He is all the time wrapped up in thoughts about the task, and at its bidding sets himself to it for a long time, enduring all kinds of bodily and mental pain. The remainder should hereafter be explained in the same manner as the dominant intention above.

Again, a few words about unintelligent men: When they are confronted with such a task, they become blinded. They know not how to begin, nor how to go on with the work, nor how to bring it to its end. They feel as if they had entered the dark where not a single light of inclination towards its performance has been set up to guide them. On the other hand—to take the more intelligent case—when a person of this type has to tackle such a great task he feels as if he were lifted up to the summit of his intellect, whereupon he discerns whence to start and whither to end. He also knows what advantage and blessing will accrue to him from its performance. He invents many devices for its easy accomplishment. He continues on with the work for a long time, and so on and so forth. The rest should be explained in the same manner as the dominant effort—only inserting the words "with an enormous amount of investigation" in place of "unswerving efforts."

Thus, when there arise great and difficult manly enterprises, these four dominants become predominant among the means of their accomplishment. Owing to the existence of these four dominants, there exist distinguished or dignified persons (personages) such as the Omniscient Buddhas, the Pacceka Buddhas,[14] the most eminent disciples, the great disciples and the ordinary disciples. Owing to the appearance of such personages, there also appear, for the general prosperity and welfare of mankind, numerous arts and sciences, as well as general articles of furniture to suit and serve human needs and wants under the canopy of civilization.

End of the Adhipati-relation.

4. *Anantara-paccaya*: The Relation of Contiguity

What is the *anantara-paccaya*? All classes of consciousness and their mental concomitants which have just ceased (in the immediately preceding instant) are *anantara-paccaya*. Which are those that are related by this *paccaya*? All classes of consciousness and their mental concomitants which have just arisen (in the immediately succeeding instant) are related by this *paccaya*.

In one existence of a being, the rebirth-consciousness is related to the first life-continuum (*bhavaṅga*) by way of contiguity, and the first life-continuum is again so related to the second life-continuum, and so on with the rest.

Now with reference to the text, "When the second immoral consciousness arises to the Pure (those of Pure Abodes, i.e. *suddhāvāsa*), etc." which is expounded in the Dhamma-Yamaka, the ninth chapter of the Sixth Book of Abhidhamma, we understand that as he becomes aware of his new body, the first process of

14. That is, those who attain Nibbāna unaided.

thought which occurs to a being in his new life is the process of immoral thought accompanied by a strong desire to live the new life, with the idea, "This is mine; this am I; this is myself." When this process is about to occur, the life-continuum vibrates first for two moments. Next comes the mind-door apprehension, and then follows a series of seven apperceptives (*javana*), accompanied by a strong desire to live the new life. Thereafter, life continua begin to flow again. In fact, this being[15] does not know anything of his present new life he lives, reflecting on what he had experienced in the previous existence. The basis of mind, however, is too weak, so that the object also cannot be clearly reflected. The object being thus indistinct, there generally arise only such classes of consciousness as are conjoined with perplexity.

After two months or so from the time of impregnation, during which period the individual is gradually developing, the controlling powers of the eyes, ears, etc. complete their full development. But there being no light, and so on, in the womb of the mother, the four classes of cognition—visual, auditory, and so on—do not arise. Only the tactile cognition and the mind-cognition arise. The child suffers much pain and distress at every change of the mother's bodily posture, and much more so while he is being born. Ever after he has come into the outer world, he has to lie very feebly on his back until the delicate body becomes strong enough (lit. reaches the state of maturity) to bear itself. During this period, he cannot cognize present objects, but his mind generally turns towards the objects of his previous existence. If he comes from the hell world, he generally presents an unpleasant face, for he still feels what he had experienced in the hell world. If he comes from the abode of *devas*, his pleasant face not only shines with smiles, but in its joyous expression of laughter, he shows his happiness at some thought of the objects of the *deva* world.

Furthermore, the members of his body steadily become stronger, and his sense-impressions clearer. So he is soon able to play joyfully in his own dear little ways. A happy life is thus begun for him, and he begins to take an interest in his new life. He takes to and imitates his mother's speech. He prattles with her. Thus his senses almost entirely turn to the present world, and all

15. Ledi Sayādaw here seems to explain the life term of a womb-born being.

his recollections of the previous life fade away. That is to say, he forgets his previous existence.

Do all beings forget their previous existences only at this period of life? No, not all beings. Some who are very much oppressed with the pain of conception forget their previous existences during the period of pregnancy, some at the time of birth, some at the aforesaid period, some during the period of youth, and some in old age. Some extraordinary men do not forget for the whole of their lifetime, and there are even some who are able to recollect two or three previous existences. They are called *jātissara-satta*, beings gifted with the memory of their previous existences.

Now, to return to our subject: Though the six-door processes of thought begin to work after the child has been born, yet the six-door processes work themselves out in full action only when the child is able to take up present objects. Thus, in every process of thought, every preceding consciousness that has just ceased is related to every succeeding consciousness that has immediately arisen, by way of contiguity. And this relation of contiguity prevails throughout the whole span of the recurring existences of an individual, right from the untraceable beginning, with unbroken continuity. But only after he has attained the path of Arahantship and has entered the *khandha-parinibbāna* (i.e. the final extinction of the five aggregates) does this continuum break, or more strictly speaking, cease forever.

Why is *anantara* so called, and why *paccaya*? *Anantara* is so called because it causes such states of phenomena as are "similar to itself" to succeed in the immediately following instant. *Paccaya* is so called because it renders help. In the phrase similar to itself, the word "similar" is meant to express similarity in respect of having the faculty of being conscious of an object. And *sārammaṇa* means a phenomenon which does not occur without the presence of an object. So it has been rendered as "similar in respect of having the faculty of being conscious of an object."

Also the above explanation expresses the following meaning: Though the preceding thought ceases, the faculty of consciousness does not become extinct until it has caused the succeeding thought to arise.

Here it should be borne in mind that the series of *paccaya-dhamma* of this relation resembles a series of preceding mothers, and the series of *paccayuppanna-dhamma* resembles a series of succeeding daughters. This being so, the last dying thought of an Arahant should also cause the arising of a rebirth-consciousness. But it does not do so, for at the close of the evolution of existence all activities of volitions and defilements (*kamma-kilesa*) have entirely ceased, and the last dying-thought has reached the final, ultimate quiescence.

End of the Anantara-relation.

5. *Samanantara-paccaya*: The Relation of Immediate Contiguity

The classification of the *paccaya-dhamma* and *paccayuppanna-dhamma* of this relation is the same as those of the *anantara-paccaya*.

In what sense is *samanantara* to be understood? *Samanantara* is to be understood in the sense of "thorough immediateness." How? In a stone pillar, though the groups of matter therein seem to unite into one mass, they are not without the material quality of limitation or space which intervenes between them, for matter is substantial and formative. That is to say, there exists an element of space, called mediacy or cavity, between any two units of matter. But it is not so with immaterial qualities. There does not exist any space, mediacy or cavity between the two consecutive groups of mind and mental concomitants. That is to say, those groups of mind and mental concomitants are entirely without any mediacy, because the mental state is not substantial and formative. The mediacy between two consecutive groups of mind and mental concomitants is also not known to the world. So it is thought that mind is permanent, stable, stationary, and immutable. Hence, *samanantara* is to be understood in the sense of "thorough immediateness."

Anantarattha has also been explained in the foregoing relation as *attano anantare attasadisassa dhammantarassa uppādanatthena* that is because it causes such states of phenomena as are similar to itself to succeed in the immediately following instant. This being so, some such suggestion as follows might be put forward. At the time of sustained cessation (*nirodhasamāpatti*),[16] the preceding

16. *Nirodha-samāpatti* has been rendered as "sustained cessation." Here the

consciousness is that of neither-consciousness-nor-unconsciousness, and the succeeding consciousness is that of the ariyan fruit. Between these two classes of consciousness, the total suspension of thought occurs either for one day, or for two, or three ... or even for seven days. Also in the abode of unconscious beings, the preceding consciousness is that of decease (*cuticitta*, the dying-thought) from the previous *kāmaloka*; and the succeeding one is that of rebirth (*paṭisandhicitta*) in the following *kāmaloka*. Between these two classes of consciousness, the total suspension of thought of the unconscious being occurs for the whole term of life amounting to five hundred *kappas* or great aeons.

Hence, is it not correct to say that the two classes of preceding consciousness are without the faculty of causing to arise something similar to themselves in the immediately following instant? The reply to this is: No, they are not without this faculty. The faculty has only been retarded in its operation for a certain extended period, through certain highly cultivated contemplations and resolutions. When the preceding thoughts cease, they cease together with the power, which they possess, of causing something to arise similar to themselves. And the succeeding thoughts, being unable to arise in continuity at that immediate instant, arise only after the lapse of the aforesaid extent of time. It cannot be rightly maintained that the preceding thoughts do not possess the faculty of causing to arise something similar to themselves, or that they are not *anantara*-relations only because of a suspension of operation of the faculty. For we do not say that a king has no armies when they are not actually in a battle or in the very act of fighting, or while they are roaming about not being required to fight by the king, who at such time may say, "My men, it is not the proper time for you yet to fight. But you shall fight at such and such a time." We do not then say that they are not armies or that they have no fighting qualities. In precisely the same way, the relation between the two aforesaid preceding thoughts is to be understood.

Here some might say, "It has just been said in this relation that both the relating and the related things, being incorporeal qualities having no form whatever and having nothing to do with

cessation is that not only of consciousness but also of mental concomitants and mental qualities born of mind. (Translator) any material quality of limitation (space) intervening between, are entirely without mediacy or cavity. If this be so, how shall we believe the occurrence at every moment of the arising and ceasing of consciousness, which has been explained in the *ārammaṇa-paccaya* by the illustration of the sound of a gong and of a violin?" We may answer this question by asserting the fact, which is quite obvious in the mental world, that the various classes of consciousness are in a state of continual flux, i.e. in a continuous succession of change. It has also been explained, in detail, in the essays on Citta Yamaka.[17]

End of the Samanantara-relation.

6. *Sahajāta-paccaya*: The Relation of Co-Existence

The classifications of the *paccaya* and *paccayuppanna-dhamma* of this relation will now be dealt with. All co-existent classes of consciousness and their mental concomitants are each mutually termed *paccaya* and *paccayuppanna-dhamma*. So also are the mental aggregates of rebirth and the physical basis of mind which co-exists with rebirth; and so also are the Great Essentials mutually among themselves. All the material qualities born of *kamma* at the moment of rebirth, and all the material qualities which are born of mind during life at the nascent instant of each momentary state of consciousness which is capable of producing material quality, are merely termed the *paccayuppanna-dhamma*, of that co-existent conscious-ness. All the material qualities derived from the Great Essentials are, however, termed the *paccayuppanna-dhamma* of the Great Essentials or the four Great Primary Elements (*mahābhūta*)—earth, water, fire and air, representing the properties of extension, cohesion, heat, and motion.

In what sense is *sahajāta* to be understood, and in what sense *paccaya*? *Sahajāta* is to be understood in the sense of co-existence,

17. Perhaps these are in the Sayādaw's *Yamaka-puccha-visajjana* or in *London Pāḷi Devī Visajjana Pāḷi* (which might be identical with the former). The latter consists of answers to questions by Mrs. C.A.F. Rhys-Davids about knotty points, etc., in the Yamaka and was published in the article "Some Points in Buddhist Doctrine" and "A Pali Dissertation on the Yamaka" in the *Journal of the Pali Text Society,* 1913–14 and also in an appendix to Mrs. Rhys-Davids' translation of the Yamaka. (BPS Ed.)

and *paccaya* in the sense of rendering help. Here, co-existence means that when a phenomenon arises, it arises together with its effect; or, in other words, it also causes its effect to arise simultaneously. Such is the meaning of co-existence implied here. For example, when the sun rises, it rises together with its heat and light. And when a candle is burning, it burns together with its heat and light. So also, this relating thing, in arising, arises together with related things. In the above example, the sun is like each of the mental states; the sun's heat is like the co-existing mental states; and the sun's light is like the co-existing material qualities. Similarly, the sun is like each of the Great Essentials, its heat like the co-existing Great Essentials, and its light like the co-existing material qualities derived from them. In the example of the candle, it should be understood in a similar way.

End of the Sahajāta-relation.

7. *Aññamañña-paccaya*: The Relation of Reciprocity

What has been spoken of as the *paccaya-dhamma* in the classifications of the relation of co-existence is here (in this relation) the *paccaya* as well as the *paccayuppanna-dhamma*. All states of consciousness and their mental concomitants are, reciprocally, the *paccaya* and the *paccayuppanna-dhamma*; so are the co-existing Great Essentials; so are the mental aggregates of rebirth; and so is the basis of mind or heart-base, which co-exists with the mental aggregates of rebirth.

As to the sense implied here, it is easy to understand. However, an illustration will not be uninteresting. When three sticks are set upright leaning against one another at their upper ends, each of them depends on, and is depended on by, the other two. As long as one of them remains in such an upright position, so long will all remain in the same position. And, if one of them falls, all will fall at the same time. Exactly so should this relation of reciprocity be understood.

Here, if any one should assert that the mental properties are not able to arise without consciousness rendering them service as their base, we would acknowledge that this is so. Why? Because the function of knowing is predominant among the functions of contact, and so forth, of the mental properties, and in the

Dhammapada as expounded by the Omniscient Buddha, "mind is predominant" (*manopubbaṅgamā dhamma*, etc.). And again if anyone holds that consciousness also is not able to arise without the mental properties as a correlative, we will support this view. For the mental properties are concomitant factors of consciousness; therefore, consciousness also is not able to arise without its accompanying mental properties. In a similar way are the four Great Essentials to be understood. But the material qualities derived from them should not be counted as concomitant factors, for they are only derivatives. Then are the material qualities of life and those born of food not concomitant factors, seeing that they can exercise, individually, the causal relation of control and that of food? No, they are not. They may be taken as concomitant factors only when the development is in full swing, but not when things are only at the state of genesis. In this relation of reciprocity, the arising of concomitants at the stage of genesis is a necessary factor.

End of the Aññamañña-relation.

8. *Nissaya-paccaya*: The Relation of Dependence

The relation of dependence is of three kinds: co-existent dependence, basic pre-existent dependence, and basic objective pre-existent dependence.

Of these, what is the relation of co-existent dependence? The relation of co-existent dependence embraces all those that are already comprised in the relation of co-existence. Hence the classifications of relation and related things ought here to be understood in the same way as those that have already been set out in the section on the relation of co-existence.

And what is the relation of basic pre-existent dependence? There are six bases—eye, ear, nose, tongue, body and heart. These six bases, during life, are causally related, by way of basic pre-existent dependence, to the seven elements of cognition. The material base itself pre-exists and serves as a standing ground or substratum, and it is therefore called "basic pre-existent dependence." Here "basic" is so called because of its being a standing ground or substratum for mind and mental properties. "To pre-exist" means to exist beforehand—one thought-moment earlier than its related thing.

Here the rebirth consciousness arises in dependence upon the heart-base[18] that co-exists with it, for there is no pre-existent physical base at that moment. And the first life-continuum arises in dependence upon the same heart-base which co-exists with the rebirth-consciousness. The second life-continuum arises also in dependence upon the heart-base which co-exists with the first life-continuum, and so on with the rest, that is, the third life-continuum arises in dependence upon the heart-base that co-exists with the second life-continuum, and so on and on, until comes the moment of death. Thus should be understood the basic pre-existent dependence which relates to the two elements of cognition, the element of apprehension and the element of comprehension.

Just as a violin sounds only when the violin-bow moves across its strings, and not otherwise, so also the five senses awaken only when the five kinds of sense-objects enter the five avenues known as five bases, and not otherwise.

The impression is possible only at the static period of the object and of the base. On account of the impression, the life-continuum vibrates for two moments; and, on account of the vibration of the life-continuum, apprehension occurs. On account of apprehension, the five sense-cognitions are able to arise. Therefore, the five sense-bases (eye, ear, etc.) which have arisen at the nascent instant of the past sub-consciousness, are the basic pre-existent dependence of the five elements of sense-cognition.

Now, at the time of death all the six bases come into being only at the nascent instant of the seventeenth sub-consciousness, reckoned backward from the dying-consciousness. No new bases occur after that seventeenth sub-consciousness. So, at the time of death, all subconsciousness, all six-door-process-cognitions and consciousness of decease arise in dependence upon these, their respective bases that came into being together with the seventeenth sub-consciousness which had arisen previously to them. This is the causal relation of basic pre-existent dependence.

What is the causal relation of basic objective pre-existent dependence? When one is reflecting and holding the view that "My mind locates itself in dependence upon matter which is

18. "Heart base" (*hadaya-vatthu*) is a figurative expression for the physical base of mental activities. It is not the physical heart that is meant. (Editor)

mine, or I, or myself," through craving, conceit, and error; or when one is reasoning or speculating thus: "My mind locates itself in dependence upon matter which is impermanent, ill, and no soul," there arise mind door cognitions, such as determining, and so forth. During that time, each of the material bases becomes the standing ground for, and also the object of, each of the mind door cognitions. Therefore, such and such a heart-base is causally related to such and such a consciousness and its concomitants, by way of basic objective pre-existent dependence. This is the causal relation of basic objective pre-existent dependence. Hence the relation of dependence is of three different kinds.

Here, the dependence by way of Suttanta should also be mentioned. We know that men, animals, trees, and so forth, stand or rest on the earth; the earth in turn, on the great mass of air; and the air, on the limitless, empty space underneath. We also know that men establish themselves in houses; bhikkhus in vihāras or monasteries; *devas* in celestial mansions; and so on with the whole universe. Thus should we understand that everything is causally related to something else by way of dependence.

End of Nissaya-relation.

9. *Upanissaya-Paccaya*: The Relation of Sufficing Condition

The relation of sufficing condition is of three kinds: objective sufficing condition, contiguous sufficing condition and natural sufficing condition. Of these three, the first is the same as objective dominance, and the second as contiguity.

What is natural sufficing condition? All past, present and future, internal and external, classes of consciousness together with their concomitants, all material qualities, Nibbāna and concepts (*paññatti*) are natural sufficing conditions, severally related, as the case may be, to all the present classes of consciousness and their concomitants.

Here, the Buddha who passed away and has entered Nibbāna, his Dhamma, the Fraternity of his sanctified disciples, and the successions of the recognized Fraternity, are causally related to us, of later generations, by way of natural sufficing condition for the cultivation of good. In the same way, our forefathers, in their respective capacities as parents, teachers, wise monks and brahmins, eminent philosophers, and powerful and august kings, are also causally related to the succeeding generations by way of natural sufficing condition, either for the cultivation of good or of evil, or for the experience of pleasure or of pain. For this reason they established or propounded various laws and sayings, moral and immoral, and also worldly institutions—both for the welfare and otherwise of the succeeding generations.

The future generations also follow their paths and adopt their customs by doing acts of charity, by observing the precepts, and so forth, by practicing the moral and social laws of the world, by adhering to various religious beliefs, by taking up various kinds of occupations, by studying various branches of arts and science, by governing hamlets, villages and towns, by being agriculturists in the field and on the farm, by digging lakes, ponds and wells, by building houses, by making carriages and carts, by building boats, steamers and ships, and by seeking for and accumulating wealth, such as silver, gold, precious, stones, pearls, and so forth and so on. Thus the world has developed unceasingly.

The future Buddha (Metteyya), his Dhamma and his Fraternity are natural sufficing conditions, being causally related to the present generation, for the acquirement of virtues and the gaining of merit. Supremacy, wealth, power, prosperity—which are to be gained in the future—are also natural sufficing conditions, related to the present generation for the putting forth of efforts of all sorts. The acquirement of happy existence and wealth and the attainment of path, fruition and Nibbāna, which are to be enjoyed in the future, are also natural sufficing conditions related to the present generation of men for the development of such forms of merit as charity, virtue and so on.

With the hope of reaping crops in winter, men till the soil and sow seeds in the rainy season, or they do various kinds of work which incur labour and intellect, with the hope of getting money upon their completion of the work. Now, the crops to be reaped and the money to be got, are future natural sufficing conditions, related to the acquisition of crops and money. In the same manner, most people in the present life do many good deeds, realizing that they will reap the fruits of their deeds in some life hereafter. In this case, the fruits which will be reaped in the future are future natural sufficing conditions, related to the deeds done in the present life. Deeds done before are also past natural sufficing conditions, related to the fruits which are to be reaped in the future. Thus we see that the future natural sufficing condition is as large and wide as the past.

The present Buddha, his Dhamma, and so on, are present natural sufficing conditions, being related to the present living men, *devas* and Brahmas, and so are living parents to living sons and daughters, and so on. The present natural sufficing condition is thus obvious and easy to understand.

Internal natural sufficing conditions are those that exist in an animate person, such as the Buddha, and so forth. External natural sufficing conditions are conditions, such as lands, mountains, rivers, oceans and so on, which serve as resting places for the existence of life (sentient beings); or such as forests, woods, trees, grasses, grains, beans and so forth; or such as the moon, the sun, the planets, the stars and so on; or such as rain, fire, wind, cold, heat, and so forth, which are useful and advantageous to life in one way or another. All these are the more powerful sufficing conditions, either for the accomplishment of good or for the spreading of evil, either for the enjoyment of pleasures or for the suffering of pains. Those with an earnest desire to enter Nibbāna in the present life work out the factors of enlightenment and those with an ardent hope to enter Nibbāna in the lives to come when Buddhas will appear, fulfil the perfections. Here, Nibbāna is the more powerful sufficing condition for the cultivation of these tasks.

A large variety of concepts or names-and-notions, commonly employed or found in the teachings of the Buddha, are also sufficing conditions for the understanding of many things.

In fact, all conditioned things here come to be only when there are present causes or conditions for the same, and not otherwise. And they stand only if there are present causes for their standing; otherwise they do not. Therefore, causes or conditions are needed for their arising as well as for their maintenance. However, Nibbāna and concepts are unconditioned things, without birth and genesis, everlasting and eternal. Therefore no causes are needed for their arising and maintenance.[19]

---

19. That is to say, Nibbāna and concepts (or more properly, concept-terms)

The moral is causally related to that which is moral by way of sufficing condition. A clear exposition of this is given in the Paṭṭhāna, where it is said: "Through faith one gives charity, observes the precepts, and so on." Similarly, the immoral is causally related to immoral—and unspecified or amoral[20] to amoral—by way of sufficing condition is made clear by these expositions: "Through lust one commits murder, theft and so on" and "Through suitable climate and food, one enjoys physical health and so forth." The moral is also causally related to that which is immoral by way of more powerful sufficing condition. This is to be understood from the following exposition: "One may give charity and thereupon exalt oneself and revile others. In the same manner, having observed the precepts, having attained concentration of mind, and having acquired learning, one may exalt oneself and belittle others."

The moral is also causally related to that which is amoral by way of more powerful sufficing condition. All good deeds done in the four planes (these four planes are the spheres of *kāma*, *rūpa*, *arūpa* and *lokuttara*), and all actions connected with doing good, are related, by way of more powerful sufficing condition, to amorals of the resultant kind, producible at a remote period. Those who practise for the perfection of charity suffer much physical and mental pain. Similarly, those who practise for such other perfections (*pāramitā*) as morality, abnegation, wisdom, perseverance, patience, sincerity, resolution, love, and resignation, suffer the same. It is likewise with those who practise the course of *jhāna* and *magga* (meditative absorption and the path).

---

do not enter time, and therefore are not subject to time's nature—change. They do not arise; therefore, they do not cease. They are "everlasting and eternal" in the sense of being extra temporal, not in the vulgar sense of being endlessly continuous in time. (Translator)

20. Here *abyākatā* is rendered as "unspecified or amoral." It is explained in the commentary as *kusala-akusala-bhāvena akathitā, añña-bhāvena kathitā*, i.e. not to be called either moral or immoral, but to be called "apart-from both," i.e. morally unspecified. The *abyākata dhammas* are all classes of resultant and inoperative consciousness and all material qualities, as well as Nibbāna. (Translator). Other suggested renderings: karmically indeterminate or karmically neutral. (Editor)

Immorals are also causally related, by way of more powerful sufficing condition, to morals. For instance, some on this earth, having done wrong, repent their deeds and better themselves to shun all such evil deeds, by cultivating such moral acts as engaging in charity, observing the precepts, practising *jhāna* and *magga*. Thus the evil deeds they have done are related, by way of stronger sufficing condition, to the moral acts they cultivate later.

Immorals are also causally related, by way of more powerful sufficing condition, to amorals. For instance, many people in this world, having been guilty of evil deeds, are destined to fall into one of the four planes of misery, and undergo the pains of suffering which prevail there. Even in the present life, some, through their own misdeeds or the misdeeds of others, have to bear a great deal of distress. Some, however, enjoy a large variety of pleasures with the money they earn by their misconduct. There are also many who suffer much on account of lust, hate, error, conceit, and so forth.

Amorals are also causally related by way of more powerful sufficing condition to morals. Having become possessed of great wealth, one engages in charity, practises for the perfection of good morals, fosters wisdom and practises the religious exercises in a suitable place, such as a monastery, a hollow place, a cave, a tree, a forest, a hill, or a village, where the climate is agreeable and food is available.

Amorals are also causally related by way of more powerful sufficing condition to immorals. Being equipped with eyes, many evils are born of sight within oneself. A similar explanation applies to our equipment with ears, etc., so also as regards hands, legs, swords, arms, etc. It is thus that sufficing condition is of three kinds.

Sufficing condition by way of Suttanta[21] may also be mentioned here. It is found in many such passages in the Piṭakas as, "through intercourse with virtuous friends," "through association with sinful companions," "by living in the village," "by dwelling in the forest," and so forth. In short, the five cosmic orders (*pañca-niyāma-dhammā*) are the stronger sufficing conditions relating to the three worlds—the animate world, the

21. That is, sufficing condition as set forth in the manner of the suttas or general discourses of the Buddha, as distinguished from the manner in which it is dealt with in the Abhidhamma section of the scriptures.

inanimate world, and the world of space—to go on unceasingly through aeons of time. This also has been expounded at length by us in the *Niyāma-dīpanī*.[22]

Why is *ārammaṇūpanissaya* so called? It is so called because the dominant object acts as a main basis for subjects (*ārammaṇika*).

Why is *anantarūpanissaya* so called? It is so called because the preceding consciousness acts as a main basis for the arising of its immediately succeeding consciousness. The preceding consciousness is just like the mother, and the succeeding one like the son. Here, just as the mother gives birth to the son, who owes his existence to her in particular, so also the preceding consciousness gives birth to the succeeding one, which owes its existence particularly to its predecessor.

Why is *pakatūpanissaya* so called? It is so called because it is naturally known to the wise as a distinct sufficing condition. Here, something further is required to be said. The influence of a sufficing condition in contiguity pervades only its immediate successor, but that of a natural sufficing condition can pervade many remote ones. Therefore, what in this present life has been seen, heard, smelt, tasted, touched and experienced in days, months, years, long gone by, takes form again at the mind door, even after a lapse of a hundred years, if a sufficient cause is available. And so people remember their past, and can utter such expressions as "I saw it before," "I heard it before," and so on. Those beings, whose birth is apparitional,[23] also remember their former existences; likewise, some among men, who are gifted with the memory of their former existences, can do so. If one out of a hundred thousand objects experienced before be met with afterwards, many or, it may be, all of them reappear in the process of thought.

End of the Upanissaya-relation.

---

22. *Niyāma-dīpanī* was written by the late Ven. Ledi Sayādaw and translated into English by Ven. U Nyāna and Dr. Barua.

23. Beings whose coming into existence takes place in any other mode than the ordinary one of birth from parents; what occidentals might call "supernatural beings" though not all of them are to be understood as superior to man in any vital respect. Many are inferior to man, in power and faculty, as well as in the opportunities open to them of winning Nibbāna. (Translator)

10. *Purejāta-paccaya*: The Relation of Pre-Existence

The relation of pre-existence is of three kinds: basic pre-existence, objective pre-existence, and basic objective pre-existence.

Of these, the first and the last have already been dealt with under the heading of *Nissaya* in the foregoing section on the *Nissaya*-relation.

Objective pre-existence is the name given to the present eighteen kinds of material qualities of the determined class (*nipphanna*). Of these, the present five objects (visible form, sound and so forth) are causally related, always by way of objective pre-existence, to those thoughts which are capable of taking part in the five-door processes. Just as the sound of the violin only arises when it is played with a bow, and the sounding necessitates the pre-existence of both the violin strings and the violin bow, so also those thoughts which take part in the five-door processes spring into being owing to the presentation of the five objects of sense at the five doors, which are no other than the five bases. The presentation is possible only when the door and the object are in their static stages.

Those five objects not only present themselves at the five doors of the five senses at that static period, but they also present themselves at the mind-door. On this account, the life-continuum vibrates for two moments, and then ceases; and the cessation of the life-continuum gives rise to a consciousness-series. This being so, the consciousness-series in any process cannot arise without the pre-existence of the objects and of the bases. The eighteen kinds of determined material qualities are either past, because they have ceased, or future, because they have not yet arisen, or present, inasmuch as they are still existing. All of them, without distinction, may be objects of the mind-door cognitions. But among them, only the present objects act as objective pre-existence. And if a thing in any distant place or concealed from sight, itself existing, becomes an object of mind, it also may be called a present object.

End of the Purejāta-relation.

11. *Pacchājāta-paccaya*: The Relation of Post-Existence

Every posterior consciousness that springs into being causally relates to the still existing group of prior corporeal qualities born of the four origins[24] (*kamma, citta, utu, āhāra*), by way of post-existence, in helping them to develop and thrive (*vuddhi-virūḷhiya*). For example, the rainwater that falls every subsequent year, renders service by way of post-existence to such vegetation as has grown up in previous years, in promoting its growth and development.

Here, by "every posterior consciousness" is meant all classes of consciousness beginning from the first life-continuum to the final dying-thought. And, by "prior corporeal qualities" is meant all corporeal qualities born of four origins starting from the group of material qualities born of *kamma*, which co-exist with the rebirth-conception.

The fifteen states of the life-continuum, starting serially from the first life-continuum which has arisen after the rebirth-conception, causally relate by way of post-existence to the group of material qualities born of *kamma*, which co-exist with the rebirth-conception. As to the rebirth-conception, it cannot be a causal relation by way of post-existence, for it co-exists with the group of corporeal qualities born of *kamma*. Similarly, the sixteenth life-continuum cannot become a causal relation by way of post-existence, for it comes into existence only when that group of material qualities reaches the stage of dissolution. Therefore, these are the fifteen states of the life-continuum which causally relate as above.

At the static moment of the rebirth-conception, there spring up two groups of material qualities, born of *kamma* and born of temperature,[25] and the same at the arrested moment. But at the nascent moment of the first life-continuum, three groups spring up: that born of *kamma*, that born of temperature, and that born of mind. When *oja* (the nutritive essence) of the food eaten spreads

24. Here, the origins of material qualities are meant. The four are *kamma*, mind, temperature and nutriment.

25. Here, *utu* (lit., season) has been rendered as temperature. It may also be rendered by popular acceptance as physical change, caloric energy, heat and cold etc.

all through the body, the corporeal nutritive essence absorbs the stimulant and produces a group of material qualities. From that time onward, the groups produced by the four origins spring up incessantly, like the flame of a burning lamp. Leaving out the nascent moment, so long as these groups stand at their static stage, every one of the posterior fifteen classes of consciousness renders them help by way of post-existence.

Vuddhi-virūḷhiya means "for the gradual development and progress of the series of corporeal qualities born of the four origins." Therefore, if they, the four kinds of corporeal groups, are repeatedly related by (lit., do repeatedly obtain) the causal relation of post-existence, then they leave behind them, when their physical life-term has expired, a powerful energy—an energy adequate to produce the development, progress and prosperity of the subsequent series of groups.

End of the Pacchājāta-relation.

12. *Āsevana-paccaya*: The Relation of Habitual Recurrence

The forty-seven kinds of mundane apperception (*javana*) comprising the twelve classes of immoral consciousness, the seventeen mundane classes of moral consciousness, and the eighteen classes of inoperative consciousness (obtained by excluding the two classes of consciousness called "turning towards," *āvajjana*, from the twenty) are here termed the causal relation of habitual recurrence. When any one of these arrives at the apperceptional process (i.e., the sequence of seven similar states of consciousness in a process of thought), every preceding apperception causally relates itself by way of habitual recurrence to every succeeding apperception. The related things, *paccayuppanna-dhamma*, comprise the succeeding apperceptions as stated above, as well as the four paths.

In what sense is the term *āsevana* to be understood? It is to be understood in the sense of habituating by constant repetition or of causing its *paccayuppanna-dhamma* to accept its inspiration, for them to gain greater and greater proficiency, energy and force. Here "proficiency" (*paguṇabhāva*) means the proficiency of the succeeding apperceptional thoughts in their apperceptive functions and stages, just as one who reads a lesson many times becomes more proficient with each new reading.

Parivāso literally means perfuming, or inspiring. Just as a silk cloth is perfumed with sweet scents, so also is the body of thought, so to speak, perfumed, or inspired, with lust, hate, and so forth; or with non-lust (*arajjana*), amity (*adussana*), and so on. Although the preceding apperception ceases, its apperceptional force does not cease, that is, its force pervades the succeeding thought. Therefore, every succeeding apperception, on coming into existence, becomes more vigorous on account of the habituation of the former. Thus the immediately preceding thought habituates or causes its immediate successor to accept its habituation. However, the process of habitual recurrence usually ceases at the seventh thought, after which either resultant thought-moments of retention follow, or subsidence into the life-continuum takes place.

Here, habitual recurrence, as dealt with in the Suttanta too, ought to be mentioned. Many passages are to be found in several parts of the Sutta Piṭaka. Such are: *satipaṭṭhānaṃ bhāveti*: one cultivates the earnest applications in mindfulness; *sammāppadhānaṃ bhāveti*: one cultivates the supreme effort; *sati-sambojjhaṅgaṃ bhāveti*: one cultivates mindfulness, a factor of enlightenment; *dhammavicaya-sambojjhaṅgaṃ bhāveti*: one cultivates the "investigation of truth," a factor of enlightenment; *sammādiṭṭhiṃ bhāveti*: one cultivates right view; *Sammāsaṅkappaṃ bhāveti*: one cultivates right aspiration and so on. In these passages, by *bhāveti* is meant to repeat the effort either for one day, or for seven days, or for one month, or for seven months, or for one year, or for seven years.

Moral and immoral actions, which have been repeatedly performed, cultivated or done many times in former existences causally relate by way of habitual recurrence to moral and immoral actions of the present existence for their greater improvement and worsening respectively. The relation which effects the improvement and the worsening, respectively, of such moral and immoral actions at some other distant time or in some future existence is called sufficing condition, but the one which effects this only during the apperceptional process is called habitual recurrence.

In this world, many incidental results or consequences are clearly seen to follow upon great achievements in art, science, literature and so forth, carried out continuously, repeatedly and incessantly in thought, word and deed.

As such a relation of habitual recurrence is found among all transient phenomena, strong zeal and effort, exerted for a long period of time, have developed to such a high degree that many great and difficult labours have reached complete accomplishment and even Buddhahood has been attained.

End of Āsevana-relation.

13. *Kamma-paccaya*: The Relation of Kamma

The relation of *kamma* is of two kinds: co-existent *kamma* and asynchronous *kamma*.

Of these two, all volitions, moral, immoral, and amoral, which consist of three time-phases, constitute the causal relation of co-existent *kamma*. Their related things are: all classes of consciousness and their mental concomitants in co-existence with volition, material qualities born of *kamma* which arise simultaneously with the rebirth, conception, and material qualities produced by mind during the term of life.

Past moral and immoral volitions constitute the causal relation of asynchronous *kamma*. Their related things are the thirty-seven classes of mundane resultant conscious-ness and their mental concomitants, and all the mental qualities born of *kamma*.

Why is *kamma* so called? It is so called on account of its peculiar function. This peculiar function is nothing but volition (or will) itself, and it dominates every action. When any action of thought, word, or body takes place, volition (or will) determines, fashions, or causes its concomitants to perform their respective functions simultaneously. For this reason, volition is said to be predominant in all actions. Thus *kamma* is so called on account of its peculiar function. Or, to define it in another way, *kamma* is that by which creatures do (or act). What do they do then? They do physical work, vocal work, and mental work. Here, by physical work is meant standing, sitting, and so forth; stepping forward and backward, and so on; and even the opening and the shutting of the eyelids. Vocal work means producing vocal sounds. Mental work means thinking wisely or badly, and, in short, the functions of seeing, hearing, and so forth, with the five senses. Thus all the actions of beings are determined by this volition. Therefore it is called *kamma*.

Sahajāta is that which comes into being simultaneously with its related things. *Sahajātakamma* is a co-existent thing as well as a *kamma*. *Sahajātakamma-paccaya* is a causal relation standing (to its effects) by way of co-existent *kamma*.

Nānākkhaṇika is a thing differing in point of time from its effects. That is to say, the time when the volition arises is one, and the time when its effects take place is another, or, in other words, the volition is asynchronous. Hence asynchronous volition is a volition that differs in point of time from its effects. So *nānākkhaṇika-kamma-paccaya* is a causal relation standing (to its effects) by way of asynchronous *kamma*. The volition which co-exists with the ariyan path, only at the moment of its ceasing, immediately produces its effect, and so it also is asynchronous.

Here, a moral volition such as predominates in charity, for instance, is causally related to its co-existent mind and mental qualities, together with the material qualities produced by the same mind, by way of co-existent *kamma*. It is also causally related, by way of asynchronous *kamma*, to the resultant aggregates of mind and material qualities born of that *kamma*, which will be brought into existence at a distant period in the future. Thus a volition, which is transmuted into a course of action entailing moral and immoral consequences, is causally related to its related things by way of two such different relations at two different times.

In this asynchronous *kamma* relation, the *kamma* signifies quite a peculiar energy. It does not cease, though the volition ceases, but latently follows the sequences of mind. As soon as it obtains a favourable opportunity, it takes effect immediately after the dying-thought has ceased, by transmuting itself into the form of an individual in the immediately following existence. But if it does not obtain any favourable opportunity, it remains in the same latent mode for many hundreds of existences. If it obtains a favourable opportunity, then what is called sublime *kamma* takes effect, upon the next existence in the Brahma-loka, by transmuting itself into the form of Brahma-*deva*, and it is so matured that it exhausts itself at the end of this second existence, and does not go any further.

End of Kamma-relation.

14. *Vipāka-paccaya*: The Relation of Effect

Thirty-six classes of resultant consciousness and their concomitants are the relation of effect. As they are mutually related to one another, the related things embrace all of them, as well as the material qualities born of *kamma* at the time of conception, and those produced by the resultant consciousness during life.

In what sense is *vipāka* applied? It is applied in the sense of *vipaccana*, which means a change of state from infancy or youth to maturity. Whose tenderness and maturity are meant? What is meant by the former is the infancy of the past volition, which is known as asynchronous *kamma*. By maturity, also, is meant the maturity of the same *kamma*.

Here, it should be understood that each volition has four *avattha* or time-phases: *cetanāvattha* or the genesis of volition; *kammāvattha*, or the continuance of volition, *nimittāvattha*, or the representation of volition; and *vipāka-vattha*, or the final result. Here, although the volition itself ceases, its peculiar function does not cease, but latently follows the series of thought. This is called *kammāvattha*, or the continuance of volition.

When it obtains a favourable opportunity for fruition, the *kamma* represents itself to the person about to die. That is to say, he himself feels as if he were giving charity, or observing the precepts, or perhaps killing some creatures. If this *kamma* fails to represent itself, a symbol of it is represented. That is to say, he himself feels as if he were in possession of the offerings, the gifts, the weapons, and so on, or anything with which he had committed such *kamma* in the past. Or, sometimes, there is represented to him the sign of the next existence where he is destined to open his new life. That is to say, such objects as the abodes or palaces of the *devas* or the fires of the *niraya*-worlds, or anything else which will be his lot to obtain or experience in the existence immediately following, enters the fields of presentation through the six doors. These are called *nimittāvattha*; the representation of the volition.

Now, how are we to understand the *vipākāvattha*? If a person dies with his attention fixed upon one of these three classes of objects, either on the *kamma* itself, or on the sign of it, or on the sign of destiny, it is said that *kamma* has effected itself, or has come to fruition, in the immediately new existence. It has transmuted itself into a personality, and appears, so to speak, in the form of a being in the new existence. This is called the *vipākāvattha* or the final result. Here, in the first three *āvattha* the volition is said to be in the state of infancy or youth.[26] The last one shows that the volition has arrived at maturity, and can effect itself. Therefore, as has been said, *vipaccana* means a change of state from infancy or youth to maturity. Thus *vipāka* is the name assigned to the states of consciousness and their concomitants, which are the results of the volitions, or to the matured volitions themselves.

Just as mangoes are very soft and delicate when they are ripe, so also the resultant states are very tranquil, since they are inactive and have no stimulus. They are so tranquil that the objects of sub-consciousness are always dim and obscure. On reviving from sub-consciousness, one has no consciousness of what its object was. For this reason, there is no possibility of occurrence of a process of thought, which can reflect the object of the sub-consciousness thus: "Such and such an object has been met with in the past existence," although in sleep at night the sub-consciousness takes for its object one of the three classes of objects (*kamma*, the symbols of *kamma*, and the symbols of one's future destiny), which had been experienced before, at the time of approaching death, in the immediately preceding existence. Hence it is that one knows nothing about any object from a past existence, either in sleep or in waking. Thus the mutual relationship by way of inactivity, non-stimulation and tranquillity is termed the function of *vipāka*.

End of Vipāka-relation.

15. *Āhāra-paccaya*: The Relation of Food

The relation of food is of two kinds: material and immaterial. Of these, material food connotes the nutritive essence (or what is called edible food), which again is subdivided into two kinds: internal and external.

26. Ledi Sayādaw has not explained the *cetanāvattha*. But it is easy enough to understand, since it is the commission of the initial volition or *kamma*. (Translator)

All the natural qualities born of the four causes,[27] pertaining to those creatures who live on edible food, are here the *paccayuppanna-dhamma* related to the two kinds of material food.

As to immaterial food, it is of three different kinds: contact, volitional activity of mind, and consciousness. These kinds of immaterial food, or *paccaya-dhamma*, are causally related to the co-existent properties, both mental and material, which are their corresponding *paccayuppanna-dhamma*.

In what sense is *āhāra* to be understood? *Āhāra* is to be understood in the sense of holding up strongly, which means causing to exist firmly. That is to say, a relating thing nourishes its related thing so as to enable it to endure long, to develop, to flourish, and to thrive, by means of support. Though the causal relation of food possesses a producing power, the power of support is predominant here.

Here, the two material foods are called *āhāra*, because they strongly hold up the group of the internal material qualities born of the four causes, by nourishing them so that they may exist firmly, endure long, and reach uncurtailed the bounds (or limits) of their life-term. Contact is an *āhāra* also, because it strongly holds up its co-existent things, and enables them to stand firmly and endure long by nourishing them with the essence extracted from desirable and undesirable objects. Volitional activity of mind, or (in a word) will, is an *āhāra* in that it furnishes courage for the execution of deeds, words, and thoughts. And consciousness is an *āhāra* also, inasmuch as it predominates in all thinking about an object. These three immaterial foods, in supplying nourishment to the co-existent mental qualities, also effect the co-existent material qualities.

Āhāra here may also be explained after the Suttanta method. Just as birds, ascertaining where their quarters are, fly with their wings through the air from tree to tree and from wood to wood, and peck at fruits with their beaks, thus sustaining themselves through their whole life, so also beings—with the six classes of consciousness, ascertaining objects, with the six kinds of volitional activity of mind, persevering to get something as an object; and with the six kinds of contact, making the essence of objects

27. The four causes (or origins) are (1) *kamma*, (2) *citta* (consciousness), (3) *utu* (temperature), (4) *āhāra* (nutriment).

appear—either enjoy pleasure or suffer pain. Or, solely with the six classes of consciousness, comprehending objects, they avail themselves of forming or becoming, body and mind. Or, solely with the contacts, making objects appear in order that feelings may be aroused through the same, they cultivate craving. Or, committing various kinds of deeds through craving accompanied by volitions, they migrate (so to speak) from existence to existence. Thus it should be understood how extensive the functioning of the different foods is.

End of the Āhāra-relation.

16. *Indriyā-paccaya*: The Relation of Control

The relation of control is of three kinds: co-existence, pre-existence and physical life (*rūpajīvita*).

Of these, the *paccaya-dhamma* of the first kind[28] are the fifteen co-existent controls, namely, life, consciousness, pleasure, pain, joy, grief, equanimity, faith, energy, mindfulness, concentration, wisdom, the thought: "I shall-come-to-know-the-unknown (Nibbāna)," the thought: "I know," and the thought: "I-have-known." The *paccayuppanna-dhamma* are their existent properties, both mental and material.

The *paccaya-dhamma* of the second kind are the five sense organs: the eye, the ear, the nose, the tongue, the body. The *paccayuppanna-dhamma* are the five classes of sense consciousness together with their concomitants.

The *paccaya-dhamma* of the third kind is only one, namely, physical life itself. And all *kamma*-born material qualities, with the exception of physical life itself, are its *paccayuppanna-dhamma*.

In what sense is *indriya* to be understood? It is to be understood in the sense of "exercising control over."

Over what does it exercise control? It exercises control over its *paccayuppanna-dhamma*.

---

28. Of these, the last three are confined to the supramundane (*lokuttara*) alone. And of these three, the first is the knowledge pertaining to the first path, the second that pertaining to the last three paths and the first three fruitions, and the third that pertaining to the last fruition only.

In what function? In their respective functions. Psychic life exercises control over its co-existent mental properties in infusing life, that is, in the matter of their prolongation by continuity. Consciousness exercises control in the matter of thinking about an object. The functioning of the rest has been explained in our recent *Indriya-Yamaka-Dīpanī*.

Here some may ask a question like this: "Why are the two sexes—the female and the male—which are comprised in the category of controls, not taken in this relation as *paccaya-dhamma*?" The answer is: Because they have none of the functions of a *paccaya*. A *paccaya* has three kinds of functioning, namely, producing, supporting and maintaining. Here, if A is causally related to B in B's arising, A's functioning is said to be that of producing; for had A not occurred the arising of B would have been impossible. The functioning of *anantara* may be instanced here. Again, if A is causally related to B in B's existence, development and prosperity, A's functioning is said to be that of supporting; for if A did not happen B would not stand, develop and flourish. The relation of *pacchājāta* will serve here as an example. And if A is causally related to B in B's prolongation by continuity, A's functioning is said to be that of maintaining; for if A did not exist, B's prolongation would be hampered, and its continuity would also be broken. The functioning of physical life will illustrate this.

Now the two sexes do not execute any one of the above three functions. Therefore, they are not taken as a *paccaya-dhamma* in this relation of control. If this be so, must they still be called controls? Yes, they must be called controls. Why? Because they have something of controlling power. They control the body in its sexual structure (*liṅga*), in its appearance (*nimitta*), in its character (*kutta*), and in its outward disposition (*ākappa*). Therefore, at the period of conception, if the female sex is produced in a being, all its personality—i.e. the five aggregates produced by the four causes (*kamma*, and so forth)—tends towards femininity. The whole body, indeed, displays nothing but the feminine structure, the feminine appearance, the feminine character, and the feminine outward disposition. Here, the female sex does not produce those qualities, nor support them, nor maintain them. But when the body (i.e. the five aggregates) has come into existence, the sex exercises control over it as if giving it the order to become so and so. All the aggregates also develop in conformity with the sex, and never out of conformity. Such is the controlling power of the female sex in the feminine structure. In the same manner the male sex exercises control in the masculine structure. Thus the two sexes have controlling functions in the structures, and hence they may be called controls.

With regard to the heart-base, though it acts as a base for the two elements of mind-cognition, it does not control them in any way, for whether the heart is limpid or not, the elements of mind-cognition in a person of well-trained mind never conform to it.

End of the Indriya-relation.

17. *Jhāna-paccaya*: The Relation of Jhāna

The seven constituents of *jhāna* are the *paccaya-dhamma* in the relation of *jhāna*. They are: *vitakka* (initial application), *vicāra* (sustained application), *pīti* (pleasurable interest), *somanassa* (joy), *domanassa* (grief), *upekkhā* (equanimity) and *ekaggatā* (unification of mind, concentration in the sense of capacity to individualise). All classes of consciousness except the five senses, along with their concomitants and material qualities in co-existence with the seven constituents, are the *paccayuppanna-dhamma* here.

In what sense is *jhāna* to be understood? *Jhāna* is to be understood in the sense of closely viewing or actively looking at, that is, going close to the object and looking at it mentally. Just as an archer, holding the arrow firmly in his hand making it steady, directing it towards the mark, keeping the target in view, and attentively aiming at it, sends the arrow through the bull's eye of a small distant target, so also a yogi or one who practises *jhāna*, directing his mind towards the object, making it steadfast; and keeping the object in view, thrusts his mind into it by means of these seven constituents of *jhāna*. Thus, by closely viewing them, a person carries out his action of body, word and mind without failure. Here, "action of body" means going forward and backward, and so forth; "action of word" means making vocal expressions, such as the sounds of the alphabet, words and so forth; "action of mind" means being conscious of objects of any kind. So no deed, such as giving charity or taking life, can be executed by a feeble mind lacking the necessary constituents of *jhāna*. It is the same with all moral and immoral deeds.

To have a clear understanding of its meaning, the salient characteristic mark of each constituent of *jhāna* should be separately explained. *Vitakka* has the characteristic mark of directing the concomitant properties towards the object, and it therefore fixes the mind firmly on the object. *Vicāra* has the characteristic mark of reviewing the object over and over, and it thus attaches the mind firmly to the object. *Pīti* has the characteristic mark of creating interest in the object, and makes the mind happy and content. The three kinds of feeling, i.e. joy, grief and indifference, have the characteristic marks of feeling the object, and they also enable the mind to experience the essence of desirable, undesirable, and neutral objects. *Ekaggatā* has the characteristic mark of concentration and it also keeps the mind steadfastly fixed on the object.

End of the Jhāna-relation.

18. *Magga-paccaya*: The Relation of Path

The twelve path-constituents are the *paccaya-dhamma* in this relation of *magga*. They are: right views, right aspiration, right speech, right action, right livelihood, right endeavour, right mindfulness, right concentration, wrong views, wrong aspiration, wrong endeavour, and wrong concentration. There are, however, no distinct mental properties to which to assign the terms wrong speech, wrong action and wrong livelihood. These are but other names for the four immoral aggregates (*akusala-khandha*) which appear under the names of lying and so forth. Therefore, they are not taken as distinct path-constituents. All classes of consciousness and mental concomitants conditioned by *hetu*, and all material qualities in co-existence with the *hetu*-conditioned mind, are *paccayuppanna-dhamma*.

In what sense is *magga* to be understood? It is to be understood in the sense of path, that is, as the means of reaching the realm of misfortune or the realm of Nibbāna. The eight path-constituents (right view and so on) lead to Nibbāna. The four wrong path-constituents lead to the realm of misfortune.

Now the functioning of *jhāna* is to make the mind straight, steadfast, and ecstatic[29] in the object. "Ecstatic mind" means mind that sinks into the object like a fish in deep water. The functioning of *magga* is to make kammic volition in the "way-in" to the circle of existence, and meditative volition in the "way-out" of the circle, straight and steadfast. It makes them issue in a course of action, develop, flourish and prosper, and reach a higher plane. This is the distinction between the two relations.

Here the kammic volition which can produce a rebirth—since it has been worked out in moral and immoral acts such as taking life, and so forth—is spoken of as "a pathway of *kamma*." And the meditative volition, which arrives at the higher stages—that is, which proceeds through a succession of stages from the sensuous stage to the transcendental one by the power of an orderly succession of training-practices, even within the brief period occupied by one bodily posture, is spoken of as "attaining to different stages."

To understand this relation, the characteristic mark of each of the path-constituents should also be separately explained in the manner shown in the Relation of *Jhāna*.

End of the Magga-relation.

19. *Sampayutta-paccaya*: The Relation of Association

The relations of association and dissociation form a pair. So also do the relations of presence and absence, and of abeyance and continuance. These three pairs of relations are not special ones. They are only mentioned to show that, in the foregoing relations, some *paccaya-dhamma* causally relate themselves to their *paccayuppanna-dhamma* by association and others by dissociation; some by presence and others by absence; some by abeyance and others by continuance.

Here also in such passages as "*atthī ti kho, Kaccāna, ayaṃ eko anto; natthī ti kho dutiyo anto ti*" [30] the words *atthi* and

29. Standing out of, or going beyond, its normal mode.

30. "Certainly, O Kaccāna, (the self) exists is one extreme, and (the self) does not exist is the second extreme" (SN 12:15). This is a passage where the

natthi are meant to indicate the heretical views of eternalism and annihilationism. Therefore, in order to prevent such interpretations, the last pair of relations is mentioned.

All classes of consciousness and mental properties mutually relate themselves to one another by way of association. In what sense is *sampayutta* to be understood? *Sampayutta* is to be understood in the sense of association or coalescence by the four associative means, namely, simultaneous arising, simultaneous cessation, the same base, and the same object. Here, by "coalescence" what is meant is that the consciousness of sight coalesces with its seven mental properties so thoroughly that they are all "unitedly" spoken of as sight. These eight mental states are no longer spoken of by their special names, for it is indeed a difficult matter to know them separately. The same explanation applies to the other classes of consciousness.

End of the Sampayutta-relation.

20. *Vippayutta-paccaya*: The Relation of Dissociation

The relation of dissociation is of four different kinds: co-existence, basic pre-existence, basic objective pre-existence, and post-existence. Of these four, the *paccaya* and *paccayuppanna-dhamma* of the co-existent dissociation may be either mental or physical in accordance with what has been shown in the relation of co-existence. Therefore a mental is causally related to a physical by way of co-existent dissociation, and vice versa. A mental here, when spoken of as a *paccaya* means the four mental aggregates, namely, feeling, perception, mental functions and consciousness during life; and a physical, when spoken of as *paccayuppanna*, means material qualities produced by mind. Again, a physical when spoken of as a *paccaya* means the heart-base at the moment of conception, and a mental when spoken of as *paccayuppanna* means the four mental aggregates belonging to rebirth.

The remaining three kinds of dissociation have already been explained.

End of the Vippayutta-relation.

problem of soul, self or ego is discussed as to its existence or non-existence as a real personal entity.

21. *Atthi-paccaya*: The Relation of Presence

The relation of presence is of seven different kinds: co-existence, basic pre-existence, objective pre-existence, basic objective pre-existence, post-existence, material food, and physical life-control.

Of these, the relation of co-existent presence is that of mere co-existence. A similar interpretation should be made for the remaining six, for which the equivalent relations that have already been explained are to be referred to. The classifications of relating and related things have already been dealt with above in each of the relations concerned.

Why is *atthi-paccaya* so called? *Atthi-paccaya* is so called because it causally relates itself to its effect by being present along with the effect in the three phases of each moment: nascent, static, and dissolution.

End of the Atthi-relation.

22. *Natthi-paccaya*: The Relation of Absence

23. *Vigata-paccaya*: The Relation of Abeyance

24. *Avigata paccaya*: The Relation of Continuance

The relation of absence is the same as the relation of contiguity; so is the relation of abeyance. The relation of continuance is the same as the relation of presence. The words *atthi* and *avigata* have the same meaning; so also the words *natthi* and *vigata*.

End of the Natthi, the Vigata, and the Avigata-relations.

End of the Exposition of Relations.

The Synthesis of Relations (*Paccaya-sabhāga*)

The relation of *sahajāta* (co-existence) may be specified as being of fifteen kinds, i.e. four superior *sahajāta*, four medium *sahajāta*, and seven inferior *sahajāta*. The four superior *sahajāta* comprise ordinary *sahajāta*, *sahajāta-nissaya* (dependence-in-co-existence), *sahajātatthi* (co-existent presence), and *sahajāta-avigata* (co-existent continuance). The four medium *sahajāta* comprise *aññamañña* (reciprocity), *vipāka* (effect), *sampayutta* (association), and *sahajāta-vippayutta* (coexistent dissociation). The seven inferior *sahajāta* comprise *hetu* (condition), *sahajātādhipati* (co-existent dominance), *sahajāta-kamma* (co-existent *kamma*), *sahajātāhāra* (co-existent food), *sahajātindriya* (co-existent control), *jhāna*, and *magga* (way).

Rūpāhāra, or material food, is of three kinds: *rūpāhāra* (ordinary material food), *rūpāhāratthi*, and *rūpāhāravigata*. *Rūpa-jīvitindriya*, or physical life-control, is of three kinds: *rūpa-jīvitindriya*, *jīvitindriyatthi*, and *rūpa-jīvitindriya-avigata*.

The relation of *purejāta* (pre-existence) may be specified as of seventeen kinds: six *vatthu-purejāta* (basic pre-existence), six *ārammaṇa-purejāta* (objective pre-existence), and five *vatthārammaṇa-purejāta* (basic objective pre-existence). Of these, the six *vatthu-purejāta* are: *vatthu-purejāta*, *vatthu-purejāta-nissaya*, *vatthu-purejātindriya*, *vatthu-purejāta-vippayutta*, *vatthu-purejātatthi*, and *vatthu-purejāta-avigata*. The six *ārammaṇa-purejāta* are: *ārammaṇa-purejāta*, some *ārammaṇa*, some *ārammaṇādhipati*, some *ārammaṇa-ārammaṇūpanissaya*, *ārammaṇa-purejātatthi*, and *ārammaṇa-purejāta-avigata*. The word "some" in "some *ārammaṇa*," and so forth, is used in order to take in only the present *nipphanna-rūpa* (material qualities determined by *kamma* and environment). The five *vatthārammaṇa-purejāta* are: *vatthārammaṇa-purejāta*, *vatthārammaṇa-purejāta-nissaya*, *vatthārammaṇa-purejāta-vippayutta*, *vatthārammaṇa-purejāta-nissaya*, *vatthārammaṇa-purejāta-vippayutta*, *vatthārammaṇa-purejātatthi*, and *vatthārammaṇa-purejāta-avigata*.

The relation of *pacchājāta* or post-existence may be specified as of four kinds: *pacchājāta*, *pacchājāta-vippayutta*, *pacchājātatthi*, and *pacchājāta-avigata*.

The relation of *anantara* (contiguity) is of seven kinds: *anantara*, *samanantara*, *anantarūpanissaya*, *āsevana*, *anantarakamma*, *natthi*, and *vigata*. Of these, *anantarakamma* is the volition which appertains to the ariyan path. It produces its effect, i.e. the ariyan fruit, immediately after it ceases.

There are five relations which do not enter into any specification. These are: the remaining *ārammaṇa*, the remaining *ārammaṇādhipati*, the remaining *ārammaṇūpanissaya*, all *pakatūpanissaya*, and the remaining kind of *kamma* which is asynchronous *kamma*.

Thus the relations expounded in the Paṭṭhāna (Treatise) are altogether of fifty-four kinds.

Of these relations, all species of *purejāta*, all species of *pacchājāta*, material food, and physical life-control are present relations. All species of *anantara* and of *nānākkhaṇika-kamma* are past relations. Omitting Nibbāna and term-and-concept (*paññatti*), the relations of *ārammaṇa* and *pakatūpanissaya* may be classified under the three periods of time: past, present and future. But Nibbāna and term-and-concept are always outside time.

These two things—Nibbāna and concepts—are both termed *appaccaya* (void of causal relation), *asaṅkhata* (unconditioned).[31] Why? Because they are absolutely void of becoming. Those things or phenomena which have birth or genesis are termed *sappaccaya* (related things), *saṅkhata* (conditioned things), and *paṭiccasamuppanna* (things arising from a conjuncture of circumstances). Hence those two things, being void of becoming and happening, are truly termed *appaccaya* and *asaṅkhata*.[32]

Among things related and conditioned, there is not a single phenomenon which is permanent, lasting, eternal and unchangeable. In fact, all are impermanent, since they are liable

---

31. Here, the word *appaccaya* is not a *kammadhāraya* compound, but is of the *bahubbīhi* class; thus: *natthi paccayā etesan-ti appaccayā. Asaṅkhata* is a *kammadhāraya* compound; thus: *saṅkhāriyante ti saṅkhatā; na saṅkhatā ti asaṅkhatā.*

32. See note to Preface. (Editor)

to dissolution. Why? Because in coming into existence they are related to some causes, and their causes are also not permanent.

Are not Nibbāna and concepts *paccaya-dhamma* or relating things? Are they not permanent and lasting? Yes, they are, but no phenomenon happens entirely through Nibbāna or concepts alone as sole cause. Phenomena happen through, or are produced by, many causes which are not permanent and lasting.

Those things which are not permanent are always distressing and hurtful to beings with the three kinds of afflictions. Therefore, they are looked upon as ill by reason of their being dreadful. Here the three kinds of afflictions are *dukkha-dukkhatā* (ill due to suffering), *saṅkhāra-dukkhatā* (ill due to conditioning), and *viparināma-dukkhatā* (ill due to changeability). All things are impermanent, and are dissolving at every moment, even while one occupies one posture.[33] Therefore, how can there be any essential self or core in creatures and persons, even though through all their life through they imagine themselves to be permanent? Everything is also subject to ill. Therefore, how can there be any essential self or core in creatures and persons who are under the oppression of ills and who nevertheless yearn for happiness? Hence all things are void of self by reason of the absence of a core.

To sum up, by expounding the twenty-four relations, the Buddha reveals the following facts: all conditioned things owe their happening and becoming or existence to causes and conditions, and none to the mere desire or will or command of creatures. And among all the things subject to causes and conditions, there is not one that comes into being through a few causes. They arise, indeed, only through many causes. Therefore this exposition reaches its culminating point in revealing the doctrine of no-soul.

End of the Synthesis of Relations

33. There are four postures: sitting, standing, walking and lying down.

The Synchrony of Relations (*Paccaya-ghaṭana-naya*)

The concurrence of causal relations in one related thing is called synchrony of relations. All phenomena are called *sappaccaya* (related to causes), *saṅkhata* (conditioned by causes), and *paṭiccasamuppanna* (arising from a conjuncture of circumstances), because in arising and in standing they are conditioned by these twenty-four causal relations. What, then, are those phenomena? They are: one hundred and twenty-one classes of consciousness, fifty-two kinds of mental properties, and twenty-eight kinds of material qualities.

Of these, the one hundred and twenty-one classes of consciousness may be classified into seven, under the category of elements (*dhātu*):

1. element of visual cognition (*cakkhuviññāṇadhātu*)
2. element of auditory cognition (*sotaviññāṇadhātu*)
3. element of olfactory cognition (*ghāṇaviññāṇadhātu*)
4. element of gustatory cognition (*jivhāviññāṇadhātu*)
5. element of tactile cognition (*kāyaviññāṇadhātu*)
6. element of apprehension (*manodhātu*)
7. element of comprehension (*manoviññāṇadhātu*)

Of these:

the two classes of sight-consciousness are called the element of visual cognition;

the two classes of sound-consciousness are called the element of auditory cognition;

the two classes of smell-consciousness are called the element of olfactory cognition;

the two classes of taste-consciousness are called the element of gustatory cognition;

the two classes of touch-consciousness are called the element of tactile cognition;

the adverting of mind towards any of the five doors (*pañca-dvārāvajjana*) and the

two classes of acceptance of impressions (*sampaṭicchana*) are called the element of apprehension;

the remaining one hundred and eight classes of consciousness are called the element of comprehension.

The fifty-two kinds of mental properties are also divided into four groups:

1. seven universals
2. six particulars
3. fourteen immorals
4. twenty-five radiants.[34]

Of the twenty-four relations, fifteen relations are common to all the mental states: *ārammaṇa, anantara, samanantara, sahajāta, aññamañña, nissaya, upanissaya, kamma, āhāra, indriya, sampayutta, atthi, natthi, vigata* and *avigata*. There is not a single class of consciousness or mental property which arises without the causal relation of *ārammaṇa* (object). The same holds good as regards the remaining causal relations of *anantara, samanantara, sahajāta* and so on.

Eight relations only—*hetu, adhipati, purejāta, āsevana, vipāka, jhāna, magga* and *vippayutta*—are common to some mental states. Of these, the relation of *hetu* is common only to the classes of consciousness conditioned by *hetu*; the relation of *adhipati* is also common only to the apperceptions (*javana*) co-existing with dominance (*adhipati*); the relation of *purejāta* is common only to some classes of mind; the relation of *āsevana* is common only to apperceptive classes of moral, immoral, and inoperative consciousness; the relation of *vipāka* is also common only to the resultant classes of mind; the relation of *jhāna* is common to those classes of consciousness and mental concomitants made up of the elements of apprehension and comprehension; the relation of *magga* is common to the classes of mind conditioned by *hetu*; the relation of *vippayutta* is excluded from the classes of mind in *arūpaloka*; only one particular relation, *pacchājāta*, is common to material qualities.

Here is the exposition in detail. The seven universal mental properties are: *phassa* (contact), *vedanā* (feeling), *saññā* (perception), *cetanā* (volition), *ekaggatā* (unification of mind), *jīvita* (life) and *manasikāra* (attention).

34. *Sobhana*, also translated as beautiful or lofty mental properties.

Of these, consciousness may be the relation of *adhipati*; it may be the relation of *āhāra*, and it may also be the relation of *indriya*; contact is the relation of *āhāra* alone; feeling may be the relation of *indriya*, and may also be the relation of *jhāna*; volition may be the relation of *kamma*, and may be the relation of *āhāra*; *ekaggatā* may be the relation of *indriya*; it may be the relation of *jhāna*, and it may be the relation of *magga* also; *jīvita* is the relation of *indriya* alone; the two remaining states—perception and attention—do not become any particular relation.

Synchrony of Relations in the Five Senses

Consciousness by way of sight obtains seven universal mental concomitants, and so they make up eight mental states. All of them are mutually related to one another by way of the seven relations: four superior *sahajāta* and three of the medium *sahajāta* excluding the relation of dissociation. Among these eight mental states, consciousness causally relates itself to the other seven by way of *āhāra* and *indriya*. Contact causally relates itself to the other seven by way of *āhāra*; feeling to the rest by way of *kamma* and *āhāra*; *ekaggatā* by way of *indriya* alone; and *jīvita* to the other seven, by way of *indriya*. The basis of eye causally relates itself to these eight states by way of six species of *vatthu-purejāta*. The present visual objects, which enter the avenue of that eye-base, causally relate themselves to those eight by way of four species of *ārammaṇa-purejāta*. The consciousness of turning-towards-the-five-doors, at the moment of cessation just before the arising of sight consciousness, causally relates itself to these eight mental states by way of five species of *anantara*. Moral and immoral deeds which were done in former births causally relate themselves to these eight resultant states of good and evil respectively, by way of asynchronous *kamma*. Nescience (*avijjā*), craving (*taṇhā*) and grasping (*upādāna*)—which co-operated with volition (*kamma*) in the past existence—and dwellings, persons, seasons, foods and so forth, of this present life, causally relate themselves to these eight states by way of *pakatūpanissaya* (natural sufficing condition). The six relations—*hetu*, *adhipati*, *pacchājāta*, *āsevana*, *jhāna* and *magga*—do not take part in this class of consciousness, but only the remaining eighteen relations take part. Just as the six relations do not take part—and only the eighteen relations do—in consciousness by way of sight, so do they in consciousness by way of hearing, smell, and so on.

End of the Synchrony of Relations in the Five Senses.

Synchrony of Relations in Consciousness Not Accompanied by *Hetu*

There are six mental properties termed particulars (*pakiṇṇaka*): *vitakka* (initial application), *vicāra* (sustained application), *adhimokkha* (decision), *viriya* (effort), *pīti* (pleasurable interest) and *chanda* (desire-to-do). Of these, initial application takes part in the relation of *jhāna* and in the relation of *magga*. Sustained application takes part in that of *jhāna* alone. Effort takes part in the relation of *adhipati*, in the relation of *indriya*, and in the relation of *jhāna*. Desire-to-do takes part in the relation of *adhipati*. Decision does not take part in any particular relation.

The ten concomitants—the seven universals and initial application, sustained application, and decision from the particulars—obtain in the five classes of consciousness, i.e. turning-towards-the five-doors, the twofold class of acceptance, and the twofold class of investigation accom-panied by equanimity. They form eleven mental states in one combination. Jhānic function obtains in these five classes of consciousness. Feeling, unification (*ekaggatā*), initial application, and sustained application perform the function of *jhāna* relation. Consciousness turning towards the five-doors belongs to the inoperative class, and so does not obtain in the relation of *vipāka*. Asynchronous *kamma* serves in place of *upanissaya*. So, leaving out *jhāna* from, and inserting *vipāka* in, the relations which have been shown above are not obtainable in the five senses, there are also six unobtainable and eighteen obtainable in the consciousness of turning-towards-the-five-doors. As for the remaining four resultant classes of consciousness, by omitting *vipāka*, five relations are unobtainable, and by adding *vipāka* and *jhāna*, nineteen are obtainable.

Investigating consciousness accompanied by joy obtains eleven mental concomitants, namely, the above ten together with pleasurable interest. With the consciousness of turning-towards-the-mind-door, eleven concomitants co-exist, and they are accompanied by effort. They make up twelve mental states together with the consciousness. Twelve concomitants, i.e. the above ten together with pleasurable interest and effort, co-exist with the consciousness of aesthetic pleasure. They make up thirteen mental states in combination with the consciousness. Of the three classes of investigating consciousness, the one accompanied by joy has one more mental property (i.e. pleasurable interest) than the other two, in respect of the *jhāna* factors; therefore, the unobtainable five and the obtainable nineteen relations are the same as in the two classes of investigating consciousness accompanied by equanimity. In the consciousness of turning-towards-the-mind-door, the predominant property is merely effort, which performs the functions of *indriya* and *jhāna*, but not the functions of *adhipati* and *magga*. This consciousness, being of the inoperative class, does not obtain the *vipāka*-relation. Therefore, the unobtainable six including *vipāka*, and the obtainable eighteen including *jhāna*, are the same as in the consciousness of turning-towards-the-five-doors. The relation of *vipāka* is also not obtained in the consciousness of aesthetic pleasure, since it belongs to the inoperative class. But being of the apperceptive class, it obtains the relation of *āsevana*. Therefore, five relations including *vipāka* are not obtainable, and nineteen relations including *āsevana* are obtainable.

End of the Synchrony of Relations in Consciousness Not Accompanied By Hetu.

Synchrony of Relations in the Immoral Classes of Consciousness

There are twelve classes of immoral consciousness: two rooted in nescience, eight rooted in greed, and two rooted in hate. There are fourteen immoral mental properties: *moha* (delusion), *ahirika* (shamelessness), *anottappa* (recklessness of consequences), and *uddhacca* (distraction)—these four are termed the delusion-quadruple; *lobha* (greed), *diṭṭhi* (wrong view), and *māna* (conceit)—these three are termed the greed-triple; *dosa* (hate), *issā* (envy), *macchariya* (selfishness), and *kukkucca* (worry)—these four are termed the hate-quadruple; *thīna* (sloth), *middha* (torpor), and *vicikicchā* (perplexity)—these three are termed the miscellaneous-triple. Of these, the three roots—greed, hate, and delusion—are *hetu*-relations. Error is a *magga*-relation. The remaining ten mental properties do not become any particular relation.

Here, the two classes of consciousness rooted in delusion are: consciousness conjoined with perplexity and consciousness conjoined with distraction. With the first of these two, fifteen mental concomitants co-exist. There are the seven universals, initial application, sustained application, effort (from the particulars), the delusion-quadruple, and perplexity (from the immorals). They make up sixteen mental states in combination with consciousness. In this consciousness, i.e. the consciousness conjoined with perplexity, the relations of *hetu* and *magga* are also obtained.

That is, delusion acts as the *hetu*-relation; initial application and effort as the *magga*; and, as to *ekaggatā* (unification of mind), as its function would be interfered with by perplexity, it does not perform the functions of *indriya* and *magga*, but it does the function of *jhāna*. Therefore, the three relations (*adhipati*, *pacchājāta*, *vipāka*) are not obtainable; and the remaining twenty-one are obtainable in this consciousness which is conjoined with perplexity.

In consciousness conjoined with distraction, there are also fifteen mental properties—omitting perplexity and adding decision. They also make up sixteen mental states together with the consciousness. In this consciousness, *ekaggatā* performs the functions of *indriya*, *jhāna* and *magga*. Therefore, three relations are not obtainable, whereas twenty-one are obtainable.

Seven universals, six particulars, the delusion-quadruple, the greed-triple, sloth and torpor—altogether twenty-two in number—severally co-exist with the eight classes of consciousness rooted in greed. Among these, the two roots—greed and delusion—are *hetu*-relations; and the three mental states—desire-to-do, consciousness itself and effort—are *adhipati*-relations. *Ārammaṇādhipati* is also obtained here. Volition is the relation of *kamma*. The three foods are the relations of *āhāra*. The five mental states—mind, feeling, unification, life and effort—are relations of *indriya*. The five *jhāna* factors, i.e. initial application, sustained application, pleasurable interest, feeling and concentration, are *jhāna*-relations. The four *magga* constituents, i.e. initial application, concentration, error, and effort, are *magga*-relations. Therefore only the two relations (*pacchājāta* and *vipāka*) are not obtained. The remaining twenty-two are obtained.

End of the Synchrony of Relations in the Immoral Classes of Consciousness.

Synchrony of Relations in the Radiant Classes of Consciousness

There are ninety-one radiant classes of consciousness. They are: twenty-four radiant classes of *kāma* consciousness, fifteen classes of *rūpa*-consciousness, twelve classes of *arūpa*-consciousness and forty classes of transcendental consciousness. Of these, the twenty-four radiant classes of *kāma*-consciousness are: eight classes of moral consciousness, eight classes of radiant resultant kind, and another eight classes of radiant inoperative kind.

There are twenty-five kinds of radiant mental properties: *alobha* (non-greed or dispassionateness), *adosa* (non-hate or amity), *amoha* (non-delusion or intelligence)—these three are termed moral *hetu*—*saddhā* (faith), *sati* (mindfulness), *hiri* (prudence), *ottappa* (discretion) *tatramajjhattatā* (balance of mind), *kāyapassaddhi* (composure of mental properties), *cittapassaddhi* (composure of mind), *kāyalahutā* (buoyancy of mental properties), *cittala-hutā* (buoyancy of mind), *kāyamudutā* (pliancy of mental properties), *cittamudutā* (pliancy of mind), *kāyakammaññatā* (fitness of work of mental properties), *citta-kammaññatā* (fitness of work of mind), *kāya-pāguññatā* (proficiency of mental properties), *citta-pāguññatā* (proficiency of mind), *kāyujukatā* (rectitude of mental properties), *cittujukatā* (rectitude of mind), *sammā-vācā* (right speech), *sammā-kammantā* (right action), *sammā-ājīva* (right livelihood)—these last three are called the three abstinences; *karuṇā* (compassion) and *muditā* (sympathetic appreciation)—these last two are called the two illimitables.

Of these, the three moral *hetu* are *hetu-paccaya*. *Amoha* appears under the name of *vīmaṃsā* in the *adhipati*-relation; under the name of *paññā* in the *indriya*-relation; and under the name of *sammā-diṭṭhi* in the *magga*-relation. *Saddhā* or faith is the *indriya*-

relation. *Sati* or mindfulness is *satindriya* in the *indriya*-relation, and *sammā-sati* in the *magga*-relation. The three abstinences (right speech, right action and right livelihood) are *magga*-relations. The remaining seventeen mental states are not particular relations.

Thirty-eight mental properties enter into combination with the eight moral classes of *kāma*-consciousness: seven universals, six particulars, and twenty five radiants. Of these, pleasurable interest enters into combination only with the four classes of consciousness accompanied by joy. Non-delusion also enters into combination only with the four classes connected with knowledge. The three abstinences enter into combination only when moral rules or precepts are observed. The two illimitables arise only when sympathising with the suffering, or sharing in the happiness, of living beings. In these eight classes of consciousness, the dual or triple roots are *hetu*-relations. Among the four kinds of *adhipati*, i.e. desire-to-do, mind, effort, and investigation, each is an *adhipati* in turn. Volition is the relation of *kamma*. The three foods are the relations of *āhāra*. The eight mental states, i.e. mind, feeling, concentration, life, faith, mindfulness, effort and intelligence, are relations of *indriya*. The five *jhāna* factors, i.e. initial application, sustained application, pleasurable interest, feeling and concentration, are relations of *jhāna*. The eight path-constituents, i.e. intelligence, initial application, the three abstinences, mindfulness, effort and concentration, are relations of *magga*. Therefore, only the two relations of *pacchājāta* and *vipāka* are not obtained in these eight classes of consciousness; the remaining twenty-two are obtained. The three abstinences do not obtain in the eight radiant classes of inoperative consciousness. As in the moral consciousness, two relations are unobtainable and twenty-two are obtainable here. The three abstinences and the two illimitables also do not obtain in the eight radiant classes of resultant consciousness. The relations unobtainable are three in number, namely, *adhipati*, *pacchājāta* and *āsevana*; the remaining twenty-one are obtainable.

The higher classes of *rūpa*, *arūpa* and transcendental consciousness do not obtain more than twenty-two relations. The synchrony of relations should be understood as existing in the four moral classes of *kāma*-consciousness connected with knowledge. If this be so, then why are those classes of consciousness more supreme and transcendental than the *kāma*-consciousness? Because of the greatness of *āsevana*. They are fashioned by marked exercises, and so *āsevana* is superior to them; for this reason, *indriya*, *jhāna*, *magga* and other relations also become superior. When these relations become supreme—each higher and higher than the other—those classes of consciousness also become more supreme and transcendental than *kāma*-consciousness.

End of the Synchrony of Relations in the Radiant Classes of Consciousness.

Synchrony of Relations in the Groups of Material Qualities

There are twenty-eight kinds of material qualities.

A. Four essential material qualities:
1. the element of solidity (*paṭhavī*)
2. the element of cohesion (*āpo*)
3. the element of kinetic energy (*tejo*)
4. the element of motion (*vāyo*)

B. Five sensitive material qualities:
1. the eye (*cakkhu*)
2. the ear (*sota*)
3. the nose (*ghāna*)
4. the tongue (*jivhā*)
5. the body (*kāya*)

C. Five material qualities of sense-fields:
1. visible form (*rūpa*)
2. sound (*sadda*)
3. odour (*gandha*)
4. taste (*rasa*)
5. the tangible (*phoṭṭhabba*)[35]

35. In computing the number of material qualities, the tangible is generally omitted, since the physical objects of body-sensitivity are identical with the afore-mentioned elements of solidity, kinetic energy and motion. When these three elements are considered, seven qualities of sense fields are counted. (Editor)

D. Two material qualities of sex:
  1. female sex (*itthibhāva*)
  2. male sex (*puṃbhāva*)

E. One material quality of life (*jīvita*)

F. One material quality of heart-base (*hadaya-vatthu*)

G. One material quality of nutrition (*āhāra*)

H. One material quality of space (*ākāsadhātu*)

I. Two material qualities of communication:
  1. intimation by the body (*kāyaviññatti*)
  2. intimation by speech (*vacīviññatti*)

J. Three material qualities of plasticity:
  1. lightness (*lahutā*)
  2. pliancy (*mudutā*)
  3. adaptability (*kammaññatā*)

K. Four material qualities of salient features:
  1. integration (*upacaya*)
  2. continuance (*santati*)
  3. decay (*jaratā*)
  4. impermanence (*aniccatā*)

Of these, six kinds of material qualities—the four essentials, the material quality of life, and the material quality of nutrition—causally relate themselves to the material qualities. Here also the four essentials are mutually related among themselves by way of five relations: *sahajāta*, *aññamañña*, *nissaya*, *atthi*, and *avigata*; and they are related to the coexistent material qualities derived from the latter by way of four relations, i.e. excluding *aññamañña* in the above five. The material quality of life causally relates itself to the co-existent material qualities produced by *kamma* by way of *indriya*. The material quality of nutrition causally relates itself to both the coexistent and the non-co-existent material qualities which are corporeal by way of *āhāra*.

Again, thirteen kinds of material qualities causally relate themselves to the mental states by some particular relations. These material qualities are: the five kinds of sensitive material qualities, the seven kinds of sense-fields, and the heart-base. Of these, just as a mother is related to her son, so also the five kinds of sensitive material qualities are causally related to the five sense-cognitions by way of *vatthu-purejāta*, by way of *vatthu-purejātindriya*, and by way of *vatthu purejāta-vippayutta*. And just as a father is related to his son, so also the seven sense-fields are causally related to the five sense-cognitions and the three elements of apprehension by way of *ārammaṇa-purejāta*. In the same way, just as a tree is related to the *deva* who inhabits it, so also the heart-base causally relates itself to the two elements of apprehension and comprehension by way of *sahajāta-nissaya* at the time of rebirth, and by way of *vatthu-purejāta* and of *vatthu-purejāta-vippayutta* during life.

There are twenty-three groups of material qualities. They are called groups (*kalāpa*) because they are tied up with the material quality of production (*jāti-rūpa*) into groups, just as hair or hay is tied up with a string.[36] Of these, the eight kinds of material qualities, such as the four essentials—colour, odour, taste, and nutritive essence—make up the primary octad of all material qualities.

There are nine groups produced by *kamma*: the vital-nonad, the heart-decad, the body-decad, the female-decad, the male-decad, the eye-decad, the ear-decad, the nose-decad, and the tongue-decad. Of these, the primary octad together with the material quality of life is called the vital-nonad. This primary nonad together with each of the eight material qualities, i.e. heart-base and so forth, makes up analogously the other eight decads, i.e. base-decad, and so forth. Here the four groups—vital-nonad, body-decad, and two-fold sex-decad—locate themselves in a person, pervading the whole body. Here vital-nonad is the name of the maturative fire (*pācakaggi*) and of the bodily fire (*kāyaggi*). The maturative fire is that which locates itself in the stomach and matures or digests the food that has been eaten, drunk, chewed and licked. The bodily fire is that which locates itself by pervading the whole body, and it refines the impure bile, phlegm and blood. Through the inharmonious action of these two elements, people

36. Ledi Sayādaw here makes the number of groups twenty-three instead of twenty-one, as in the *Compendium of Philosophy* (*Abhidhammatthasaṅgaha*), tr. by S. Z. Aung (PTS), p. 164. He also makes the groups of material qualities produced by thought number eight instead of six, as in the *Compendium*; thus they are here increased by two. (Cf. *Paramatthadīpanī*, page 273.) (Translator)

become unhealthy, and by their harmonious action they become healthy. It is this dual fire (or that vital-nonad) that gives life and good complexion to people. The body-decad makes available pleasurable and painful contact. The two-fold sex-decad makes available all the feminine characteristics to females and all the masculine characteristics to males. The remaining five decads are termed partial decads. Of these, the heart-decad, locating itself in the cavity of the heart, makes available many various kinds of moral and immoral thoughts. The four decads, i.e. eye-decad and so forth, locating themselves respectively in the eyeball, in the interior of the ear, in the interior of the nose, and on the surface of the tongue, make available sight, hearing, smell, and taste.

There are eight groups produced by mind. The first four are the primary octad, the sound-nonad, the nonad of body communication, the sound-decad of speech-communication. Taking these four together with lightness, pliancy and adaptability, they make up another four: the undecad of plasticity, the sound-dodecad of plasticity, the dodecad of body-communication together with plasticity, and the sound-tredecad of speech communication together with plasticity. The first four are termed primary groups, and the last four are termed plastic groups.

Of these, when the elements of the body are not working harmoniously, only the four primary groups occur to a sick person. His material qualities then become heavy, coarse and inadaptable, and consequently it becomes difficult for him to maintain the bodily postures as he would wish, to move the members of the body, and even to make a vocal reply. But when the elements of the body are working harmoniously—there being no defects of the body, such as heaviness and so on, in a healthy person—the four plastic groups come into existence. Among these four, two groups of body communication occur by means of mind or by moving any part of the body. The other two groups of speech communication occur also on account of mind, when wishing to speak; but when non-verbal sound is produced through laughing or crying, only the two ordinary sound-groups occur. At other times the first two groups, the primary octad and the sound-nonad, occur according to circumstances.

There are four groups produced by physical change: the two primary groups (the primary octad and the sound-nonad) and the two plastic groups (i.e. the undecad of plasticity and the sound-dodecad of plasticity). Now this body of ours maintains itself right on throughout the whole life, through a long course of bodily postures. Hence, at every moment, there occur in this body the harmonious and inharmonious workings of the elements, through changes in the postures, through changes in its temperature, through changes of food, air, and heat, through changes of the disposition of the members of the body, and through changes of one's own exertion and of others. Here also, when working harmoniously, two plastic groups occur; and when working inharmoniously, the other two primary groups occur. Of the four groups, two sound groups arise, when there occur various kinds of sound other than that produced by mind.

There are two groups produced by food: the primary octad and the undecad of plasticity. These two groups should be understood as the harmonious and inharmonious occurrences of material qualities produced respectively by suitable and unsuitable food.

The five material qualities, namely, the element of space and the four salient features of matter, lie outside the grouping. Of these, the element of space lies outside the grouping because it is the boundary of the groups. As to the material qualities of the salient features, they are left aside from grouping because they are merely the marks or signs of conditioned things through which we clearly know them to be really conditioned things.

These twenty-three groups are available in an individual. The groups available in external things are only two, which are no other than the two primary groups produced by physical change. There are two locations of material qualities, the internal and the external. Of these two, the internal location means a sentient being and the external location means the earth, hills, rivers, oceans, trees, and so forth. Therefore we have said that, in an individual twenty-three groups, or all the twenty-eight kinds of material qualities, are available.

Now the rebirth-conception and its mental concomitants are causally related to the groups produced by *kamma* at the moment of conception by way of six different relations, the four superior *sahajāta*, *vipāka*, and *vippayutta*. But to the heart-base alone, they are causally related by seven relations: the above together with the relation of *aññamañña*. Among the mental states at the moment of rebirth, the roots are causally related by way of the *hetu*-relation; the volition by way of *āhāra*; the controls by way of *indriya*; the *jhāna* constituents by way of *jhāna*; and the path-constituents, by way of *magga*, to the *kamma*-produced groups. The past moral and immoral volitions are causally related by way of *kamma* alone. The first posterior life-continuum, the second, the third, and so on, are causally related to the prior material qualities produced by *kamma*, by way of *pacchājāta*. By "*pacchājāta*" is meant all the species of *pacchājāta*. The past volitions are causally related by way of *kamma* alone. Thus the mental states are causally related to the material qualities produced by *kamma* by fourteen different relations. Here, ten relations are not obtained: *ārammaṇa*, *adhipati*, *anantara*, *samanantara*, *upanissaya*, *purejāta*, *āsevana*, *sampayutta*, *natthi* and *vigata*.

During the term of life, mental states capable of producing material qualities are causally related to the co-existent material qualities produced by them, by five different relations: the four superior *sahajāta* and *vippayutta*. Among these mental states: *hetu* are causally related by way of *hetu*, the dominances by way of *adhipati*, the volition by way of *kamma*, the resultants by way of *vipāka*, the foods by way of *āhāra*, the controls by way of *indriya*, the *jhāna* factors by way of *jhāna*, the path-constituents by way of *magga*, to the mind-produced material qualities. All the posterior mental states are causally related to the prior material qualities produced by mind by way of *pacchājāta*. Thus the mental states are causally related to the material groups produced by mind by fourteen different relations. Here also ten relations are not obtainable: *ārammaṇa*, *anantara*, *samanantara*, *aññamañña*, *upanissaya*, *purejāta*, *āsevana*, *sampayutta*, *natthi* and *vigata*.

During a lifetime, starting from the static phase of conception, all mental states are causally related both to the material groups produced by food and to those produced by physical change solely by way of *pacchājāta*. Here again, by "*pacchājāta*" is meant all the four species of *pacchājāta*. The remaining twenty relations are not obtainable.

Among the twenty-three groups of material qualities, the four essentials are mutually related among themselves by way of five different relations: four superior *sahajāta* and one *aññamañña*; but to the co-existent derivative material qualities they are related by way of the four superior *sahajāta* only. The material quality of nutritive essence is causally related by way of *āhāra*, both to the co-existent and the non-coexistent material qualities which are corporeal. The material quality of physical life in the nine groups produced by *kamma* is causally related only to the co-existent material qualities by way of *indriya*. Thus the corporeal material qualities are causally related to the corporeal material qualities by seven different relations. As for the external material qualities, they are mutually related to the two external groups produced by physical change, by way of five different relations.

End of the Synchrony of Relations in the Groups of Material Qualities.

The Meaning of Paṭṭhāna

The meaning of the term *paṭṭhāna* also will now be explained: *padhānaṃ ṭhānaṃ ti paṭṭhānaṃ*. "*Paṭṭhāna* is the pre-eminent or principal cause." In this definition *padhāna* means "pre-eminent" and *ṭhāna* means "condition" or "cause." Hence the whole expression means the pre-eminent cause, the actual cause or the ineluctable cause. This is said having reference to its ineluctable effect or result.[37]

There are two kinds of effect, the direct and the indirect. By "the direct" is meant the primary or actual effect, and by "the indirect" is meant the consequent or incidental effect. Of these two kinds, only the direct effect is here referred to as ineluctable, and for this reason: that it never fails to arise when its proper cause is established or brought into play. And the indirect effect is to be understood as eluctable since it may or may not arise even though its cause is fully established. Thus the ineluctable cause is so named with reference to the ineluctable effect. Hence the ineluctable or principal cause alone is meant to be expounded in this "Great Treatise (*Mahāpakaraṇa*)." For this reason the name *paṭṭhāna* is assigned to the entire collection of the twenty-four relations, and also to the "Great Treatise."

And now, to make the matter clearer and simpler: Say that greed springs into being within a man who desires to get money

37. Elsewhere I have rendered the word *paccayuppanna* as "related thing."

and grain. Under the influence of greed, he goes to a forest where he clears a piece of land and establishes fields, yards and gardens, and starts to work very hard. Eventually he obtains plenty of money and grain by reason of his strenuous labours. So he takes his gains, looks after his family, and performs many virtuous deeds, from which also he will reap rewards in his future existences. In this illustration, all the mental and material states co-existing with greed are called direct effects.

Apart from these, all the outcomes, results and rewards, which are to be enjoyed later on in his future existences, are called indirect effects. Of these two kinds of effects, only the former is dealt with in the Paṭṭhāna. However, the latter kind finds its place in the Suttanta discourses: if this exists, then that happens; or, because of the occurrence of this, that also takes place. Such an exposition is called "expounding by way of Suttanta" In fact, the three states (greed, hate and ignorance) are called the *hetu* or conditions, because they are the roots whence spring the defilements of the whole animate world, of the whole inanimate world, and of the world of space. The three other opposite states (dispassionateness, amity, and intelligence) are also called *hetu* or conditions, since they are the roots whence springs purification. In the same manner the remainder of the relations are to be understood in their various senses. Thus must we understand that all things that happen, occur, take place, or produce changes, are solely the direct and indirect effects, results, outcomes, or products of these twenty-four relations or causes.

Thus ends the *Paṭṭhānuddesa Dīpanī*, "The Concise Exposition of the Buddhist Philosophy of Relations," written by The Most Venerable Ledi Araññavihāravāsi Mahāthera of Monywa, Burma.

Anāthapiṇḍika

The Great Benefactor

by

Hellmuth Hecker

WHEEL PUBLICATION NO. 334

Prologue

"Thus have I heard: One time the Blessed One was staying at Sāvatthī in the Jeta Grove, in Anāthapiṇḍika's Monastery ..." Numerous discourses of the Buddha begin with these words, and hence the name of that great lay devotee, Anāthapiṇḍika is well known. His name means: "One who gives alms (*piṇḍa*) to the unprotected (*a-nātha*)" and is the honorific of the householder Sudatta of the city of Sāvatthī. Who was he? How did he meet the Buddha? What was his relationship to the teaching? The answers to these questions may be found in the many references to him which occur in the traditional texts.

1. How Anāthapiṇḍika Became a Disciple of the Buddha

In the first year after Siddhattha Gotama's enlightenment, his Order, found in Rājagaha, the capital of the kingdom of Magadha, consisted then of only a few people who, after hearing the Four Noble Truths, had become Arahats. Being liberated ones, they lived homeless in field and forest, on mountains, and in meadows. When a wealthy merchant, the brother-in-law of Anāthapiṇḍika, became a faithful lay follower of the Buddha and saw how they lived, he suggested to the monks that they ask their Master whether he would allow them to have a permanent dwelling.

When the Buddha gave his permission, the merchant at once set about to erect no fewer than sixty dwellings for the monks, explaining that he needed to gain merit. With the building of that first Buddhist monastery, the foundation for the spread of the Teaching began, for now there would be a training centre for the Order in which to educate those who were not yet Arahats (Cv 1).

One day Anāthapiṇḍika, the richest merchant in Sāvatthī was travelling on business in the neighbouring state of Magadha and came to Rājagaha. As usual, his way led him first to his brother-in-law, to whom he was bound by a warm friendship. As he entered the house, he found to his astonishment that the household hardly noticed him. Hitherto, he had been accustomed to his brother-in-law's full attention and to the other residents of the house receiving him gladly. But now he saw that they were busy, eagerly making elaborate preparations. He asked his preoccupied brother-in-law what this meant: "A wedding? A major sacrifice? A visit from the king?" But the brother-in-law explained, "Tomorrow the Order of monks with the Enlightened One is coming here, for I have invited them."

Anāthapiṇḍika became attentive. "Did you say the 'Enlightened One'?" "Indeed," answered the brother-in-law, "tomorrow the Enlightened One is coming." And Anāthapiṇḍika asked a second time and a third time, "Did you say the 'Enlightened One'?" Then, breathing a deep sigh of relief, he said, "Even the sound alone of these words is indeed rare in this world—the Enlightened One—can one really see him?" His brother-in-law answered that while today was not the time, tomorrow would be.

Moved by many kinds of thoughts and feelings, Anāthapiṇḍika lay down to sleep. Yet he awoke three times in that night, thinking it was already daytime, so strong was his anticipation of the next day's meeting. Finally he arose even before dawn and went out of the city to the monastery. In the darkness, however, fear overcame him, doubts arose within him, and all his worldly instincts told him to turn back, but an inner voice assured him that it would be best to continue on. And so through the rest of the night he walked resolutely on. After a while he saw in the misty dawn a figure walking silently to and fro. Anāthapiṇḍika stopped. Then the figure called to him in an indescribably harmonious voice: "Come, Sudatta!"

Anāthapiṇḍika was startled at being addressed in this manner, for no one there knew him by his original name. He was only known as Anāthapiṇḍika, and besides, he was unknown to the Buddha and had come unexpectedly. Now he was certain that he was in the presence of the Enlightened One. Overwhelmed by the gravity of the encounter, he fell at the feet of the Blessed One, and asked him in a stammering voice about his well-being. With the answer to this conventional question, Anāthapiṇḍika came a little closer to the supramundane reality, since the Enlightened One explained that the Arahats were always well, for they were beyond all possibilities for suffering. And then the Enlightened One, leading him step by step, spoke to him of giving, of virtue, of the heavens, of the perils, vanity, and defiling nature of sensual pleasures, and of the benefits of renunciation.

When the Blessed One saw that Anāthapiṇḍika the householder was ready in heart and mind, pliable, unobstructed, uplifted and serene, he gave him the explanation of the Teaching which is unique to the Enlightened Ones: the noble truth of suffering, its cause, its cessation, and the path. With that, the pure eye of truth (*dhammacakkhu*) opened for Anāthapiṇḍika: "Whatever has arisen must also cease." Anāthapiṇḍika, who had understood the truth of the Teaching, had overcome all doubts and was without any wavering, certain in mind, and relying on no one else in the Master's Dispensation. He had achieved the attainment of stream-entry (*sotāpatti*).

He then invited the Blessed One for a meal the next day at the home of his brother-in-law, and the Master accepted. After the meal, Anāthapiṇḍika asked the Enlightened One if he might build a monastery for the Order in his hometown of Sāvatthī. The Buddha answered: "The Enlightened Ones love peaceful places." "I understand, O Master, I understand," answered Anāthapiṇḍika, overjoyed with the acceptance of his offer (SN 10:8 = Cv 6.4).

When Anāthapiṇḍika returned to Sāvatthī he encouraged the people along the route to receive the Buddha in a respectful manner. In this way he prepared the way along the Rājagaha-Sāvatthī road for the Buddha's journey. Once he arrived in Sāvatthī he immediately searched for an appropriate location for the monastery. It had to be neither too close to the city, nor too far. The site should not be one that would be overrun by people in the daytime, nor should there be noise at night. It should be suitable for access by devoted visitors and also fit for those bent on seclusion. At last, in the chain of hills surrounding the city, he found a beautiful forest glade, ideal for the purpose. The area belonged to Prince Jeta, a son of King Pasenadi.

Anāthapiṇḍika visited Prince Jeta in his palace and asked if the forest were for sale. The prince answered that the large tract of land was not for sale, not even for the appropriate price of eighteen million. "I will give you that much, right now," replied Anāthapiṇḍika, but they were not able to come to terms and went to an arbitrator. The arbitrator ruled that the price should amount to as many gold pieces of the eighteen million as could be laid next to each other on the land. One this basis an agreement of sale was reached.

Anāthapiṇḍika had many carts filled with gold coins, and had them spread out upon the site. Finally only one small patch of ground at the entrance remained bare. He gave the instructions that more gold be brought, but the Prince Jeta announced that he was prepared to build a mighty gate-tower on that spot at his own expense. This imposing bastion and gate protected the monastery from the outside world, shielded it from the noises of the road, and emphasised the dividing line between the realms of the sacred and the worldly. Anāthapiṇḍika then spent another eighteen million for buildings and furnishings. He built individual cells, a meeting hall, a dining hall, storerooms, walkways, latrines, wells, and lotus ponds for bathing as well as a large surrounding wall. Thus the forest glade was transformed into a monastery and stood apart as a religious sanctuary (Cv 6.4).

When everything had been completed, the Enlightened One, with his monks, came to Sāvatthī to take up the residence at the new monastery. On their arrival, Anāthapiṇḍika invited them for an alms meal. After the meal he addressed the Buddha and asked: "How should I proceed with the offering of this Jetavana?"—"You may dedicate it to the Sangha of the four quarters, present and future." And so Anāthapiṇḍika did. Then the Buddha expressed his appreciation to him in the following verses:

"They ward off cold and heat and beasts of prey from there
And creeping things and gnats and rains in the wet season.
When the dreaded hot wind arises, that is warded off.
To meditate and obtain insight in a shelter and at ease—

A dwelling-place is praised by the Awakened One as chief gift to an Order.
Therefore a wise man looking to his own weal,
Should have dwelling-places built, so that
Learned ones can stay therein.

To these food and drink, raiment and lodgings
He should give, to the upright, with mind purified.
Then these will teach him Dhamma dispelling every ill;
He, knowing that Dhamma, here attains Nibbāna, cankerless."

(Translated by I.B. Horner).

The alms-meal for the monks was followed by a sumptuous celebration for the laity with gifts for everyone. This cost another eighteen million, so altogether Anāthapiṇḍika spent fifty-four million on the headquarters for the Order. Therefore, he stands at the head of the benefactors (AN 1:19).

2. Anāthapiṇḍika as a Wealthy Patron

Anāthapiṇḍika continued to feel responsible for the monastery which he had established. He supplied the monks who lived there with all necessities. Each morning he sent rice gruel to the monastery, and each evening he supplied all the requirements of clothing, alms bowls, and medicines; all repairs and upkeep in the Jeta Grove were undertaken by his servants. Above all, several hundred monks came daily to his home—a seven story palace—to receive the noon meal. Every day during meal-times his home was filled with saffron-coloured robes and the feeling of saintliness.

When King Pasenadi learned of Anāthapiṇḍika's generosity, he wished to emulate him and so he supplied alms food for five hundred monks daily. One day, as he was on his way to talk with the monks, he learned from his servants that the monks were taking the food away with them and giving it to their supporters in the city, so that these friends could offer it to them. The king was mystified, for he had always provided very tasty food, and so he asked the Buddha the reason for the monks' behaviour. The Buddha explained to the king that in the palace the courtiers distributed the food without any inner feeling, just following orders as if they were cleaning out a barn or taking a thief to court. They lacked faith and had no love for the monks. Many of them even felt that the monks were idlers who had to be supported by the working population. When anything was given in that spirit, no one could feel good—even when receiving the most expensive meal. On the other hand, with the faithful householders in the city, like Anāthapiṇḍika and Visākhā, the monks were welcome and were regarded as spiritual friends who lived for the welfare and benefit of all beings. A humble meal provided by a friend would be worth much more than the most sumptuous meal provided by someone who was indifferent or who did not give in the right spirit: "Even sour rice gruel becomes sweet when given by a friend." (J 465) The Buddha added a verse for the king to remember:

A dish may be coarse, savoury or sweet,
It may be meagre or it may abound,
Yet if offered with friendship and with love,
Then a delicious meal is always found (*J 346*).

Anāthapiṇḍika and Visākhā were not only the foremost donors in Sāvatthī (J 337, 346, 465), but their help was frequently solicited by the Buddha whenever something needed to be arranged with the lay community.

Yet even the wealth of Anāthapiṇḍika was not inexhaustible. One day treasures worth eighteen million were swept away by a flash flood and washed into the sea. Moreover, he had loaned about the same amount of money to business friends who did not repay him. He was reluctant, however, to ask for the money. Since his fortune amounted to about five times eighteen million, and he had already spent three-fifths of this for the forest monastery, his money was now running out. Anāthapiṇḍika, once a millionaire, had become poor. Nevertheless, he still continued to provide some food for the monks, even though it was only a modest serving of thin rice gruel.

At that time a spirit lived in the seven-storied palace, above the gate-tower. Whenever the Buddha or a holy disciple entered the house, the spirit, following the laws of his realm, was obliged to step down from his place in order to honour the Great Ones. However, this was very inconvenient for the spirit. And so he tried to think of a way to keep the Holy Ones out of the house. He appeared to a servant and suggested the stopping of the alms giving. But the servant paid no attention to these urgings. Then the spirit tried to turn the son of the house against the monks, but this also failed.

Finally, the spirit appeared in his supernatural aura to the householder himself and tried to persuade him to stop the giving of alms since he was now impoverished. Anāthapiṇḍika explained, however, that he knew only three treasures: the Buddha, the Enlightened One; the Dhamma, the Teaching; and the Sangha, the Order of Noble Disciples. He was looking after these treasures, and told the spirit to leave his house as there was no place in it for enemies of the Buddha.

Thereupon, the spirit, again following the laws of his realm, had to abandon that place. He betook himself to the deity who was the divine protector of the city of Sāvatthī and requested an assignment to a new shelter, but was referred to a higher court, that of the Four Great Kings. But these four also did not feel qualified to make a decision where Holy Ones were concerned and sent the homeless spirit to Sakka, the king of the gods.

In the meantime, however, the spirit had become aware of his wrong conduct and asked Sakka to seek forgiveness on his behalf. The king of the gods required that as a penance the spirit help Anāthapiṇḍika regain his fortune. First of all, the spirit had to retrieve the sunken gold; moreover, he had to procure unclaimed buried treasure, and finally, he had to persuade Anāthapiṇḍika's debtors to repay their debts.

With a great deal of effort, the spirit fulfilled these tasks. In doing so, he appeared to the debtors in dreams and demanded repayment. Forthwith Anāthapiṇḍika again had fifty-four million and was able to be as generous as before.

The spirit appeared now before the Enlightened One and asked forgiveness for his malevolent behaviour. He received forgiveness, and after the Enlightened One had explained the Teaching to him, he became a disciple. The Enlightened One taught him, moreover, that a person who strove for perfection in giving could not be kept from it by anything in the world, by neither bad nor holy spirits, nor gods, nor devils, nor threat of death (J 140; J 340).

After Anāthapiṇḍika had become as wealthy as before, a Brahman became jealous of his good fortune and decided to steal from him what, in his opinion, had made him so wealthy. He wanted to abduct the manifestation of Siri, the goddess of fortune, because he thought that then fortune would leave Anāthapiṇḍika and come to him. He could then force her to do his bidding. This strange perception was based on the idea that so-called favours of fate, while a reward for earlier good deeds, are nevertheless dispensed by deities, who force them to dwell in the beneficiary's house.

So the Brahman went to Anāthapiṇḍika's house and looked around to see where the spirit of fortune might be found. Like many Indians of his day, he had clairvoyant powers and he saw "Fortune" living in a white cock which was kept in a golden cage in the palace. He asked the master of the house to give him the cock to waken his students in the morning. Without hesitation, the generous Anāthapiṇḍika granted his wish. However, just at that moment, "Fortune" wandered into a jewel. The Brahman also requested this as a present and received it. But then the spirit hid in a staff, a weapon used for self-defence. After the Brahman had successfully begged this, the manifestation of Siri settled down on the head of Puññalakkhana, the first wife of Anāthapiṇḍika, who was truly the good spirit of this house and therefore had the protection of the gods. When the Brahman saw this, he recoiled in fright: "His wife I cannot request from him!" He confessed his evil intentions, returned the presents, and deeply ashamed, left the house.

Anāthapiṇḍika went to the Enlightened One and told him of this strange encounter which he had not understood. The Buddha explained the connection to him—how the world is changed through good works and how, for those with right insight through moral purification, everything is attainable, even Nibbāna (J 284).

Every time the Buddha stayed in Sāvatthī Anāthapiṇḍika visited him. At other times, however, he felt bereft without a tangible support for worship. Therefore, one day he told Ānanda of his wish to build a shrine. When Ānanda reported this to the Enlightened One, he answered that there are three types of shrines; memorials, monuments, and holy places. The first type was based upon a corporeal relic, which, after the death of an Enlightened One, was stored in a stupa; the second was based on an object which had a connection with the Enlightened One and had been used by him (often an alms bowl); the third was a symbol without a material object. Of these three visible supports for worship, the first was not yet a possibility as long as he was living. The third possibility would not be appropriate for those who could not content themselves with a mere picture or a symbol. There remained only the second possibility.

The Tree of Enlightenment—the Bodhi tree in Uruvelā—seemed the best object to serve as a memorial to the Blessed One. Under it the Enlightened One had opened the door to the Deathless, to salvation; under it he had taught and had remained in absorption. So it was decided to plant a small shoot of this tree in Sāvatthī.

Mahā Moggallāna brought a cutting from the tree which was to be planted at the gate-tower of the Jeta Grove in the presence of the court and the most distinguished of the monks and laity. Ānanda presented the sapling to the king for the ceremonial planting. But King Pasenadi replied, with princely humility, that he served in this life merely as a steward for the office of the king. It would be more appropriate that someone with a closer relationship to the Teaching consecrate the tree. So he presented the shoot to Anāthapiṇḍika who was standing next to him.

The tree grew and became an object of devotion for all the pious laity. At the request of Ānanda, the Enlightened One spent a night sitting under the tree in order to bestow on it another more distinguished consecration. Anāthapiṇḍika often sought out the tree and used the memories associated with it and the spiritual upliftment which he received there to focus his thoughts on the Enlightened One (J 479).

3. The Family of Anāthapiṇḍika

Anāthapiṇḍika was happily married. His wife, Puññalakkhaṇa, which means "the one who has the mark of merit," lived up to her name, and as the good spirit of the house, she took care of the servants and of the monks who came at midday. She too, was devoted to the Teaching. Through her brother, who had been one of the first lay disciples of the Buddha, she had become familiar with the Teaching.

Anāthapiṇḍika had four children, three daughters and a son. Two of the daughters, Little Subhadda and Big Subhadda, were steeped in the Dhamma like their father and had attained stream-entry. And just as they took after their father in spiritual matters, so they did in worldly affairs; they were both happily married. But the youngest daughter, Sumana, surpassed even the rest of her family in her deep wisdom. Upon hearing the Buddha, she had quickly attained the second step of purification, becoming a once-returner. She did not marry, but not because she had renounced marriage. In fact, when she saw the happiness of her two sisters, she became sad and lonely. Her spiritual strength did not suffice to overcome her depression. To the deep sorrow of her family, she wasted away, eating nothing, starving to death. She was reborn in the Tusita heaven, the highest form of existence in the sensual realm, and there she had to purge herself of the residue of dependence on other people, her last desire directed outwardly (Dhp Comy).

The only son of Anāthapiṇḍika, Kala the Dark One, was at first a strain on his father's house. He did not want to know anything of the Teaching, immersing himself completely in his business affairs. Then one day his father urged him to observe a holy day, offering him one thousand pieces of gold if he would keep the Uposatha day. Kala consented, and soon found it relaxing to take one day of the week off from business to enjoy himself in the company of his family. Because of this, the fasting regulations of the Uposatha day did not weigh too heavily on him. Then his father made a second request and offered him another thousand if he would come to the monastery with him one holiday afternoon in order to listen to the Teaching. Kala gladly agreed and it became the turning point of his life. Through the discourse of the Enlightened One, he attained stream-entry. His daily life became ennobled, just as in his father's case, and he also became a major benefactor of the Order, known by the name of "Little Anāthapiṇḍika" (Dhp Comy).

Kala was married to Sujātā, a sister of the famous lay devotee Visākhā, the mother of Migara.[1] She was very proud of her family background and her wealth on both sides. Because her thoughts revolved around nothing else but these trifles, she could not arouse any noble thoughts. She was unfulfilled, dissatisfied and peevish, and she vented her unhappiness on others. This was seen in the hostile and angry way in which she treated everyone. She would beat her servants, and whenever she appeared she spread fear and terror. Nor did she follow the rules of propriety in her relations with her parents-in-law and her husband. Thus she increasingly made herself an object to be scorned.

One day after a meal, as the Buddha was giving a discourse, much shouting and yelling was heard in the house as Sujātā was again scolding the servants. The Enlightened One interrupted his discourse and asked Anāthapiṇḍika what kind of a commotion this was, that sounded like the noisy shouts of fisher folk. The householder answered that it was his own daughter-in-law, who

1. Actually, Visākhā was Migara's daughter-in-law. But because she taught him the Dhamma, she became know as his mother.

did not behave properly towards her husband or his parents, who did not give alms, who was faithless and unbelieving, and who was forever causing conflict.

Then an unusual thing happened: the Buddha asked that she be called. When she appeared before him, he asked her which of the seven types of wives she wanted to be. She replied that she did not understand the meaning of this, and asked for more explanation. So the Enlightened One described the seven kinds of wives to her in verse:

Who, with mind corrupted, is unfeeling
Loves other men but her husband despises,
He who with wealth has gained her
She even seeks to kill—a Slayer is such a wife.
Whatever her husband gets for her by trade,
By skilled profession or a farmer's work,
She tries to filch a little just for herself.
Such a wife may well be called a Thief.
The slothful glutton, bent on idling,
A woman rude and fierce with coarse speech,
He who supports her, she dominates.
Such a wife a Tyrant must be called.
She who always for her husband cares
With sympathy, like a mother for her son,
Who carefully guards his stored-up wealth,
Such a wife may Motherly be called.
She who holds her husband in the same regard
As younger sister holds the elder born,
Who humbly serves her husband's every wish,
As Sisterly is such a wife known.
She whom her husband's sight will always please,
Like friends who see each other after long a time,
Who nobly bred and virtuous, devoted to her husband,
A Friend is she as well as wife.
From anger free, afraid of punishment,
Who bears with her husband with patient heart,
And without grudge obeys his every wish,
A Handmaid is she and a wife.
Who is called a Slayer, a Tyrant, or a Thief,

Who is rude, unvirtuous, and disrespectful,
Such kinds of wives will on their death
To hellish worlds of misery depart.
But wives like Mother, Sister, Friend and Handmaid,
Firm in virtue, imbued with long termed self-control,
Such kinds of wives will on their death
To happy destinies depart.

"These, Sujātā, are the seven kinds of wives a man may have," said the Blessed One, "and which of them are you?"

Deeply moved, Sujātā replied that from then on she would strive to be a handmaid to her husband. The words of the Enlightened One had shown her how to conduct herself as a wife. Later she became a faithful disciple of the Buddha, to whom she was ever grateful for her salvation.

News of the conversion of Sujātā quickly spread. One evening when the Buddha came into the lecture hall and asked what conversation the monks were having, they reported that they were discussing the miracle of the Dhamma. They had been praising the mighty power of an Awakened One who had made such a charming wife out of the former house dragon Sujata. Thereupon the Buddha told them how he had already tamed her once in an earlier existence. That time, she had been his mother, and he had stopped her scolding and domineering through a comparison between the odious crows and the sweet songbirds (J 269; AN 7:59).

Finally, mention is made of a nephew of Anāthapiṇḍika. He had inherited a fortune of forty million but lived a wild life, squandering, drinking, and gambling everything away. He gave away thousands to various entertainers, women, and obliging friends. When he had exhausted his inheritance, he asked his wealthy uncle for support. His uncle gave him a thousand gold pieces and told him that he should use this to start a business. But again he wasted all of his money, and appeared once more at the palace of Anāthapiṇḍika, who this time gave him five times as much as before, without a single condition, but as a severance. But even the warning that this would be the last of the money did not keep the nephew from his wasteful ways. For the third time he begged his uncle for money. Anāthapiṇḍika gave the young man two pieces of clothing, but he wasted these, too, and was shameless enough to call on his uncle for a fourth time. This time, however, he was told to leave. If he had come as one of the many beggars and not as a demanding nephew, he certainly would not have asked in vain for sustenance from the house of Anāthapiṇḍika. But this he did not do, for he did not want alms food but money to squander.

Because he was too lazy and stubborn to earn his own living, yet was not willing to beg, he died wretchedly. His body was found at the city wall and was thrown onto the refuse pile. When Anāthapiṇḍika heard of this, he asked himself whether he could have prevented this sad ending. He told the Buddha the story and asked if he should have acted differently. The Buddha, however, resolved his misgivings, and in his omniscience explained how that nephew belonged to the fortunately small number of insatiable people who were like bottomless vats. He had perished because of real external needs, and this same situation had already occurred in earlier lives (J 291).

4. Anāthapiṇḍika's Associations with Friends

Once Anāthapiṇḍika had attained stream-entry, he was unswervingly committed to observing the precepts, to purity of mind, to the endeavour to influence those around him toward good. So he lived in purity amongst like-minded people. Not only his immediate family, but also his employees and servants strove to practise generosity, to keep the five precepts, and to observe the holy days (J 382). His home became a centre of kindness and goodwill, and this attitude spread to his environment, to his friends and associates. He did not force his ideas on them, nor did he evade the problems of everyday life. Some details of his life in those days are contained in the scriptures.

Once a group of drinking companions in Sāvatthī ran out of money. They wondered how they could get more brandy, and one of them thought of drugging the wealthy Anāthapiṇḍika and then, when he had become unconscious, robbing him. They knew that he always took a particular route to visit the king, and so they set up a small brandy shop along the way. When Anāthapiṇḍika came along, they invited him to have a drink with them. But thinking to himself: "How can a devout follower of the Exalted One drink brandy?" he declined the invitation and continued on to the palace.

The depraved drinkers, however, tried to entice him once again on his return trip. Then he faced them directly and said that even they did not want to drink their own brew since it stood just as untouched as on the earlier trip. Were they planning to make him unconscious and then rob him? When he bravely confronted them with these words, they fled in terror (J 53).

Anāthapiṇḍika knew how to differentiate between his own observance of the precept not to drink alcohol and the behaviour of others, as is shown in the following example:

One of Anāthapiṇḍika's friends dealt in spirits. In spite of this, Anāthapiṇḍika maintained their friendship. Once when the wine dealer suffered a major loss of merchandise through the carelessness of an employee, Anāthapiṇḍika was entirely sympathetic and treated his friend no differently than any other friend who had met with misfortune. He himself set a good example, but forced his ways on no one and reproached no one (J 47).

Once when Anāthapiṇḍika was in a region where there was danger of falling into the hands of robbers, he preferred the inconvenience of travelling without a night's rest rather than expose himself to the risk of an attack (J 103). He was true to the instructions of Lord Buddha, that one may overcome some things by fleeing from them, without a display of false heroism.

Anāthapiṇḍika avoided being robbed in other ways. He had a friend with the unfortunate name "Unlucky Bird," who had been his friend since childhood. When this friend needed money, Anāthapiṇḍika helped him generously and appointed him to a job in his own household. His other friends criticised him for this—the fellow had an inauspicious name and he came from rather low origins. But Anāthapiṇḍika rebuffed them, "What's in a name? The wise pay no attention to superstition." When Anāthapiṇḍika went on a business trip, he entrusted his house to this friend. Some thieves heard of the departure of the wealthy man and planned a burglary. When they had surrounded the house, the vigilant "Unlucky Bird" beat drums and made so much noise that it sounded as if a celebration were in progress. This convinced the thieves that the head of the house had not really left, so they threw away their tools and fled. When Anāthapiṇḍika heard of this he said to his friends, "See, that 'Unlucky Bird' has done me a great service. Had I listened to you, I would have been robbed" (J 83, 121).

Most of Anāthapiṇḍika's friends were religious people, although some of them revered the various wandering ascetics who represented the many sects and diverse beliefs prevalent in India at that time. One day Anāthapiṇḍika suggested that a large group of his friends come to listen to the Buddha. They went willingly and were so stimulated by the Enlightened One's Teaching that they professed themselves to be his followers. From then on they regularly visited the monastery, gave donations, and observed the precepts and the holy days. But as soon as the Buddha left Sāvatthī they deserted the Teaching and once again followed the other ascetics with whom they had daily contact.

Several months later, when the Buddha was again at Sāvatthī Anāthapiṇḍika again brought his friends to see him. This time the Awakened One not only presented the edifying aspects of the Doctrine, but also warned the apostates that there was no better or more comprehensive protection against suffering in the world than the Threefold Refuge in the Buddha, the Dhamma, and the Sangha. This opportunity was seldom available in this world, and whoever forfeited it would be extremely sorry. Whoever, though, took the Three Refuges would escape the hell regions and would attain to one of the three happy destinies: a good human rebirth, one of the heavenly abodes, or Nibbāna. Then he summarised this exhortation in these verses:

Who in the Buddha refuge take,
They shall not go to realms of woe.
When they lay aside the human frame,
They shall fill up the hosts in heaven.
Who in the Dhamma refuge take,
They shall not go to realms of woe.
When they lay aside the human frame,
They shall fill up the hosts in heaven.
Who in the Sangha refuge take,
They shall not go to realms of woe.
When they lay aside the human frame,

They shall fill up the hosts in heaven.[2]
To mountains and to forests many go for refuge,
To shrines and trees and groves, by fear impelled.
Not one is a safe refuge, not one a refuge that is final,
Not by going to such a refuge can one find the freedom from all suffering,
But he who takes in Buddha, Dhamma, Sangha, his refuge,
Who sees with right wisdom the Fourfold Noble Truth—
Of suffering, its cause and its transcending,
And of the Noble Eightfold Path which to the stilling of all suffering leads—
He finds a refuge that is safe, a refuge that is final.
Going to such a refuge leads to freedom from all suffering.[3]

The Buddha stimulated these merchants to think along different lines and made their minds so receptive for hearing what is particular to the Buddhas, the teaching of the Four Noble Truths, that they all attained stream-entry. In this way, Anāthapiṇḍika's attainment also became a blessing for his friends (J 1).

5. Discourses by the Blessed One

Of the forty-five rainy seasons[4] of his life as a teacher, the Buddha spent nineteen in Sāvatthī in Anāthapiṇḍika's monastery in the Jeta Grove. Whenever he spent the three or four months of the rainy season there, Anāthapiṇḍika would usually visit him twice a day, often just to see him, but frequently to hear a discourse. Anāthapiṇḍika was reticent about asking the Exalted One questions. As the most generous benefactor of the Order, he did not want to create the impression that he was merely bartering his contributions for personal advice. The donations were for him a matter of the heart, a joy, given without any thought of reward—they were in themselves sufficient for him. He thought that the monks and the Buddha would not regard the instruction as an

2. Dīgha Nikāya, 20.
3. Dhammapada, vv 188–192.
4. Rainy season (*vassa*): the monsoon season when the monks and nuns remain in their monasteries and practise meditation intensively.

obligation or a compensation for the benefactor, but that they would be a heart-felt joy for them, too.

Therefore, when Anāthapiṇḍika came to the Buddha, he would sit quietly off to one side and wait to see whether the Exalted One would give him any instruction. If the Awakened One said nothing, Anāthapiṇḍika would sometimes relate one of the episodes of his life, of which several have been recounted. He would wait to see whether the Exalted One had any comments to offer, approving or criticising his behaviour, or whether he would use that special event as a point of departure for a discourse. In this way he connected all that he experienced in his everyday life with the Teaching.

Many of the occasions when the Buddha gave instructions to Anāthapiṇḍika have been recorded in the Pali canon. They constitute a comprehensive code of conduct for the conscientious lay follower of the Buddha, so that Anāthapiṇḍika has also become a benefactor to all those in future times who are trying to follow the Teaching. These discourses, which are contained in the Aṅguttara Nikāya,[5] range from the simplest message to the most profound. A few are mentioned here, beginning with the most basic advice to the laity:

"Housefather, possessed of four things, the noble disciple has entered on the householder's path of duty, a path which brings good repute and leads to the heaven world. What are the four?

"Herein, housefather, the noble disciple waits upon the order of monks with the offer of a robe, alms food, lodging ... and medicines for use in sickness. These are the four things" (AN 4:60).

"Housefather, there are these four kinds of bliss to be won by the householder: ... the bliss of ownership, the bliss of wealth, the bliss of debtlessness, the bliss of blamelessness.

"... A man has wealth acquired by energetic striving, amassed by strength of arm, won by sweat, lawful and lawfully gotten. At the thought: 'Wealth is mine acquired by energetic striving ...,' bliss comes to him, satisfaction comes to him. This, housefather, is called, 'the bliss of ownership.'

"... A man by means of wealth acquired by energetic striving

5. *Aṅguttara Nikāya*, "*The Discourses Collection in Numerical Order*," trans. by Nyanaponika, The Wheel, Part I No. 155–157; Part II No. 208–211; Part III No. 238–240, BPS.

... both enjoys his wealth and does meritorious deeds therewith. At the thought: 'By means of wealth acquired ... I both enjoy my wealth and do meritorious deeds,' bliss comes to him, satisfaction comes to him. This, housefather, is called 'the bliss of wealth.'

"... A man owes no debt great or small to anyone. At the thought: 'I owe no debt, great or small, to anyone,' bliss comes to him, satisfaction comes to him. This, householder, is called 'the bliss of debtlessness.'

"... The noble disciple is blessed with blameless action of body, blameless action of speech, blameless action of mind. At the thought: 'I am blessed with blameless action of body, speech, and mind,' bliss comes to him, satisfaction comes to him. This is called 'the bliss of blamelessness.'

"Such, housefather, are the four kinds of bliss to be won by the householder ..." (AN 4:62).

"There are, O householder, five desirable, pleasant, and agreeable things which are rare in the world. What are those five? They are long life, beauty, happiness, fame and (rebirth in) a heaven. But of those five things, O householder, I do not teach that they are to be obtained by prayer or by vows. If one could obtain them by prayer or vows, who would not do it?

"For a noble disciple, O householder, who wishes to have long life, it is not befitting that he should pray for long life or take delight in so doing. He should rather follow a path of life that is conducive to longevity. By following such a path he will obtain long life, be it divine or human.

"For a noble disciple, O householder, who wishes to have beauty ... happiness ... fame (rebirth in) a heaven, it is not befitting that he should pray for them or take delight in so doing. He should rather follow a path of life that is conducive to beauty ... happiness ... fame ... (rebirth in) a heaven. By following such a path he will obtain beauty, happiness, fame, and (rebirth in) a heaven" (AN 5:43).

"Householder, there are five reasons for getting rich. What five?

"... A noble disciple with riches gotten by work and zeal, gathered by the strength of the arm, earned by the sweat of the brow, justly obtained in a lawful way, makes himself happy, glad, and keeps that happiness; he makes his parents happy, glad, and keeps them so; so likewise his wife and children, and his servants.

"... When riches are thus gotten, he makes his friends and companions happy, glad, and keeps them so.

"... When riches are thus gotten, ill-luck ... is warded off, and he keeps his goods in safety.

"... When riches are thus gotten, he makes the five oblations to kin, guests, spirits, kings and deities.

"... When riches are thus gotten, the noble disciple institutes offerings of lofty aim, celestial, ripening to happiness, leading heavenward, for all those recluses and good men who abstain from pride and indolence, who bear all things in patience and humility, each mastering self, each calming self, each perfecting self.

"Now if the wealth of that noble disciple, heeding these five reasons, comes to destruction, let him consider thus: 'At least I've heeded those reasons for getting rich, but my wealth has gone!'—thus he is not upset. And if his wealth increases, let him think: 'Truly, I've heeded those reasons and my wealth has grown!'—thus he is not upset in either case" (AN 5:41).

The importance of the preceding discourses is further emphasised by the fact that the Buddha impressed them again on Anāthapiṇḍika on another occasion in a slightly different form. On that occasion he said to him:

"Housefather, there are these four conditions (to realise which is) desirable, dear, delightful, hard to win in the world. What four?

"(The wish:) 'Oh may wealth by lawful means come to me!'

"'Wealth being gotten by lawful means, may good report attend me along with my kinsmen and teachers!'

"'... May I live long and reach great age!'

"'... When the body breaks up, on the other side of death may I attain the heaven world!'

"Now, housefather, to the winning of these four conditions, four conditions conduce. What four?

"Perfection of faith, perfection of virtue, perfection of generosity, and perfection of wisdom" (AN 4:61).

Faith can only be won if one fully acknowledges the Blessed One and his message about the nature of existence. One can only attain virtue if one fulfils the five minimum precepts for the moral life. Generosity is possessed by one who is free from the defect of avarice. One achieves wisdom when one realises that if the heart is riddled with worldly passions, malevolence, lassitude, agitation, absent-mindedness, and doubt, then one does what should not be done and fails to do what should be done.

But one who does evil and neglects good, will lose his reputation and his good fortune. On the other hand, one who constantly investigates and observes his inner impulses and motives, is one who begins to overcome the five hindrances.[6] Hence their conquest is a consequence of wisdom. If the noble disciple—through faith, virtue, generosity, and wisdom—is well on the way to obtaining the four desired things, namely, wealth, good reputation, long life, and a path to a good rebirth, then he uses his money to accomplish four good deeds. He makes himself, his family, as well as his friends happy; he avoids accidents; he performs the five above-mentioned duties; and he supports genuine ascetics and priests. By whomever wealth has been spent in other than these four ways, those riches have not fulfilled their purpose, and they have been senselessly squandered. But whoever has diminished his wealth because of spending it for these four purposes, has used it in a meaningful way (AN 4:61).

On yet another occasion, the Buddha explained the difference between right and wrong conduct for the lay disciple in the discourse on people who indulge in worldly pleasures. There he says: The most foolish kind of person is one who, having obtained possessions in dishonest ways, does not even enjoy the use of them himself, and neither does he use them to benefit others. Slightly more sensible is the person who at least derives happiness and joy from ill-gotten gains. Still more sensible is the one who uses them to make others happy. Even on these lowest planes of forcible and illegal acquisition of money and goods which the ordinary person indignantly and indiscriminately condemns, the Awakened One sees fine distinctions in the behaviour and attitudes of people.

The person who recognises that the elementary purpose of grasping for wealth is at least to obtain some comfort for himself, could be made to see how, through having an honest income, he can obtain more benefit. And one who derives additional pleasure

---

6. Sensual desire, ill will, sloth and torpor, restlessness and worry, and sceptical doubt. See Nyanaponika, *The Five Mental Hindrances and Their Conquest*, The Wheel No. 26, BPS.

by giving some pleasure to others too, will readily understand that he has obviously given no joy to those whom he has cheated or robbed, while by making money honestly, he does not hurt anyone.

The second group of people are those who earn money entirely in dishonest ways but at least partly through honest work. Among these, too, are those who bring joy neither to themselves nor to others; those who at least enjoy their wealth; and those who also gladden others. Finally, the third group consists of those people who earn their living entirely in honourable ways and likewise fall under the four groups.

In the last case, there are again two types: those who are strongly attached to their wealth and being infatuated are unaware of its inherent danger, not seeking a way out of it; and there are those who are not attached to their wealth and not infatuated by it, but are aware of its inherent dangers and know the way out of it. So there are ten types of people who enjoy worldly pleasures concerned with wealth (AN 5:91).

Once the Buddha asked Anāthapiṇḍika whether alms were provided in his house. This refers, according to the Commentary, only to alms given to the needy. The Buddha knew, of course, that alms were generously given to the Order of Monks (the Sangha) in Anāthapiṇḍika's house. From this arose a talk on the qualitative grades of excellence in giving. The Buddha explained: "Whether one gives coarse or choice alms, if one gives it without respect and politeness, not with one's own hand, gives only leftovers, and without belief in result of actions, then wherever he is reborn as a result of his giving of alms, his heart will have no inclination for fine food and clothing, fine vehicles, for the finer five sense-objects. His children, wife, servants and labourers will not obey him, not listen to him, and not pay him attention. And why is that so? Because this is the result of actions done without respect."

In connection with this, the Buddha told how, in an earlier life, as a rich Brahman called Velāma, he himself had distributed an enormous amount of alms but none of the recipients had been worthy of the gifts. Far more meritorious than large donations to unworthy people would be a single feeding of noble disciples, from stream-winners to Arahats. Even more meritorious would be the feeding of a Paccekabuddha or of a hundred Paccekabuddhas, and even more so the giving of alms to a Buddha, or the building of a monastery.

But better yet would be taking refuge in the Buddha, the Dhamma and the Sangha. And this deed would be perfected if one observed the five precepts. It would be still better if one could imbibe a slight fragrance, if only for a moment, of an all-encompassing radiation of love. The best of all, however, the ultimate, would be to cultivate, even for the time of a finger-snap, the thought of impermanence (AN 9:20).

This speech shows the gradations of practise: of giving, of virtue, of the excellence of universal love, and finally, the unwavering realisation of the impermanence of all conditioned things. Without making efforts in giving, in virtue, and in impartial love for all fellow creatures, the concentrated contemplation of impermanence is not possible; for in peace and quiet which this practise requires, pangs of conscience or other dark thoughts can arise.

This exposition on the kinds of giving recalls another short discourse. It is the only one in which Anāthapiṇḍika himself asks a question, namely, how many were there worthy of receiving gifts. The Buddha answered that there were two kinds: those who were on the way to liberation, and those who had already attained it (A 2:27).

While in the talks mentioned thus far the purification of the heart has been more or less indirectly stressed, at another time the subject was directly approached. On that occasion the Buddha said to Anāthapiṇḍika: "If the heart is corrupted, then all actions, words, and thoughts are tainted, too. Such a person will be carried away by his passions and will have an unhappy death, (just as) gables, rafters, and walls of a badly roofed house are unprotected and will decay because they will rot when drenched with rain" (AN 3:107–108).

One time Anāthapiṇḍika went with several hundred lay followers to the Buddha, who spoke to them thus: "To be sure, you householders provide the monastic community with clothing, food, shelter, and medicine, but you should not be satisfied with that. May you also from time to time strive to enter and abide in the joy of (inner meditative) seclusion![7]"

---

7. *Pītiṃ pavivekaṃ.* Joy (*pīti*) is present in the first and second of the meditative absorptions (*jhāna*).

After these words the venerable Sāriputta added the following:

"At a time when the noble disciple dwells in the joy of (meditative) seclusion, five things do not exist in him: there is no pain and grief connected with the senses;[8] no pleasure and gladness connected with the senses; no pain and grief connected with what is unwholesome;[9] no pleasure and gladness connected with what is unwholesome;[10] no pain and grief connected with what is wholesome[11]" (AN 5:176).

On another occasion when Anāthapiṇḍika and many lay followers again visited the Buddha, the blessed One said to Sāriputta:

"A white-clad householder who is restrained in his actions according to the five precepts and who can, easily and without difficulty, obtain at will the four lofty mental abidings which bring happiness in the present—such a householder may, if he so wishes, declare of himself: 'Destroyed for me is (rebirth in) hell, destroyed is animal rebirth, destroy the realm of ghosts; destroyed for me are the lower worlds, the unhappy destinies, the abysmal realms; I have entered the stream, no more subject to fall into the states of woe, affirmed, assured of final enlightenment.'

"In what five precepts are his actions restrained? A noble disciple abstains from killing, from taking what is not given, from wrong sensual behaviour, from lying, and from intoxicants that cause indolence.

"And what are the four lofty mental abidings bringing happiness in the present, which he can obtain at will?

"A noble disciple has unshakable faith in the Buddha, unshakable faith in the Teaching, unshakable faith in the Order; and he is possessed of virtues beloved by the Nobles—virtues that are unbroken, unviolated, untarnished, without blemish, bringing freedom, praised by the wise, uninfluenced, conducive to concentration.

"These are the four lofty mental abidings bringing happiness in the present, which purify the impure mind and cleanse the

---

8. "Connected with the senses," i.e., with sense-desire and the sense-objects.
9. This in the case of the failure when intentions or actions are unwholesome.
10. This in the case of success in unwholesome intentions or actions.
11. This in the case of failure in wholesome intentions or actions.

unclean mind. These he obtains at will, easily and without difficulty" (AN 5:179).

At another time the attainment of stream-entry was explained to Anāthapiṇḍika in three different ways—but only to him alone. The Buddha said:

"When in the noble disciple the five fearsome evils have disappeared, when he possesses the four attributes of stream-entry, and if he understands wisely and well the noble method, then he can regard himself as a stream-enterer. However, one who kills, steals, engages in sexual misconduct, lies, and takes intoxicants, generates five fearsome evils both in the present and in the future, and experiences pain and grief in his mind. Whosoever keeps away from the five vices, for him the five fearsome evils are eliminated. Secondly, he possesses—as attributes of stream-entry—unshakable trust in the Buddha, in the Dhamma, in the Sangha, and he keeps his virtue unbroken. And thirdly, he has fully seen and penetrated the noble method, that is, the dependent origination" (AN 10:92).

One incident is reported where Anāthapiṇḍika wanted to visit the Buddha one morning, but because it was still too early, he went to the monastery of some Brahman pilgrims. Since they knew him as a follower of the Buddha, they asked him which views the ascetic Gotama held. He replied that he didn't know all the views of the Exalted One. To the question of which views the monks held, he replied again that he did not know all their views. Thereupon he was asked what view he himself held. He replied:

"What views I hold, O honourable ones, would not be difficult for me to explain. But may I first ask the honourable ones to present their own views. After that it will not be difficult for me to explain what kind of views I hold."

The pilgrims explained their notions of the world. One held it to be eternal, another held it not to be eternal; one held it to be finite, another held it to be infinite; one believed that body and life were identical, others supposed them to be distinct; some believed that Enlightened Ones endured after death, others said that they were destroyed.

Then Anāthapiṇḍika spoke: "Whichever of these views held, it could only come from one of two sources: either from one's own unwise musings, or through the words of another. In either case, the view has arisen conditionally. Conditioned things, however, are transitory; and things of a transitory nature involve suffering. Hence, one who holds views and opinions clings to suffering, succumbs to suffering."

Then the pilgrims wished to know what views Anāthapiṇḍika held. He answered: "Whatever arises is transitory; the transitory is of the nature of suffering. But suffering does not belong to me, that is not me, that is not my self."

Seeking a rebuttal, the pilgrims argued that he himself was involved in as much as he clung to the view he had just expressed. He replied that that was not the case, for he had perceived those facts in accordance with reality, and besides that, he knew the escape from it, as it really is—in other words, he used the view only as a means and in time would also discard it. Thereupon the pilgrims were unable to respond, felt defeated, and sat in silence.

Anāthapiṇḍika went quietly to the Blessed One, reported the conversation to him, and heard the Buddha's praise: "You were right, householder. You should guide those deluded ones more often into harmony with the truth." And then he delighted and encouraged him with a discourse. After Anāthapiṇḍika had left, The Blessed One said to the monks that even a monk who had lived one hundred years in the Order would not have been able to speak better to the pilgrims than Anāthapiṇḍika the householder had done (AN 10:93).

Finally, two other incidents can be reported: Anāthapiṇḍika was ill and requested a visit from a monk in order to receive consolation. Because Anāthapiṇḍika had done so much as a benefactor of the Order, there was no question that his request would be fulfilled. The first time, Venerable Ānanda came to him; the second time, Venerable Sāriputta. The Venerable Ānanda said that one of untrained mind was afraid of death and of what came after it, because it lacked four kinds of trust: he did not believe in the Buddha, the Dhamma, the Sangha, nor did he possess the virtues which were dear to the noble ones. But Anāthapiṇḍika replied that he had no fear of death. He possessed unshakable trust in the Buddha, in the Dhamma, and in the Sangha. As for the rules for householders, he knew of none which he was still violating. Then Venerable Ānanda praised him and said that he had just declared the fruit of stream-entry (SN 55:27).

When Venerable Sāriputta visited, he said to Anāthapiṇḍika that, unlike the untrained worldling for whom hell was imminent, he had faith in the Three Jewels and had not yielded to vice. If he were now to concentrate very strongly on his faith in the Buddha, the Dhamma, and the Sangha, and on his own virtue, then his sickness would disappear through this meditation. He did not, like those who were untrained, have wrong views, wrong intentions, wrong speech, wrong action, wrong livelihood, wrong effort, wrong mindfulness, wrong absorption, wrong knowledge, or wrong liberation. If he would consider the fact that he, as a stream-winner, was in possession of the ten noble factors, flowing in the direction of right liberation, then through this meditation his illness would vanish. Through the strengthening power of this contemplation, Anāthapiṇḍika recalled his great good fortune to be a noble disciple, and because of this excellent spiritual medicine, the disease disappeared immediately. He stood up, invited the Venerable Sāriputta to have his meal, and carried on a further discussion with him. At the end, the Venerable Sāriputta gave him three verses to remember:

Whoever has faith in the Tathāgata,
Unwavering and fixed,
Whose life is good,
Praised by the Noble Ones and dear to them;
Whoever is likewise loyal to the Order,
Whose views are clear and straight—
'He is not poor,' they say,
'Not lived in vain the life of such a man.'
Therefore the wise should cultivate (these three),
Faith, virtue and
Clear-seeing of the Dhamma,
Bearing the Buddha's message in their minds

(SN 55:26; adapted from F. L. Woodward's translation).

Eighteen Anāthapiṇḍika-discourses have been briefly recounted. Fourteen were given at the Exalted One's instigation; one arose when Anāthapiṇḍika posed a question; in another he reported how he had taught others; and in two he was instructed by Venerable Ānanda and Venerable Sāriputta. These eighteen discourses reveal how the Buddha made the teaching clear to the laity and inspired them to joyful endeavours.

6. The Death of Anāthapiṇḍika

The householder Anāthapiṇḍika became sick a third time with very strong pains which were getting worse and not easing. Again Anāthapiṇḍika asked Venerable Sāriputta and Venerable Ānanda for assistance. When Venerable Sāriputta saw him, he knew that Anāthapiṇḍika was nearing death, and gave him the following instructions:

He should practise freeing himself from clinging to the six sense faculties and not attach his thoughts to them; secondly, he should practise releasing himself from dependence on the six objects and not attach his thoughts to them either. Thirdly, he should stop clinging to the connecting link between the six senses and the six sense objects, as well as to the six sense contacts, the six feelings, the six elements, the five aggregates and the four formless realms, as well as to all that is seen, heard, thought, perceived, and investigated in the mind.

Anāthapiṇḍika must have followed this detailed presentation with his heart so that even as he was listening, he was already practising in the way the wise and holy Venerable Sāriputta had instructed him. At the end of the instructions, tears came to Anāthapiṇḍika's eyes. The Venerable Ānanda turned to him compassionately and asked him to calm himself and be at peace. But Anāthapiṇḍika replied: "I cannot calm myself and be at peace, O worthy Ānanda. I have served the Master and the spiritually accomplished monks for a long time, and yet I have never heard such a profound discourse."

Then Venerable Sāriputta said: "Such profound talk, O householder, will not be clear enough for white-clad lay followers; it is clear enough for ascetics."

Anāthapiṇḍika answered: "Venerable Sāriputta, let such talks on the Dhamma be given to white-clad laity, too. There are those with just a little dust on their eyes. If they don't hear such teachings, they will be lost. Some may be able to understand."

The difference from the previously presented teaching of the Buddha is significant. Here we are concerned with ultimate questions, with the highest deliverance, not just on a theoretical basis but as practise. Anāthapiṇḍika was aware, as a disciple who possessed the fruit of stream-entry, of the transitory nature the five aggregates of clinging, and he himself had expressed the fact that he knew the three characteristics of existence: impermanence, suffering, and non-self. But there is a great difference as to whether one merely hears these things and ponders them, or whether one actually practises and applies their relevance to oneself. In this distinction lies the essential difference between the methods the Buddha used to teach householders and he used to teach monks.

For the laity, insight into the nature of existence was presented as a matter of knowledge, and this teaching was given at first to the monks as well. But for the many monks who had progressed further, the Buddha introduced the practise that would lead to complete liberation even in this life. Only if one sees that Venerable Sāriputta's exposition was a practical step-by-step approach to Nibbāna, can one understand that Anāthapiṇḍika had never heard the core of the Teaching presented in quite such a manner. In his dying hour he was already far removed from his worldly concerns and, while thinking of the Dhamma, had renounced attachment to worldly possessions as well as his body; thus he found himself in a situation comparable to that of the most advanced monks. Under these circumstances, Venerable Sāriputta was able to give him such instructions as would have the most far-reaching effects.

After advising Anāthapiṇḍika in this way, Venerable Sāriputta and Venerable Ānanda left. Shortly thereafter, the householder Anāthapiṇḍika died and was reborn in the Tusita Heaven, where his youngest daughter had preceded him. Yet he was so genuinely devoted to the Buddha and the Sangha that he appeared in the Jeta Grove as a deva, filling the whole area with heavenly light. He went to the Buddha and, after paying homage to him, spoke the following verses:

O blessed is this Jeta Grove, frequented by the holy Order,
Where the Dhamma King resides, the fount of all my happiness.
By deeds, by knowledge, by righteousness,
By virtue, by the sublimest life,
By these are mortals purified, and not by lineage nor by wealth.
A wise man, therefore, seeing his own good,

Wisely will he choose the Dhamma, that he may thus be purified.
Like Sāriputta in his wisdom, in his virtue, and in highest peace,
At best a bhikkhu who has gone across, can only equal him.

(MN 143; SN 2:20).

Buddhist Stories

From the Dhammapada Commentary
Part III

Translated from the Pāli by

Eugene Watson Burlingame

Selected and revised by

Bhikkhu Khantipālo

WHEEL PUBLICATION NO. 335/336

Publisher's Note

This anthology has been compiled from Eugene Watson Burlingame's classic translation of the background stories from the Dhammapada Commentary, *Buddhist Legends.* Originally published in the Harvard Oriental Series, *Buddhist Legends* has been maintained in print since 1969 by the Pali Text Society. With the latter's permission, the Buddhist Publication Society issues this selection of these stories in booklet form in the Wheel Series, edited and arranged by Bhikkhu Khantipālo. The publisher gratefully acknowledges the kindness of the Pali Text Society for granting permission to publish this anthology. Readers who would like to obtain the complete three-volume collection of *Buddhist Legends* may contact the Pali Text Society or inquire from bookshops specializing in Asian literature.

What Novices Can Do

31. The Elder Sangharakkhita's Nephew

FARING FAR, WANDERING ALONE ... This instruction was given by the Teacher while he was in residence at Sāvatthī with reference to Sangharakkhita.

The story goes that a certain youth of respectable family living at Sāvatthī, after hearing a discourse of the Teacher, made his renunciation and went forth, obtained acceptance as a monk, and in but a few days attained arahantship. He was known as the Elder Sangharakkhita. When a nephew of the Elder Sangharakkhita came of age, he went forth under the elder, and after obtaining acceptance entered upon the rains residence at a certain monastery.[1]

Receiving two robes such as are worn by monks during the period of the rains, one seven cubits long, the other eight cubits long, he decided to present the robe eight cubits long to his preceptor and to keep the robe seven cubits long for himself. When he had completed the rains residence, he set out for the purpose of seeing his preceptor and journeyed from place to place, receiving alms along the way.

He arrived at the monastery before the elder arrived. Entering the monastery, he swept the elder's day-quarters, set out water for bathing the feet, prepared a seat, and then sat down, watching the road by which the elder would approach. When he saw the elder approach, he advanced to meet him, took his bowl and robe, seated the elder with the words, "Please be seated, reverend sir," took a palm-leaf fan and fanned him, gave him water to drink, and bathed his feet. Finally he brought forth the robe, laid it at the elder's feet, and said, "Reverend sir, please wear this robe." Having done so, he resumed fanning him. Said the elder to the nephew, "Sangharakkhita, I have a complete set of robes; you wear this robe yourself."—"Reverend sir, from the moment I

1. The "going forth" (*pabbajjā*) is the novice ordination. "Acceptance" (*upasampadā*) is full ordination as a bhikkhu.

received this robe I set my heart on giving it to you alone. Please make use of it."—"Never mind, Sangharakkhita, my set of robes is complete; you wear this robe yourself."—"Reverend sir, please do not refuse the robe, for if you wear it, great will be the fruit I shall receive thereby."

Although the younger monk repeated his request several times, the elder refused to accept the present of the robe. So, as the younger monk stood there fanning the elder, he thought to himself, "While the elder was a layman, I stood in the relation of nephew to him. Since he has been a monk, I have been his fellow-resident. But in spite of this he is not willing as my preceptor to share my possessions. If he is not willing to share my possessions with me, why should I longer remain a monk? I will become a householder once more." Then the following thought occurred to him, "It is a hard thing to live the household life. Suppose I become a householder once more; how shall I gain a living?" Finally the following thought occurred to him:

"I will sell this robe eight cubits long and buy a she-goat. Now she-goats are very prolific, and as fast as the she-goat brings forth young, I will sell them, and in this way accumulate some capital. As soon as I have accumulated some capital, I will take a wife. My wife will bear me a son, and I will name him after my uncle. I will put my son in a go-cart, and taking son and wife with me, will go to pay my respects to my uncle. As I journey by the way, I will say to my wife, 'Just bring me my son; I wish to carry him.' She will reply, 'Why should you carry this boy? Come, push this go-cart.' So saying, she will take the boy in her arms, thinking to herself, 'I will carry him myself.' But lacking the necessary strength to carry him, she will let him fall in the path of the wheels, and the go-cart will run over him. Then I will say to her, 'You would not even give me my own son to carry, although you were not strong enough to carry him yourself. You have ruined me.' So saying, I will bring down my stick on her back."

Thus pondered the younger monk as he stood fanning the elder. As he concluded his reflections, he swung his palm-leaf fan and brought it down on the head of the elder. The elder considered within himself, "Why did Sangharakkhita strike me on the head?" Immediately becoming aware of every single thought that had passed through the mind of his nephew, he said to him,

"Sangharakkhita, you did not succeed in hitting the woman; but what has an old monk done to deserve a beating?" The younger monk thought to himself, "Oh, I am ruined! My preceptor, it appears, knows every thought that has passed through my mind. What have I to do with the life of a monk any longer?" Straight away he threw his fan away and started to run off. But the young monks and novices ran after him, caught him, and led him to the Teacher.

When the Teacher saw those monks, he asked them, "Monks, why have you come here? Have you captured a monk?"—"Yes, reverend sir. This young monk became discontented and ran away, but we captured him and have brought him to you."—"Monk, is what they say true?"—"Yes, reverend sir."—"Monk, why did you commit so grievous a fault? Are you not the son of a Buddha of strenuous effort? And once having gone forth in the dispensation of a Buddha like me, though you failed through self-conquest to win for yourself the attainments of stream-entry or once-returning or non-returning, even so why did you commit so grievous a fault as this?"

"I am discontented, reverend sir."—"Why are you discontented?" In reply the younger monk related the whole story of his experiences, from the day he received the robes worn by monks in residence to the moment when he struck the elder on the head with his palm-leaf fan. "Reverend sir," said he, "That is why I ran away." Said the Teacher, "Come, monk; be not disturbed. The mind has a way of dwelling on subjects that are far off. One should strive to free it from the bonds of lust, hatred, and delusion." So saying, he pronounced the following stanza:

37. Faring far, wandering alone,
Formless and lying in a cave—
Those who restrain the mind
Are freed from Māra's bonds.

32. The Elder Tissa's Novice

Peaceful is his mind ... This instruction was given by the Teacher while he was in residence at Jetavana with reference to the novice of the Elder Tissa.

The story goes that a certain youth of good family, residing at Kosambī, went forth and obtained acceptance as a monk in the dispensation of the Teacher. After his acceptance, he was known as Elder Kosambivāsī Tissa. After he had kept the rains at Kosambī, his supporter brought a set of three robes and offerings of ghee and jaggery[2] and laid them at his feet. The elder said to him, "What are these, lay disciple?"—"Reverend sir, have you not kept residence with me during the season of the rains? Those who keep residence in our monastery always receive these offerings; please accept them, reverend sir."—"Never mind, lay disciple, I have no need of them."—"Why is that, reverend sir?"—"I have no novice to make things allowable for me, friend."[3]—"Reverend sir, if you have no novice to make things allowable, my son will become your novice."

The elder graciously accepted the offer. The lay disciple brought his own son, but seven years old, to the elder, and committed him into the elder's hands, saying "Please give him the going forth, reverend sir." The elder moistened the boy's hair, taught him the formula of meditation on the first five of the constituent parts of the body,[4] and gave him the going forth. The instant the razor touched his hair, he attained arahantship together with the analytical knowledges.

The elder, having given him the going forth, remained there for a fortnight. Then, deciding to visit the Teacher, he directed the novice to take the requisites, and set out on his journey. On the way he entered a certain monastery. The novice obtained lodging for the elder and looked after it for him.

While he was thus engaged, it grew dark and he was therefore unable to provide a lodging for himself. When the time came for

2. Brown palm sugar, usually in soft cakes, allowed to monks as a refreshment.

3. It is one of the novice's duties to offer such medicines to monks who themselves may not keep them longer than seven nights.

4. Head hairs, body hairs, nails, teeth, skin. These are traditionally taught as a meditation subject on the occasion of the novice ordination.

the novice to wait upon the elder, the novice approached the elder and sat down. The elder asked the novice, "Novice, have you not neglected to provide yourself with a lodging?"—"Reverend sir, I have had no opportunity to look after a lodging for myself."—"Well then, remain with me. It will inconvenience you to lodge outside in the place reserved for visitors." So saying, the elder, taking him with him, entered his own lodging. Now the elder had not yet attained the fruit of stream-entry, and as soon as he lay down, fell asleep. Thereupon the novice thought to himself, "Today is the third day during which I have occupied the same lodging with my preceptor. If I lie down to sleep, the elder will commit the offense of sleeping in common.[5] Therefore I will spend the night sitting up." So assuming a cross-legged posture near the bed of his preceptor, he spent the night sitting up.

The elder rose at dawn and said to himself, "I must cause the novice to go out." So he took a fan which was placed at the side of the bed, struck the mat of the novice with the tip of the palm-leaf, and then, tossing the fan into the air, said, "Novice, go out" (so as to avoid the above offence). The handle of the fan struck the novice in the eye and straightaway put out his eye. "What did you say, reverend sir?" said the novice. "Rise and go out," was the reply. The novice, instead of saying, "Reverend sir, my eye has been put out," covered his eye with one hand and went out. Moreover, when it was time for him to perform his duties as novice, he did not say, "My eye has been put out," nor did he remain seated, but covering his eye with one hand and taking a handbroom in the other, he swept out the privy and the washroom, after which, setting out water for washing the face, he swept out the elder's cell.

When he advanced to present the toothstick to the elder, he presented it to him with only one hand. His preceptor said to him, "This novice is not properly trained. Is it proper for a novice to present a toothstick to teachers and preceptors with one hand?"[6]—"Reverend sir, I know perfectly well what is the proper form, but one of my hands is engaged."—"What is the matter, novice?" Then

5. The fifth offence of expiation (*pācittiya*): "Should any bhikkhu sleep for more than two or three nights along with one not fully ordained (as a bhikkhu), this entails expiation."

6. Respectful offering is done with both hands.

the novice told him the whole story, beginning at the beginning. When the elder heard his story, he was deeply moved and said to himself, "Oh, what a grave deed I have done!" Then he said to the novice, "Pardon me, most excellent youth; I did not know this. Be my refuge." And extending his clasped hands in an attitude of reverent salutation, he crouched on the ground before the feet of the seven-year-old novice. Then said the novice to him, "It was not for this purpose, reverend sir, that I spoke. I said this for the purpose of sparing your feelings. You are not to blame in this matter and neither am I. The round of existences alone is to blame for this. It was because I wished to spare you remorse that I did not tell you the real facts."

The novice tried to comfort the elder, but he would not be comforted. Overcome with remorse, he took the novice's requisites and proceeded to the Teacher. As the Teacher sat, he observed him approaching. The elder went to the Teacher, saluted him, and exchanged friendly greetings with him. The Teacher asked him, "Monk, is everything well with you? I trust that you have suffered no excessive discomfort." The elder replied, "All is well with me, reverend sir. I have suffered no excessive discomfort. But here is a young novice whose good qualities surpass anything I have ever seen."

"Why, what has he done, monk?" Thereupon the elder told him the whole story, beginning at the beginning and concluding as follows, "Reverend sir, when I asked him to pardon me, he said this to me, 'You are not to blame in this matter and neither am I. The round of existences alone is to blame for this. Be not disturbed.' Thus he tried to comfort me, appearing to cherish neither anger nor hatred towards me. His good qualities surpass anything I have ever seen." Said the Teacher to the elder, "Monk, those who have rid themselves of the taints cherish neither anger nor hatred towards anyone. On the contrary, their senses are in a state of calm and their thoughts are in a state of calm." So saying, he joined the connection, and teaching the Dhamma, pronounced the following stanza:

96. Peaceful is his mind,
Peaceful too his speech and action,
Who, truly knowing, is released,
Perfectly tranquil and wise.

33. Paṇḍita the Novice

Irrigators lead the waters ... This instruction was given by the Teacher while he was in residence at Jetavana with reference to the novice Paṇḍita.

Story of the Past: Sakka and the Poor Man

In times past, they say, Kassapa the Supremely Enlightened One, accompanied by a retinue of twenty thousand monks freed from the taints, paid a visit to Benares. Thereupon the residents, mindful of the fame they should acquire thereby, united in bands of eight or ten and presented the visiting monks with the customary offerings. Now it happened one day that the Teacher, in rejoicing with the merits of the donors at the end of the meal, spoke as follows: "Lay disciples, here in this world one man says to himself, 'It is my bounden duty to give only that which is my own. Why should I urge others to give?' So he himself gives alms, but does not urge others to give. That man, in his future states of existence, receives the blessing of wealth, but not the blessing of a following. Another man urges others to give, but does not himself give. That man receives in his future states of existence the blessing of a following, but not the blessing of wealth. Another man neither himself gives nor urges others to give. That man, in his future states of existence, receives neither the blessing of wealth nor the blessing of a following, but lives as an eater of remnants. Yet another man not only himself gives, but also urges others to give. That man, in his future states of existence, receives both the blessing of wealth and the blessing of a following."

Now a certain wise man who stood there heard this and thought to himself, "I will straightaway act so as to obtain both blessings for myself." Accordingly he paid obeisance to the Teacher and said, "Reverend sir, tomorrow receive alms from me."—"How many monks do you wish me to bring?"—"How many monks are there in your following, reverend sir?"—"Twenty thousand monks."—"Reverend sir, tomorrow bring all your monks and receive alms from me." The Teacher accepted his invitation.

The man entered the village and announced, "Men and women, I have invited the Order of Monks presided over by the

Buddha to take a meal here tomorrow; each and all of you give to as many monks as you are able." Then he went about inquiring how many each could provide for. "We will supply ten"; "We will supply twenty"; "We will supply a hundred"; "We will supply five hundred," they replied, each giving in proportion to their means. All of the pledges he wrote down in order on a leaf.

Now at that time there lived in this city a certain man who was so poor that he was known as Prince of Paupers, Mahāduggata. The solicitor, meeting him face to face, said also to him, "Sir Mahāduggata, I have invited the Order of Monks presided over by the Buddha for tomorrow's meal; tomorrow the residents of the city will give alms. How many monks will you provide for?"—"Sir, what have I to do with monks? Monks need rich men to provide for them. But as for me, I possess not so much as a small measure of rice wherewith to make porridge tomorrow; what have I to do with monks?"

Now it behooves a man who urges others to give to be circumspect; therefore when the solicitor heard the poor man plead his poverty as an excuse, instead of remaining silent, he spoke to him as follows, "Sir Mahāduggata, there are many people in this city who live in luxury, eating rich food, wearing soft clothes, adorned with all manner of adornments, and sleeping on beds of royal splendour. But as for you, you work for your living and yet get scarcely enough to fill your belly. That being the case, does it not seem to you likely that the reason why you yourself get nothing is that you have never done anything for others?"—"I think so, sir."—"Well, why do you not do a work of merit right now? You are young, and you have plenty of strength; is it not your bounden duty while you are earning a living to give alms according to your ability?" Even as the solicitor spoke, the poor man was overcome with emotion and said, "Write my name on the leaf for one monk; no matter how little I may earn, I will provide food for one monk." The solicitor said to himself, "What is the use of writing one monk on the leaf?" and omitted to write down the name.

Mahāduggata went home and said to his wife, "Wife, tomorrow the residents of the village will provide food for the Order of Monks. I, also, was requested by the solicitor to provide food for one monk; therefore we also will provide food for one monk tomorrow." His wife, instead of saying to him, "We are poor; why did you promise to do so?" said, "Husband, what you did was quite right. We are poor now because we have never given anything; we will both work for hire and give food to one monk." So both of them went out to look for work.

A rich merchant saw Mahāduggata and said to him, "Sir Mahāduggata, do you wish to work for hire?"—"Yes, your honour."—"What kind of work can you do?"—"Whatever you would like to have done."—"Well then, we are going to entertain three hundred monks; come, split wood." And he brought an axe and a hatchet and gave them to him. Mahāduggata put on a stout girdle and, exerting himself to the utmost, began to split wood, first tossing the axe aside and taking the hatchet, and then tossing the hatchet aside and taking the axe. The merchant said to him, "Sir, today you work with unusual energy; what is the reason for it?"—"Master, I expect to provide food for one monk." The merchant was pleased at heart and thought to himself, "It is a difficult task this man has undertaken; instead of remaining silent and refusing to give because of his poverty, he says, 'I will work for hire and provide food for one monk.'"

The merchant's wife also saw the poor man's wife and said to her, "Woman, what kind of work can you do?"—"Whatever you wish to have done." So she took her into the room where the mortar was kept, gave her a winnowing-fan, a pestle, and so on, and set her at work. The woman pounded the rice and sifted it with as much joy and pleasure as if she were dancing. The merchant's wife said to her, "Woman, you appear to take unusual joy and pleasure in doing your work; what is the reason for it?"—"Lady, with the wages we earn at this work we expect to provide food for one monk." When the merchant's wife heard this, she was pleased and said to herself, "What a difficult task it is that this woman is doing!"

When Mahāduggata had finished splitting the wood, the merchant gave him four measures of rice as pay for his work and four more as an expression of goodwill. The poor man went home and said to his wife, "The rice I have received for my work will serve as a supply of provisions for us. With the pay you have earned procure curds, oil, wood, relishes, and utensils." The merchant's wife gave the woman a cup of ghee, a vessel of curds, an assortment of relishes, and a measure of clean rice. The husband and wife between them therefore received nine measures of rice.

Filled with joy and satisfaction at the thought that they had received food to bestow in alms, they rose very early in the morning. Mahāduggata's wife said to him, "Husband, go seek leaves for curry and fetch them home." Seeing no leaves in the shop, he went to the bank of the river. And there he went about picking up leaves, singing for joy at the thought, "Today I shall have the privilege of giving food to the noble monks."

A fisherman who had just thrown his big net into the water and was standing close by thought to himself, "That must be the voice of Mahāduggata." So he called him and asked, "You sing as though you were overjoyed at heart; what is the reason?"—"I am picking up leaves, friend."—"What are you going to do?"—"I am going to provide food for one monk."—"Happy indeed the monk who shall eat your leaves!"—"What else can I do, master? I intend to provide for him with the leaves I have myself gathered."—"Well then, come here."—"What do you wish me to do, master?"—"Take these fish and tie them up in bundles to sell for a shilling, sixpence and a penny."

Mahāduggata did as he was told, and the residents of the city bought them for the monks they had invited. He was still engaged in tying up bundles of fish when the time came for the monks to go on their rounds for alms, whereupon he said to the fisherman, "I must go now, friend; it is time for the monks to come."—"Are there any bundles of fish left?"—"No, friend, they are all gone."—"Well then, here are four redfish which I buried in the sand for my own use. If you intend to provide food for the monks, take them with you." So saying he gave him the redfish.

Now as the Teacher surveyed the world on the morning of that day, he observed that Mahāduggata had entered the net of his knowledge. And he considered within himself, "What is going to happen? Yesterday Mahāduggata and his wife worked for hire that they might provide food for one monk. Which monk will he obtain?" And he came to the following conclusion, "The residents will obtain monks to entertain in their houses according to the names written on the leaf; no other monk will Mahāduggata obtain, but only me." Now the Buddhas are said to show particular tenderness to poor men. So when the Teacher, very early in the morning, had attended to his bodily needs, he said to himself, "I will bestow my favour on Mahāduggata." And he went into the Perfumed Chamber and sat down.

When Mahāduggata went into his house with the fish, the Yellowstone Throne of Sakka, king of the gods, showed signs of heat.[7] Sakka looked about and said to himself, "What can be the reason for this?" And he considered within himself, "Yesterday Mahāduggata and his wife worked for hire that they might provide food for one monk; which monk will he obtain?" Finally he came to the following conclusion, "Mahāduggata will obtain no other monk than the Buddha, who is sitting in the Perfumed Chamber with this thought in his mind, 'I will bestow my favour on Mahāduggata.' Now it is Mahāduggata's intention to offer the Tathāgata a meal of his own making, consisting of porridge and rice and leaf-curry. Suppose I were to go to Mahāduggata's house and offer to act as cook?"

Accordingly Sakka disguised himself, went to the vicinity of his house, and asked, "Would anyone like to hire a man to work for him?" Mahāduggata saw him and said to him, "Sir, what kind of work can you do?"—"Master, I am a man-of-all-work; there is nothing I do not know how to do. Among other things I know how to cook porridge and boil rice."—"Sir, we need your services, but we have no money to pay you."—"What work is it you have to do?"—"I wish to provide food for one monk and I should like to have someone prepare the porridge and rice."—"If you intend to provide food for a monk, it will not be necessary for you to pay me. Is it not proper that I should perform a work of merit?"—"If that is the case, very well, sir; come in." So Sakka entered the poor man's house, had him bring the rice and other articles of food, and then dismissed him, saying, "Go and fetch the monk allotted to you."

Now the solicitor of alms had sent to the houses of the residents the monks according to the names on the leaf. Mahāduggata met him and said to him, "Give me the monk allotted to me." The solicitor immediately recollected what he had done and replied, "I forgot to allot you a monk." Mahāduggata felt as if a sharp dagger had been thrust into his belly. Said he, "Sir, why are you

7. Sakka's throne becomes hot as a portend of some event of momentous virtue about to occur in the human world.

ruining me? Yesterday you urged me to give alms. So my wife and I worked all day for hire, and today I got up early in the morning to gather leaves, went to the bank of the river, and spent the day picking up leaves. Give me one monk!" And he wrung his hands and burst into tears.

People gathered about and asked, "What is the matter Mahāduggata?" He told them the facts, whereupon they asked the solicitor, "Is it true, as this man alleges, that you urged him to hire himself out for service to provide food for a monk?"—"Yes, noble sirs."—"You have done a grave wrong in that, while making arrangements for so many monks, you failed to allot this man a single monk." The solicitor was troubled by what they said and said to him, "Mahāduggata, do not ruin me. You are putting me to great inconvenience. The residents have taken to their several houses the monks allotted to them according to the names written on the leaf, and there is no monk in my own house whom I can take away and give to you. But the Teacher is even now sitting in the Perfumed Chamber, having just bathed his face; and without are seated kings, royal princes, commanders-in-chief, and others, waiting for him to come forth, that they may take his bowl and accompany him on his way. Now the Buddhas are accustomed to show particular tenderness to a poor man. Therefore go to the monastery, pay obeisance to the Teacher, and say to him, 'I am a poor man, reverend sir. Bestow your favour on me.' If you have merit, you will undoubtedly obtain what you seek."

So Mahāduggata went to the monastery. Now on previous occasions he had been seen at the monastery as an eater of remnants of food. Therefore the kings, royal princes, and others said to him, "Mahāduggata, this is not meal time. Why do you come here?"—"Sirs," he replied, "I know it is not meal time; but I have come to pay obeisance to the Teacher." Then he went to the Perfumed Chamber, laid his head on the threshold, paid respectful obeisance to the Teacher, and said, "Reverend sir, in this city there is no man poorer than I. Be my refuge; bestow your favour on me."

The Teacher opened the door of the Perfumed Chamber, took down his bowl, and placed it in the poor man's hands. It was as though Mahāduggata had received the glory of a Universal Monarch. Kings, royal princes, and others gasped at each other.

Now when the Teacher presents his bowl to a man, no one dares take it from him by force. But they spoke thus, "Sir Mahāduggata, give us the Teacher's bowl; we will give you all this money for it. You are a poor man; take the money. What need do you have of the bowl?" Mahāduggata said, "I will give it to no one. I have no need of money; all that I desire is to provide food for the Teacher." All without exception begged him to give them the bowl, but failing to get it, desisted.

The king thought to himself, "Money will not tempt Mahāduggata to give up the bowl, and no one can take from him the bowl which the Teacher has given to him of his own free will. But how much will this man's alms amount to? When the time comes for him to present his alms, I will take the Teacher aside, conduct him to my house, and give him the food I have made ready." This was the thought in his mind even as he accompanied the Teacher.

Now Sakka, king of gods, prepared porridge, rice, leaf-curry, and other kinds of food, made ready a seat worthy of the Teacher, and sat down awaiting the arrival of the Teacher. Mahāduggata conducted the Teacher to his house and invited him to enter. Now the house in which he lived was so low that it was impossible to enter without bowing the head. But the Buddhas never bow their heads in entering a house. When they enter a house, the earth sinks or the house rises. This is the fruit of the generous alms they have given. And when they have departed and gone, all becomes as before. Therefore the Teacher entered the house standing quite erect, and having entered, sat down on the seat prepared by Sakka. When the Teacher had seated himself, the king said to Mahāduggata, "Sir Mahāduggata, when we begged you to give us the Teacher's bowl, you refused to do so. Now let us see what sort of alms you have prepared for the Teacher."

At that moment Sakka uncovered the dishes and showed the porridge, rice, and other kinds of food. The perfume and fragrance that arose enveloped the whole city. The king surveyed the porridge, rice, and other foods, and said to the Exalted One, "Reverend sir, when I came here, I thought to myself, 'How much will Mahāduggata's alms amount to? When he presents his alms, I will take the Teacher aside, conduct him to my house, and give him the food I have myself prepared.' But as a matter of fact, I have never yet seen such provisions as these. If I remain here, Mahāduggata will be annoyed; therefore I will depart." And having paid obeisance to the Teacher, he departed. Sakka presented the porridge and other food to the Teacher and faithfully ministered to his needs. After the Teacher had eaten his meal, he returned thanks, rose from his seat, and departed. Sakka made a sign to Mahāduggata, who thereupon took the Teacher's bowl and accompanied him.

Sakka turned back, stopped at the door of Mahāduggata's house, and looked up at the sky. Thereupon there came down from the sky a rain of the seven kinds of jewels. The jewels filled all the vessels in his house and the very house itself. When there was no room left in the house, they took the children in their arms, carried them outside, and stood there. When Mahāduggata returned from accompanying the Teacher and saw the children standing outside the house, he asked, "What does this mean?"—"Our whole house is filled with the seven kinds of jewels, so much that there is no room to go in." Mahāduggata thought to himself, "Today I have received the reward of the alms I have given." Thereupon he went to the king, made obeisance to him, and when the king asked him why he had come, he said, "Your majesty, my house is filled with the seven kinds of jewels; accept this wealth." The king thought, "This very day have the alms given to the Buddhas reached their consummation." And he said to the man, "What must you have to remove the jewels?"—"Your majesty, it will require a thousand carts to remove all of this wealth." The king sent out a thousand carts and had the wealth removed and dumped in the palace court. It made a heap as high as a palm tree.

The king assembled the citizens and asked them, "Is there anyone in this city who possesses so much wealth as this?"—"There is not, your majesty."—"What ought to be done for a man possessed of so much wealth as this?"—"He should be given the post of treasurer, your majesty." The king bestowed high honour upon him and gave him the post of treasurer. Then he pointed out the site of a house occupied by a former treasurer, and said to him, "Have the bushes that are growing there removed, build a house and reside in it."

As the ground was being cleared and levelled, urns of treasure came to light with their brims touching each other. When Mahāduggata reported this to the king, the latter said, "It is through your merit that these urns have come to light; you alone shall have them." When Mahāduggata had completed the house, he gave alms for seven days to the Order of Monks presided over by the Buddha. Thereafter, having lived out his allotted term of life in the performance of works of merit, Mahāduggata was reborn at the end of his life in the world of the gods. After enjoying celestial glory for the space of the interval between the appearances of two Buddhas, he passed from that state of existence in the dispensation of the present Buddha, and was conceived in the womb of the daughter of a rich merchant of Sāvatthī, a supporter of the Elder Sāriputta. (*End of Story of the Past.*)

Story of the Present: Paṇḍita the Novice

When the mother and father of the merchant's daughter learned that she had conceived a child in her womb, they saw to it that she received the treatment necessary for the protection of the embryo. After a time the longing of pregnancy came upon her and she thought to herself, "Oh, that I might make offerings of the choicest portions of redfish to the five hundred monks headed by the Marshal of the Dhamma.[8] Oh, that I might put on yellow robes, sit down in the outer circle of the seats, and partake of the food left uneaten by these monks!" She expressed her longing to her mother and father and fulfilled her longing, whereupon it subsided. Thereafter she held seven festivals more, and provided the five hundred monks headed by the Marshal of the Dhamma with the choicest portions of redfish. This was the fruit of his offering of the choicest portions of redfish in his former existence as the poor man, Mahāduggata.

Now on the day appointed for the naming of the child the mother said to the Elder Sāriputta, "Reverend sir, confer the moral precepts on your servant." Said the elder, "What is the name of this child?"—"Reverend sir, from the day this child came into existence in my womb, those of this household who were stupid and deaf and dumb became wise; therefore the name of my child shall be Young Wiseman, Paṇḍita Dāraka." The elder then conferred the moral precepts on the child.

8. Ven. Sāriputta Thera.

Now from the day of his birth his mother resolved, "I will not interfere with the desire of my son." When he was seven years old, he said to his mother, "I desire to become a monk under the elder." She replied, "Very well, dear child; long ago I made up my mind not to interfere with your desire." So she invited the elder to her house, provided him with food, and said to him, "Reverend sir, your servant desires to become a monk; I will bring him to the monastery this evening." Having seen the elder off, she gathered her kinsfolk together and said to them, "This very day I shall render the honours appropriate to the occasion of my son's leaving the life of a layman." So she prepared rich gifts, and taking the child to the monastery, committed him to the hands of the elder, saying, "Reverend sir, give him the going forth."

The elder spoke to him of the difficulties of going forth. The boy replied, "I will carry out your admonitions, reverend sir." "Well then," said the elder, "Come!" So saying, he wetted his hair, taught him the formula of meditation on the first five of the constituent parts of the body,[9] and gave him the going forth. His mother and father remained at the monastery for seven days, making offerings consisting wholly of the choicest portions of redfish to the Order of Monks headed by the Buddha. Having done so, they returned home.

On the eighth day the elder took the novice with him to the village. He did not, however, accompany the monks. Why was this? Not yet had the novice acquired a pleasing manner of taking his bowl and robe; not yet had he acquired a pleasing manner of walking, standing, sitting, and lying. Besides, the elder had duties to perform at the monastery. So when the Order of Monks had entered the village for alms, the elder went the rounds of the entire monastery, swept the places that had not been swept, filled the empty vessels with water for drinking and refreshment, and restored to their proper places the beds, chairs, and other articles of furniture that had been left in disorder. Having done so, he entered the village. It was because he did not wish to give the sectarians, who might enter the empty monastery, a chance to say, "Behold the habitations of the disciples of the Monk Gotama!" that he cleaned up the entire monastery before entering the village.

9. See p. 146, n. 4.

Therefore on that particular day, having instructed the novice how to take his bowl and robe, he entered the village somewhat later than usual.

As the novice proceeded with his preceptor, he saw a ditch by the roadside. "What is that, reverend sir?" he asked. "That is called a ditch, novice."—"What do they use it for?"—"They use it to lead the water this way and that, for irrigating their grain fields."—"But, reverend sir, has the water mind or bile?"[10] "It has not, friend."—"But, reverend sir, can they lead anything like this, which lacks reason, to whatever place they desire?"—"Yes, friend." The novice thought to himself, "If they can lead even such a thing as this, which lacks mind, to whatever place they wish, why cannot also they that have mind bring their own mind under their own control and cause it to do the monks' duty?"[11]

Proceeding farther, he saw arrow-makers heating reeds and sticks over the fire and straightening them by sighting with them out of the corner of their eye. "What are these men, reverend sir?" he asked. "They are arrow-makers, friend."—"What are they doing?"—"They are heating reeds and sticks over the fire and straightening them."—"Have these reeds a mind, reverend sir?"—"They are without mind, friend." The novice thought to himself, "If they can take reeds, which are without mind, and straighten them by heating them over the fire, why cannot also they that have mind bring their own mind under control and cause it to do the monks' duty?"

Proceeding yet farther, he saw carpenters fashioning spokes, rims, naves, and other parts of wheels. "Reverend sir, what are these men?" he asked. "These men are carpenters, friend."—"What are they doing?"—"Out of pieces of wood they make wheels and other parts of carts and other vehicles, friend."—"But do these objects possess mind, reverend sir?"—"No, friend, they are without mind." Then this thought occurred to the novice, "If they can take these logs of wood lacking mind and make wheels and so forth out of them, why cannot also they that have mind bring their own mind under control and cause it to do the monks' duty?"

---

10. "Mind or bile" (*cittaṃ vā pittaṃ vā*): an idiomatic phrase in Pāli with rhyming words, which English cannot imitate.

11. The monks' duty is the attainment of arahantship.

Having seen all these things, the novice said to the elder, "Reverend sir, if you will be so good as to take your bowl and robe, I should like to turn back." The elder, not allowing himself to think, "This young novice who has just gone forth addresses me thus!" said, "Bring them, novice," and took his bowl and robe. The novice paid obeisance to the elder and turned back, saying, "Reverend sir, when you bring me food, be kind enough to bring me only the choicest portions of redfish."—"Where shall we get them, friend?"—"Reverend sir, if you cannot obtain them through your own merit, you will succeed in obtaining them through my merit."

The elder thought to himself, "Should this young novice sit outside, some danger may befall him." Therefore he gave him a key and said to him, "Open the door of the hut where I reside, go in, and remain there." The novice did so. Sitting down, he investigated with wisdom his own physical body and thoroughly comprehended his own personality. Through the power of his virtue Sakka's seat showed signs of heat. Sakka considered within himself, "What can be the cause of this?" and came to the following conclusion, "The novice Paṇḍita has given his preceptor his bowl and robe and turned back, saying, 'I will strive for the attainment of arahantship'; therefore I also ought to go there."

So Sakka addressed the Four Great Kings,[12] saying, "Drive away the birds that make their homes in the monastery park and guard the approaches from all quarters." And he said to the moon-deity, "Hold back the disk of the moon"; and to the sun-deity, "Hold back the disk of the sun." Having so said, he went in person to the place where hung the rope for opening and closing the door and stood on guard. There was not so much as the sound of a withered leaf in the monastery. The novice's mind was tranquil, and before his meal he knew thoroughly his own personality and obtained the three lower fruits.

The elder thought, "The novice is seated in the monastery, and I can obtain food in such and such a house to assist him in his preparation." So he went to the house of a certain supporter, whose love and respect for him he well knew. Now the members

12. The four deities that rule over the realm of the Four Great Kings, the lowest of the six sense-sphere heavens.

of this household had obtained some redfish that very day and were seated, watching for the elder to come. When they saw him coming, they said to him, "Reverend sir, it is good that you have come here." And they invited him in, gave him broth and hard food, and presented him with alms consisting of the choicest portions of redfish. The elder allowed the purpose of his visit to be known, whereupon the members of the household said to him, "Eat your meal, reverend sir, and you shall also receive food to take with you." So when the elder had finished his meal, they filled his bowl with food consisting of the choicest portions of redfish and gave it to him. The elder, thinking to himself, "The novice must be hungry," hastened back to the monastery with all speed.

Very early on the morning of that day the Teacher ate his meal and went to the monastery. And he considered within himself, "The novice Paṇḍita has given his preceptor his bowl and robe and turned back, saying, 'I will strive for the attainment of arahantship.' Will he reach the goal of his religious life?" Perceiving that he had attained the three lower fruits, he considered, "Has he or has he not the necessary factors to attain arahantship?" Perceiving that he had, he considered, "Will he or will he not be able to attain arahantship even before his meal?" And straightaway he perceived that he would.

Then the following thought occurred to him, "Sāriputta is hastening to the monastery with food for the novice and may perhaps interfere with his meditations. I will therefore sit down in the battlemented chamber on guard. When Sāriputta arrives, I will ask him four questions. While these questions are being answered, the novice will attain arahantship together with the analytical knowledges."

So he went and took his stand in the battlemented chamber, and when the elder arrived, the Teacher asked him four questions, each of which the elder answered correctly. These were the questions and answers. The Teacher asked Sāriputta, "Sāriputta, what have you got?"—"Food, reverend sir."—"What does food produce, Sāriputta?"—"Sensation, reverend sir."—"What does sensation produce, Sāriputta?"—"Material form, reverend sir."—"What does material form produce, Sāriputta?"—"Contact, reverend sir."[13]

13. There is a play on words here which English can only reproduce in a

This is the meaning of these questions: When a hungry man eats food, the food banishes his hunger and brings a pleasurable sensation. As a result of the pleasurable sensation which comes to a man who is satisfied by the eating of food, his body takes on a beautiful colour; and for this reason it is said that sensation produces material form. Now when a man is satisfied by the material form which is the product of the food he has eaten, he is filled with joy and delight; and with the thought in his mind, "Now I have attained happiness," whether he lies down or sits down he obtains pleasurable contact.

While these four questions were being answered, the novice attained arahantship together with the analytical knowledges. Then the Teacher said to the elder, "Go, Sāriputta, give the food to your novice." The elder went and knocked at the door. The novice came out, took the bowl from the elder's hands, set it aside, and began to fan the elder with a palm-leaf fan. The elder said to him, "Novice, have your meal."—"But you, reverend sir?"—"I have eaten; you eat yours." Thus did a child seven years old, on the eighth day after going forth, like a freshly blossomed lotus, reflecting upon the subjects of reflection,[14] sit down for his meal.

When he had washed his bowl and put it away, the moon-deity released the moon and the sun-deity the sun; the Four Great Kings abandoned their watch over the four quarters; Sakka the king of the gods gave up his post at the rope of the door; and the sun vanished from mid-heaven and disappeared.

The monks were annoyed and said, "Unwonted darkness has come on; the sun has disappeared from mid-heaven, and the novice has only just eaten; what does this mean?" The Teacher, aware of what they were saying, came and asked, "Monks, what are you saying?"

They told him. He replied, "Yes, monks, while this novice, fruitful in good works, was striving for the attainment of arahantship, the moon-deity held back the disk of the moon and the sun-deity the disk of the sun; the Four Great Kings stood

laboured way: "Sāriputta, what have you got?"—"*Sustenance*, reverend sir."—"What does *sustenance sustain*?" etc.

14. This refers to the reflection upon the proper purpose of eating almsfood, part of the monk's discipline.

on guard over the four quarters in the monastery park; Sakka king of the gods kept watch over the rope of the door; and I myself, although a Buddha, was unable to remain in an attitude of repose, but went to the battlemented chamber and stood guard over my son. Wise men who observe ditch-diggers leading the water, arrow-makers straightening their arrows, and carpenters fashioning wood, meditate on these things, and so obtain mastery over themselves and attain arahantship." And joining the connection, he instructed them in the Dhamma by pronouncing the following stanza:

80. Irrigators lead the waters,
Arrow-makers bend the shafts,
Carpenters shape the wood:
Those who are wise tame themselves.

34. The Four Novices

AMONG THE HOSTILE UNHOSTILE ... This instruction was given by the Teacher while he was in residence at Jetavana with reference to four novices.

The story goes that the wife of a certain brahmin prepared food for four specially designated monks, and said to the brahmin, her husband, "Go to the monastery, have the steward pick out four old brahmins, and bring them here." The brahmin went to the monastery and said, "Have four brahmins picked out for me and give them to me."[15] There fell to him four seven-year-old novices who had attained arahantship: Saṅkicca, Paṇḍita, Sopāka, and Revata. The brahmin's wife had costly seats prepared and stood waiting. At sight of the novices, she was filled with rage, and sputtering as when salt is dropped on a brazier, she said to her husband, "You have gone to the monastery and brought back with you four youngsters not old enough to be your grandsons." She refused to let them sit on the seats which she had prepared,

15. It is very typical of a brahmin to wish to give only to other brahmins even if they are monks. But *brahmins*, in the Buddhist sense of the word, are arahants. They are also "old" (venerable) in the Buddhist sense due to their attainment.

but spreading some low seats for them, said to them, "Sit here!" Then she said to her husband, "Brahmin, go and look out for some old brahmins and bring them here."

The brahmin went to the monastery, and seeing the Elder Sāriputta, said to him, "Come, let us go to our house," and took him back home with him. When the elder reached the house and saw the novices, he asked, "Have these brahmins received food?"—"No, they have received no food." Knowing that food had been prepared for just four persons, he said, "Bring me my bowl," and taking his bowl, departed. The brahmin's wife asked, "What did he say?" Her husband replied, "He said, 'These brahmins sitting here ought to receive food. Bring me my bowl.' So saying, he took his bowl and departed." Said the brahmin's wife, "It must be that he did not wish to eat; go quickly, look out for another brahmin and bring him here." The brahmin went back to the monastery, and seeing the Elder Moggallāna the Great, said the same thing to him, and brought him back home with him. When the Elder Moggallāna the Great saw the novices, he said the same thing as had the Elder Sāriputta, and taking his bowl, departed. Then said the brahmin's wife to her husband, "These elders do not wish to eat; go to the brahmins' enclosure (around the brahmins' houses) and bring back with you a single old brahmin."

Now the novices had nothing to eat from early morning and sat there famished with hunger. By the power of their merit Sakka's seat showed signs of heat. Considering within himself what might be the cause, he perceived that the novices had sat there from early morning and that they were weak and exhausted. "It is my duty to go there," thought Sakka. So disguising himself as an old brahmin, worn out by old age, he went to the brahmins' enclosure and sat down in the most conspicuous seat of the brahmins. When the brahmin saw him, he thought to himself, "Now my wife will be delighted," and saying, "Come, let us go home," he took him and went back home with him. When the brahmin's wife saw him, her heart was filled with delight. She took rugs and mats which were spread over two seats, spread them over one, and said to him, "Noble sir, sit here."

When Sakka entered the house, he respectfully saluted the four novices, and finding a place for himself at the edge of the seats where the novices were sitting, sat down cross-legged on the ground.

When the brahmin's wife saw him, she said to the brahmin, "For sure, you have brought a brahmin, but you have brought back with you one old enough to be your father. He is going about saluting novices young enough to be his grandsons. What use have we for him? Put him out!"

The brahmin seized him first by the shoulder, then by the arm, finally by the waist, and tried his best to drag him out, but he refused to stir from where he sat. Then the brahmin's wife said to her husband, "Come, brahmin, you take hold of one arm and I will take hold of the other." So the brahmin and his wife both took hold of his two arms, belaboured him about the back, and dragged him through the door out of the house. Nevertheless, Sakka remained sitting in the same place in which he had sat before, waving his hands back and forth.

When the brahmin and his wife returned and saw him sitting in the very same place in which he had sat before, they screamed screams of terror and let him go. At that moment Sakka made known his identity. Then the brahmin and his wife gave food to their guests. When those five persons had received food, they departed. One of the novices broke through the circular peak of the house; the second broke through the front part of the roof; the third broke through the back part of the roof; the fourth plunged into the earth, while Sakka departed from the house by another route. Thus did those five persons depart from the house by five different routes. From that time on, so it is said, that house was known as the House with the Five Openings.

When the novices returned to the monastery, the monks asked them, "Friends, what was it like?"—"Please don't ask us," replied the novices. "The brahmin's wife fumed with rage the moment she saw us. She refused to allow us to sit on the seats which she had prepared and said to her husband, 'Make haste and bring an old brahmin.' Our preceptor came, and seeing us said, 'These brahmins who are sitting here ought to receive food.' So saying, he ordered his bowl to be brought to him and departed. Then the brahmin's wife said to her husband, 'Bring another old brahmin.' Then the brahmin brought the Elder Moggallāna the Great. When the Elder Moggallāna the Great saw us, he said the same thing as had the Elder Sāriputta and departed. Then the brahmin's wife said to her husband, 'These elders do not wish to eat; brahmin, go to the brahmins' enclosure and bring back a single old brahmin.' The brahmin went there and brought back Sakka, who came in the disguise of a brahmin. When Sakka arrived, the brahmin and his wife gave us food."

"But were you not angry with them for what they did?"—"No, we were not angry." When the monks heard their reply, they reported the matter to the Teacher, saying, "Reverend sir, when these monks say, 'We were not angry,' they say what is not true, they utter falsehood." Said the Teacher, "Monks, those who have rid themselves of the evil passions oppose not those by whom they are opposed." So saying, he pronounced the following stanza:

406. Among the hostile unhostile
Among the violent completely cool,
Detached amidst these who are attached—
That one I call a brāhmaṇa.

How Dhamma is Practised

35. Worthy of Reverence

From whomever one learns the Dhamma ... This instruction was given by the Teacher while he was in residence at Jetavana with reference to the Elder Sāriputta.

This venerable elder, we are told, first heard the Dhamma from the lips of the Elder Assaji; and from the day when he attained the fruit of stream-entry, in whatever quarter he heard that the Elder Assaji was residing, in that direction he would salute reverently with hands together, in that direction he would turn his head when he lay down to sleep. The monks said to each other, "Elder Sāriputta holds false views; on this very day he is going about doing reverence to the cardinal points." And they reported the matter to the Tathāgata.

The Teacher caused the elder to be summoned before him and asked him, "Sāriputta, is the report true that you are going about doing reverence to the cardinal points?"—"Reverend sir, you know me, and you yourself know whether or not I am going about doing reverence to the cardinal points." Then said the Teacher, "Monks, Sāriputta is not doing reverence to the cardinal points. The fact is that he first heard the Dhamma from the lips of the Elder Assaji, and from the day when he attained the fruit of stream-entry, he has reverenced his own teacher. For a monk should reverence the teacher through whom he has learned the Dhamma with the same degree of reverence with which a brahmin reverences the sacred fire." So saying, he taught the Dhamma, pronouncing the following stanza:

392. From whomever one learns the Dhamma—
The Teaching of the Perfect Buddha—
Devoutly one should honour him
As a brahmin does the sacred fire.

36. The Elder Attadattha

ONE'S OWN GOOD ONE SHOULD NOT NEGLECT ... This instruction was given by the Teacher while he was in residence at Jetavana with reference to the Elder Attadattha ("Own Good").

For when the Teacher was about to pass into Nibbāna, he said to his disciples, "Monks, four months from now I shall attain final Nibbāna." Thereupon seven hundred monks who had not yet attained the fruit of stream-entry were deeply moved, and never leaving the Teacher's side, whispered to each other, "Brethren, what are we to do?" But the Elder Attadattha thought to himself, "The Teacher says that four months from now he is to attain final Nibbāna. Now I have not yet freed myself from the power of the evil passions. Therefore so long as the Teacher yet remains alive, I will strive with all my might for the attainment of arahantship." Accordingly the Elder Attadattha no longer went with the monks.

Now the monks said to him, "Brother, why is it that you thus avoid our company and do not talk with us?" And conducting the Elder Attadattha to the Teacher, they laid the matter before him, saying, "Reverend sir, this elder does thus and so." The Teacher asked the Elder Attadattha, "Why do you act thus?" The elder replied, "Reverend sir, you have said that four months from now you are to attain final Nibbāna; and I have determined that so long as you yet remain alive, I will strive with all my might for the attainment of arahantship."

The Teacher applauded him for his wise decision and said to the monks, "Monks, whosoever sincerely loves me should be like the Elder Attadattha. For truly they honour me not who honour me only with perfumes and garlands. They only honour me who practise the Dhamma according to Dhamma. Therefore others also should follow the example of the Elder Attadattha." So saying, he pronounced the following stanza:

166. One's own good one should not neglect
For another's good however great:
Knowing well one's own good
Be intent on one's own good.

37. The Elder Ānanda's Question

The perfume of flowers goes not against the wind ... This instruction was given by the Teacher while he was in residence at Sāvatthī by way of reply to a question which the Elder Ānanda asked him.

We are told that one evening, absorbed in meditation, the elder pondered the following thought: "The Exalted One receives the three perfumes of superlative excellence: namely, the perfume of sandal, the perfume of roots, and the perfume of flowers. Each of these perfumes, however, goes only with the wind. Is there possibly a substance whose perfume goes against the wind, or is there possibly a substance whose perfume goes both with the wind and against the wind?" Then the following thought occurred to him: "What is the use of my trying to determine this question all by myself? I will ask the Teacher, and the Teacher alone." Accordingly he approached the Teacher and put the question to him. Therefore it is said:[16]

Now one evening the Venerable Ānanda arose from profound meditation and drew near to the place where the Exalted One was sitting, and when he had drawn near, he addressed the Exalted One as follows: "Reverend sir, there are these three substances whose perfume goes only with the wind and not against the wind. What are the three? The perfume of roots, the perfume of sandal, and the perfume of flowers. These, reverend sir, are the three substances whose perfume goes only with the wind and not against the wind. But, reverend sir, is there possibly a substance whose perfume goes with the wind, against the wind, and both with and against the wind?"

Said the Exalted One in answer to the question, "Ānanda, there is a substance whose perfume goes with the wind, against the wind, and both with and against the wind."—"But, reverend sir, what is that substance whose perfume goes with the wind, against the wind, and both with and against the wind?"—"Ānanda, if in any village or market-town in this world any human being, whether man or woman, seeks refuge in the Buddha, seeks refuge in the Dhamma, seeks refuge in the Order; if they refrain from

16. The following is taken from Aṅguttara Nikāya 3:79.

killing living beings, from taking that which is not given, from wrong conduct in sexual relations, and from lying, and avoid occasions of carelessness through the use of liquor or spirits or other intoxicants; if they are virtuous, if they live the life of a householder in righteousness, with a heart free from the stain of avarice, if they are liberal and generous, if they are open-handed, if they take delight in giving, if they are attentive to petitions, if they delight in the distribution of alms, in all parts of the world monks and brahmins utter their praise. If in such and such a village or market-town either a man or a woman seeks refuge in the Buddha ... if they take delight in the distribution of alms, deities and spirits utter their praise. If in such and such a village or market-town either a man or a woman seeks refuge in the Buddha ... if they take delight in the distribution of alms, such acts as these, Ānanda, are the substance whose perfume goes with the wind, whose perfume goes against the wind, whose perfume goes both with and against the wind." So saying, he pronounced the following stanzas:

54. The perfume of flowers goes not against the wind,
Neither that of sandalwood, jasmine or *tagara*;
But the perfume of the virtuous goes against the wind,
The good person suffuses all directions.

55. Sandalwood or tagara,
Lotus or the jasmine great—
Of these various kinds of perfume
Virtue's perfume is unexcelled.

38. Angry Bhāradvāja

Angerless does he endure abuse ... This instruction was given by the Teacher while he was in residence at Veḷuvana with reference to Akkosa Bhāradvāja.[17]

For Akkosa Bhāradvāja had a brother named Bhāradvāja, whose wife, named Dhānañjānī, had attained the fruit of stream-entry. Whenever she sneezed or coughed or stumbled, she would breathe forth the solemn utterance, "Homage to the Exalted

17. This story combines Saṃyutta Nikāya 7:1 and 7:2.

One, All-Worthy, Perfectly Enlightened!" One day, while distribution of food to brahmins was in progress, she stumbled, and immediately breathed forth that solemn utterance as usual with a loud voice.

The brahmin Bhāradvāja was greatly angered[18] and said to himself, "No matter where it may be, whenever this vile woman stumbles, she utters the praise of this shaveling monkling in this fashion." And he said to his wife, "Now, vile woman, I will go and worst that teacher of yours in an argument." She replied, "By all means go, brahmin; I have never seen the man who could worst the Exalted One in an argument. Nevertheless, go ask the Exalted One a question." The brahmin went to the Teacher, and without even saluting him, stood on one side and asked him a question, pronouncing the following stanza:

"What must one slay to live at ease?
What must one slay to grieve no more?
Of what one thing do you approve
The killing?—tell us, Gotama!"[19]

In answer, the Teacher pronounced the following stanza:

"To live at ease, anger must be slain.
With anger slain, one grieves no more.
Of anger with its poisoned root
And honeyed climax, brāhmaṇa,
The noble ones praise killing it:
When it is slain, one grieves no more."

Having serene confidence in the Teacher, the brahmin went forth and attained arahantship.

Now his younger brother, who was called Akkosa Bhāradvāja, heard the report, "Your brother has gone forth," and greatly angered, he went and abused the Teacher with wicked, ugly words. But the Teacher subdued him by employing the illustration of food given to guests: ["Do you sometimes have guests, brahmin?"—

18. Because all his brahmin guests were scandalized by the wife's praising the Buddha and got up and left without touching the food, which perhaps they thought was ritually impure.

19. The brahmin may have wanted the Buddha to approve of ritual sacrifice.

"Yes, Master Gotama, I sometimes do."—"Do you entertain them with various kinds of food?"—"Yes, I do."—"Now, if they do not accept your food, to whom does it then belong?"—"If they do not accept it, it again belongs to us."—"In the same way, brahmin, those words of scolding and abuse which you gave us, we do not accept; hence, brahmin, they belong to you."[20]]

Thereupon this brahmin too gained serene confidence in the Teacher, went forth and attained arahantship. Likewise Akkosa Bhāradvāja's two younger brothers, Sundari Bhāradvāja and Bilañjika Bhāradvāja, abused the Teacher, but the Teacher subdued them, and they too went forth and attained arahantship.

One day in the Hall of Truth the monks began the following discussion: "How wonderful are the virtues of the Buddhas! Although these four brothers abused the Teacher, the Teacher, without so much as saying a word, became their refuge." At that moment the Teacher drew near. "Monks," said he, "What is the subject that engages your attention now as you sit here all gathered together?"—"Such and such," replied the monks. Then said the Teacher, "Monks, because I possess the power of patience, because I am without defilements among those who are defiled, therefore I am truly the refuge of the multitude." So saying he pronounced the following stanza:

399. Angerless does he endure abuse,
Beating and imprisonment,
Patience his power and armed might—
That one I call a brāhmaṇa.

39. Patience Subdues Violence

One should not strike a brāhmaṇa ... This instruction was given by the Teacher while he was in residence at Jetavana with reference to the Elder Sāriputta.

The story goes that once upon a time several men gathered together at a certain place and extolled the noble qualities of the elder, saying, "Oh, our noble master is endowed with patience to such a degree that even when men abuse him and strike him, he

20. The bracketed passage is added from Saṃyutta Nikāya 7:2.

never gets the least bit angry!" Thereupon a certain brahmin who held false views asked, "Who is this that never gets angry?"—"Our elder."—"It must be that nobody ever provoked him to anger."—"That is not the case, brahmin."—"Well then, I will provoke him to anger."—"Provoke him to anger if you can!"—"Trust me," said the brahmin, "I know just what to do to him."

Just then the elder entered the city for alms. When the brahmin saw him, he stepped up behind him and struck him a tremendous blow with his staff on the back. "What was that?" said the elder, and without so much as turning around to look, continued on his way. The fire of remorse sprang up within every part of the brahmin's body. "Oh, how noble are the qualities with which the elder is endowed!" exclaimed the brahmin. And prostrating himself at the elder's feet, he said, "Pardon me, reverend sir."—"What do you mean?" asked the elder. "I wanted to try your patience and struck you."—"Very well, I pardon you."—"If, reverend sir, you are willing to pardon me, hereafter sit and receive your food only in my house." So saying, the brahmin took the elder's bowl, the elder yielding it willingly. The brahmin conducted him to his house and served him with food.

The bystanders were filled with anger. "This fellow," said they, "struck with his staff our noble elder, who is free from all offence; he must not be allowed to get away. We will kill him right here and now." And taking clods of earth and sticks and stones into their hands, they stood waiting at the door of the brahmin's house. As the elder rose from his seat to go, he placed his bowl in the hands of the brahmin. When the bystanders saw the brahmin going out with the elder, they said, "Reverend sir, order this brahmin who has taken your bowl to turn back."—"What do you mean, lay disciples?"—"That brahmin struck you and we are going to treat him in as he deserves."—"What do you mean? Did he strike you or me?"—"You, reverend sir."—"If he struck me, he begged my pardon; go your way." So saying, he dismissed the bystanders, and permitting the brahmin to turn back, the elder went back again to the monastery.

The monks were highly offended. "What sort of thing is this!" they exclaimed. "A brahmin struck the Elder Sāriputta a blow, and the elder straightaway went back to the house of the very brahmin who struck him and accepted food at his hands! From the moment he struck the elder, for whom will he any longer have any respect? He will go about pounding everybody right and left." At that moment the Teacher drew near. "Monks," said he, "what is the subject that engages your attention now as you sit here all gathered together?"—"This was the subject we were discussing." Said the Teacher, "Monks, no brahmin ever strikes another brahmin;[21] it must have been a householder-brahmin who struck a monk-brahmin; for when a man attains the fruit of the third path, all anger is utterly destroyed in him." So saying, he expounded the Dhamma, pronouncing the following stanzas:

389. One should not strike a brāhmaṇa,
Nor for that should he react.
Shame on one who hits a brāhmaṇa,
More shame on him should he react!

390. Nothing is better for the brāhmaṇa
Than restraining the mind from what is dear.
When he turns away from the wish to harm
Just thus does his suffering subside.

40. Sirimā

BEHOLD THIS ORNAMENTED IMAGE ... This instruction was given by the Teacher while he was in residence at Veḷuvana with reference to Sirimā.

Sirimā, the story goes, was a very beautiful courtesan of Rājagaha who had, during a certain rainy season, offended against the female lay disciple Uttarā, wife of the treasurer's son Sumana and daughter of the treasurer Puṇṇaka. Desiring to be on good terms with her again, she went to her house when the Teacher and the Order of Monks were within, and after the Teacher had finished his meal, asked him for pardon. Now on that day the Master pronounced within the hearing of Sirimā the following words of rejoicing with the merits of the donors:

223. Conquer anger by non-anger;
Conquer the evil with good;

21. Note the play on the word "brahmin" again.

By giving conquer the miserly:
By truth conquer the liar.

At the conclusion of the stanza Sirimā obtained the fruit of stream-entry. (This is a brief synopsis of the story; as for the complete story, it will be found related at length in the commentary on this stanza in the Chapter on Anger.)

Having thus attained the fruit of stream-entry, Sirimā invited the Master to be her guest, and on the following day presented rich offerings. From that time on she gave regularly eight food-tickets and from that time on eight monks came regularly to her house. "Accept ghee, accept milk," she would say, filling their bowls. What she gave to one monk would have sufficed for three or four; every day sixteen pieces of money were expended on the alms which were presented to the monks who visited her house.

Now one day a certain monk who had eaten the eight ticket-foods in her house went on a journey of three leagues and stopped at a certain monastery. In the evening, as he sat in the monastery, the monks asked him, "Friend, where did you obtain food just before you came here?"—"I have just eaten Sirimā's eight ticket-foods."—"Is the food which she gives pleasing to the taste, friend?"—"It is impossible to describe her food; it is the choicest of choice food that she gives, and a single portion would suffice even for three or four. But good as her food is, she herself is still more pleasing to look upon; such and such are the marks of beauty which she possesses." Thus did the monk describe her marks of beauty.

A certain monk heard the visiting monk describe her marks of beauty, and in spite of the fact that he had never seen her, nevertheless fell in love with her. He said to himself, "I ought to go and see her." So having declared his seniority,[22] he asked the visiting monk some questions. The visiting monk replied, "Tomorrow, friend, stand at that house, and being the most senior in the Order there, you will receive the eight ticket-foods." The monk immediately took bowl and robe and went out. Early in the morning, as the dawn rose, he entered the ticket-hall, and being the most senior in the Order there, received the eight ticket-foods in the woman's house.

22. So that the visiting monk could know that he could be the leader of the Sangha.

Now it so happened that on the day before, just as the last monk who had received food in her house went out, the female lay disciple became afflicted with a disease, and therefore removed her jewellery and lay down. When the monks came to receive the eight ticket-foods, her female slaves, seeing them, informed their mistress. Since she was unable to take their bowls in her own hands, provide them with seats, and wait upon them, she gave orders to her slaves, saying, "Women, take the bowls and provide the noble monks with seats; give them broth to drink and hard food to eat. When it is time to present boiled rice, fill their bowls and give them to the monks."

"Very well, noble lady," replied the slaves. So they invited the monks within, gave them broth to drink and hard food to eat, and when it was time to present boiled rice, they filled their bowls and gave them to the monks. When they had done so, they went and informed their mistress. She said, "Take me and carry me with you, that I may pay my respects to the noble monks." So they took her and carried her with them; and when they brought her into the presence of the monks, she paid obeisance to them, her body all of a tremble.

When that monk looked upon her, he thought to himself, "Even in sickness this woman possesses wonderful beauty. What manner of beauty must she not possess when she is well and strong and adorned with all her adornments?" Thereupon human passion, accumulated during many millions of years, arose within him. He became indifferent to all about him and was unable to take food. He took his bowl and went back to the monastery; covering his bowl, he put it away, and spreading out a corner of his robe he lay down. A certain monk who was a companion of his tried to persuade him to eat, but without success, for he absolutely refused to take food.

On that very day in the evening Sirimā died. Thereupon the king sent word to the Teacher, "Reverend sir, Jīvaka's youngest sister, Sirimā, is dead." When the Teacher received that message, he sent back the following message to the king, "Sirimā's body should not be burned. Have her body laid in the burning-ground, and set a watch that crows and dogs may not devour it." The king did so. Three days passed, one after another. On the fourth day the body began to bloat, and from the nine openings of her body, which were just like sores, there oozed forth maggots. Her whole body looked like a cracked vessel of boiled rice.

The king caused a drum to go through the city and the following proclamation to be made: "Let all approach to behold Sirimā. Except watchmen of houses, all who refuse to do so shall be fined eight pieces of money." And he sent the following message to the Teacher: "Let the Order of Monks presided over by the Buddha approach to behold Sirimā." The Teacher made proclamation to the monks, "Let us go forth to behold Sirimā."

Now that young monk had lain for four days without touching food, paying no attention to anything anyone said to him; the rice in his bowl had rotted, and his bowl was covered with mildew. The rest of the monks who were his fellows approached him and said to him, "Brother, the Teacher is going forth to behold Sirimā." When the young monk, lying thus, heard the name Sirimā, he leaped quickly to his feet. Someone said to him, "The Teacher is going forth to behold Sirimā; will you also go?"—"Indeed I will go," he replied. And tossing the rice out of his bowl, he washed it and put it in his sling and then set out with the company of monks.

The Teacher, surrounded by the Order of Monks, stood on one side of the corpse; the Order of Nuns and the king's retinue and the company of lay disciples, both male and female, stood on the other side of the corpse, each company in its proper place. The Teacher then asked the king, "Great king, who is this woman?"—"Reverend sir, it is Jīvaka's sister, Sirimā."—"Is this Sirimā?"—"Yes, reverend sir."—"Well! Send a drum through the town and make proclamation: 'Those who will pay a thousand pieces of money for Sirimā may have her'." Not a man said "hem" or "hum." The king informed the Teacher, "They will not take her, reverend sir."

"Well then, great king, put the price down." So the king had a drum beaten and the following proclamation made: "If they will give five hundred pieces of money, they may have her." But nobody would take her at that price. The king then proclaimed to the beating of a drum that anyone might have her who would give two hundred and fifty pieces of money, or two hundred, or a hundred, or fifty, or twenty-five, or ten, or five. Finally he reduced the price to a penny, then to a halfpenny, then to a farthing, then to an eighth of a penny. At last he proclaimed to the beating of a drum, "They may have her for nothing." Not a man said "hem" or "hum."

Then said the king to the Teacher, "Reverend sir, no one will take her, even as a gift." The Teacher replied, "Monks, you see the value of a woman in the eyes of the multitude. In this very city men used to pay a thousand pieces of money for the privilege of spending one night with this woman. Now there is no one who will take her as a gift. Such was her beauty who now has perished and gone. Behold, monks, this body diseased and corrupt." So saying, he pronounced the following stanza:

147. Behold this ornamented image,
A mass of sores, a congeries,
Miserable, full of desires,
Where nothing is stable, nothing persists.

The bhikkhu, hearing this, attained the fruit of stream-entry.

41. A Certain Monk

The mind is very hard to see ... This instruction was given by the Teacher while he was in residence at Jetavana with reference to a certain discontented monk.

We are told that while the Teacher was in residence at Sāvatthī, a certain treasurer's son approached an elder who resorted to his house for alms and said to him, "Reverend sir, I desire to obtain release from suffering. Tell me some way by which I can obtain release from suffering." The elder replied, "Good indeed, friend. If you desire release from suffering, give ticket-food, give fortnightly food, give lodgings during the season of the rains, give bowls and robes and the other requisites. Divide your possessions into three parts: with one portion carry on your business; with another portion support son and wife; dispense the third portion on alms to support the Teaching of the Buddha."

"Very well, reverend sir," said the treasurer's son, and did all in the prescribed order. Having done all, he returned to the elder and asked him, "Reverend sir, is there anything else I ought to do?"—"Brother, take upon yourself the Three Refuges and the Five Precepts." The treasurer's son did so, and then asked whether there was anything else he ought to do. "Yes," replied the elder, "take upon yourself the Ten Precepts."—"Very well, reverend sir," said the treasurer's son, and took upon himself the Ten Precepts. Because the treasurer's son had in this manner performed works of merit, one after another (*anupubbena*), he came to be called Anupubba. Again he asked the elder, "Reverend sir, is there anything else I ought to do?" The elder replied, "Yes, become a monk." The treasurer's son immediately went forth.

Now he had a teacher who was versed in the Abhidhamma and a preceptor who was versed in the Vinaya. After he had obtained acceptance as a monk, whenever he approached his teacher, the latter repeated questions found in the Abhidhamma, "In the dispensation of the Buddha it accords with Dhamma to do this; it does not accord with Dhamma to do that." And whenever he approached his preceptor, the latter repeated questions found in the Vinaya, "In the dispensation of the Buddha it accords with Dhamma to do this; it does not accord with Dhamma to do that; this is proper; this is improper." After a time he thought to himself, "Oh, what a wearisome task this is! I became a monk in order to obtain release from suffering, but here there is not even room for me to stretch out my hands. It is possible, however, to obtain release from suffering even if one lives the household life. I had best become a householder once more."

From that time forth, discontented and dissatisfied, he no longer rehearsed the thirty-two constituent parts of the body and received instruction. He became emaciated; his skin shrivelled up; veins stood out all over his body; weariness oppressed him, and his body was covered with scabs. The young novices asked him, "Friend, how is it that wherever you stand, wherever you sit, you are sick with jaundice, emaciated, shrivelled up, your body covered with scabs? What have you done?"—"Friends, I am discontented."—"Why?" He told them his story, and they told his teacher and his preceptor, and his teacher and his preceptor took him with them to the Teacher.

Said the Teacher, "Monks, why have you come?"—"Reverend sir, this monk is dissatisfied in your dispensation."—"Monk, is what they say true?"—"Yes, reverend sir."—"Why are you dissatisfied?"—"Reverend sir, I became a monk in order to obtain release from suffering. My teacher has recited passages from the

Abhidhamma, and my preceptor has recited passages from the Vinaya. Reverend sir, I have come to the following conclusion: 'Here there is not even room for me to stretch out my hands. It is possible for me to obtain release from suffering as a householder. I will therefore become a householder.'"

"Monk, if you can guard one thing, it will not be necessary for you to guard the rest."—"What is that, reverend sir?"—"Can you guard your mind?"—"I can, reverend sir."—"Well then, guard your mind alone." Having given this admonition, the Teacher pronounced the following stanza:

36. The mind is very hard to see,
Subtle, falling on what it wants;
Let the wise man guard his mind,
A guarded mind brings happiness.

42. The Monk from the Vajji People

Hard is the going forth ... This instruction was given by the Teacher while he was in residence at Mahāvana near Vesālī with reference to a certain Vajjian prince who became a monk. The story concerning him is as follows:[23]

A certain Vajjian prince who had become a monk took up his residence at Vesālī in a certain forest grove. It so happened that at that time there was a festival in progress at Vesālī which lasted through the night. When this monk heard the noise and tumult of the beating of drums and the playing of musical instruments at Vesālī, he wept and lamented, and uttered on that occasion the following stanza:

Alone we reside in the forest
Like a log thrown away in the wood.
On such a night as this is,
Who is worse off than we?

It appears that this monk had formerly been a prince in the kingdom of the Vajjians, and that when his turn came to rule, he renounced his kingdom and became a monk. On the night of the full moon of the month Kattikā, the entire city of Vesālī

---

23. This story is an expanded version of Saṃyutta Nikāya 9:9.

was decked with flags and banners, making it coterminous with the realms of the Four Great Kings, and the festival began. As the festival continued through the night, he listened to the noise of the beating of drums and the striking of other musical instruments and the sound of the playing of lutes. When the seven thousand and seven hundred and seven princes of Vesālī, and a like number of young princes and commanders-in-chief, all dressed and adorned in festive array, entered the street for the purpose of taking part in the festivities, he himself walked through his great meditation walk sixty cubits long, beheld the moon poised in mid-heaven, stopped near the seat at the end of the meditation walk, and surveyed his own person, for lack of festive garments and adornments resembling a log of wood thrown away in the forest. And then and there he thought to himself, "Is there any one worse off than we?"

Under ordinary circumstances he possessed the merits and virtues of a forest dweller, but on this occasion was oppressed with discontent, and therefore spoke thus. Thereupon the forest spirit who inhabited that forest grove formed the resolution, "I will stir up this monk," and uttered in reply the following stanza:

> Alone you reside in the forest
> Like a log thrown away in the wood.
> Many do envy you just as hell-dwellers
> Envy those who go to heaven.

The discontented monk heard this stanza, and on the following day approached the Teacher, saluted him, and sat down respectfully on one side. Aware of what had happened, and desiring to make plain the hardships of the household life, the Teacher summed up the five kinds of suffering in the following stanza:[24]

---

24. (1) It is hard to give up one's wealth and go forth. (2) It is hard to delight in the going forth because of the difficulties of the alms round for instance, or because one lives in remote places. (3) The suffering of household life is familiar to all who have experienced it. (4) "Unequals" among laymen means those coming from different social backgrounds, etc.; among monks, those holding different views. (5) Wandering in the round of birth and death (*saṃsāra*) is always painful.

302. Hard is the going forth, hard to delight in;
Hard and painful is household life;
Painful is association with unequals;
Painful is it to be a wanderer.
Therefore do not be a wanderer,
Do not be afflicted with pain.

The bhikkhu concerned was established in arahantship.

One Foot in the World

Buddhist Approaches to Present-day Problems

by

Lily de Silva

WHEEL PUBLICATION NO. 337/338

Preface

The dispensation of the Buddha includes not only monks and nuns, but male and female lay followers as well. All these four groups comprising the Buddhist community have but one ultimate goal. That goal is the attainment of Nibbāna.

Though Nibbāna means final liberation from the world, while walking along the path to liberation a Buddhist has to live in the world and deal with the various difficulties imposed upon him by the limiting conditions of worldly existence. This problem is likely to be felt especially acutely by the lay Buddhist, who may find that the demands and attractions of secular life tend to pull him away from the path to deliverance. However, the Buddha was not unaware of or unconcerned about this dilemma confronted by his lay disciples, but gave it his careful attention. He taught his lay followers how to organize lay life in accordance with the ethical principles of the Dhamma and how to lead successful lay lives without deviating from the path of rectitude.

As lay Buddhists, we must be ever vigilant so that in our pursuit of worldly goals such as wealth, pleasure, and success we do not lose sight of our spiritual goal.

Care should be taken especially to avoid the violation of the basic moral principles summed up in the Five Precepts, as such violation leads to regression on the path. We must often remind ourselves that the first two of the four stages of holiness can be attained by those still leading a married life; that there have been non-returners of the third stage who continued to remain in lay life though observing celibacy; and that the texts record instances of laymen who even attained Arahatship prior to their deaths. The Pali Canon contains ample evidence of exemplary laymen and laywomen, such as Anāthapiṇḍika, Visākhā, and the parents of Nakula, to mention only the most prominent. Therefore a layman should make every endeavor to follow the way to the end of suffering in this very life itself, by leading a life of moderation and self-discipline and by practicing meditation with the aim of developing insight into the ultimate truths of life and death.

The essays in this booklet explore various facets of experience from lay life which requires the attention of the lay aspirant to deliverance. They deal particularly with those which have become more pronounced and urgent in our contemporary materialistic and secularized world. My wish is to share these ideas with others who also may be attempting to follow the Buddha's path in the lay life, and are thus walking with one foot on the way to Nibbāna and one foot still in the world. I hope these essays will assist them to understand and overcome the problems they may face in their day-to-day lives.

A Layman's Happiness

Life in the modern age has become particularly trying and problematic. Though it remains a fact that the standard of living has generally improved, man is still suffering immensely under the weight of present-day living. The physical condition of man has been reduced to such a pathetic level that he succumbs to untimely death by killer diseases such as cancer, heart failure, diabetes, etc. to an unprecedented degree. Mentally, he is so tension-ridden that he has forgotten the art of relaxing, and he cannot even enjoy sound sleep without the aid of tranquilizers. In this set up interpersonal relations have become so brittle and vulnerable that the divorce rate has become alarmingly high, thus letting loose a whole series of other social problems such as uncared-for children, juvenile delinquency, suicide, etc. Thus life has become a problematic burden and a solution to make life more tolerable and enjoyable is a great pressing need.

As the word of the Buddha is of everlasting value and universal applicability, and as the Buddha preached not only to monks and nuns but also to the lay public as well, it is useful to find a teaching of the Buddha which is relevant to our present-day problems. In the *Pattakammavagga* of the Aṅguttara Nikāya (A II 69) the Buddha preached a sutta to Anāthapiṇḍika on the fourfold pleasures of a layman. It is our considered opinion that this sutta offers adequate insight to meet the demands of the present-day problems as well. The four types of pleasure listed there are: *atthisukha,* the pleasure of having material wealth; *bhogasukha,* the pleasure of enjoying material wealth; *anaṇasukha,* the pleasure of being debtless; and *anavajjasukha,* the pleasure of being blameless. Let us take these for discussion one by one and see how these sources of pleasure can be harnessed for leading a happy life in the present-day world.

Atthisukha—Man should not only have a righteous means of living, avoiding blameworthy trades such as dealing in meat, liquor, poison, firearms and slavery, he should also entertain a wholesome attitude towards his righteous occupation. For instance, if a doctor welcomes epidemics in the locality in order to make much money, or a trader hopes for natural calamities to send market prices up, the money earned by such unscrupulous individuals is not righteous money as their intentions are impure and foul. Also one should not deceive or exploit others in carrying out one's occupation. Exerting oneself with great perseverance, one should earn one's living, and such hard-earned wealth is called righteous wealth (*dhammika dhammaladdha*). Again one could have great wealth, but if one does not experience a sense of contentment with what one has, one cannot really enjoy *atthisukha* or the pleasure of having. The amassing of wealth of such a person is like trying to fill a bottomless vessel. This is one of the widespread maladies we see in the present-day society. Inordinate expansion of wealth becomes a source not of happiness, but of anxiety. Such wealth exposes the possessor to the jealousies and maneuvers of other unscrupulous individuals, hence the occurrence of blackmailing and kidnapping from time to time. But if one does have a righteous means of earning one's living and the correct attitude to wealth, one can escape many of the hazards which money brings in its wake to modern man.

Bhogasukha—Wealth has only instrumental value and the proper enjoyment of wealth is an art which is worth carefully cultivating. Buddhism deplores both extravagance and miserly hoarding. One must maintain a healthy balanced standard of living according to one's means. If, in the enjoyment of wealth, one overindulges in sense pleasures, one is bound to run into health hazards in a very short time. If, for instance, one overindulges in food just because one can afford it, one will soon be overcome by diseases such as heart failure, high blood pressure and diabetes. Such a person will be faced with the situation of "cutting his neck with his own tongue." Moderation in food is a virtue praised in Buddhism and it is a health-promoting habit. Often in the name of enjoying wealth, man cultivates unhealthy habits such as smoking and drinking. It is paradoxical that man, who actually loves himself most, should act as if he were his own worst enemy by indulging in habits which ultimately reduce him to a physical wreck. It is medically established that smoking causes the highest percentage of lung cancer, and that drinking causes irreparable damage to vital organs of the body. If only one pauses to ponder over one's own welfare, and if only one entertains at least some degree of compassion towards oneself, one would not get into the clutches of these vicious habits. Wealthy men often end up in the pitiful plight of the ant fallen in the pot of honey. Such men did not know the art of enjoying *bhogasukha.* They regard the body as an instrument for pleasure, and they wear out and debilitate the body's capacity for enjoyment in double quick time, long before the natural process of wear and tear sets in. If we love ourselves, we have to treat our bodies with proper care without taxing it with overindulgence and deprivation. It is with the body that we can enjoy not only the pleasures of the senses, but even the spiritual bliss of Nibbāna. Another aspect of the joy of wealth is the art of sharing. Without being an *Adinnapubbaka,* a "never-giver," if one learns to share one's riches with the less fortunate have-nots, one will have the noble experience of being happy at the joy of another. At the same time one will learn the love and good will of others, instead of becoming the target of jealousy and intrigue.

Anaṇasukha—The pleasure of being debtless is the third quality discussed in our sutta. Economically if one can be completely free of debt, one is indeed a very fortunate person. To be really debtless in society one has to discharge one's obligations scrupulously. As a wage earner one has to discharge one's duties for which one is paid, otherwise one can be indebted to the wage one gets. As a parent one has to fulfill one's obligations to one's children. In our society children are taught to worship and look after their parents, and it is well to bear in mind that parents too have to qualify themselves for the honor they receive by being dutiful parents. It should be emphasized that fathers who neglect their families as a result of their addiction to vices such as drinking and gambling fall far short of the ideal of debtlessness. One can have the satisfaction of being debtless only if one has fulfilled one's obligations in all social roles one has to perform.

Anavajjasukha—The satisfaction of leading a blameless life is the highest form of satisfaction that a layman can have. Every society has a code of ethics to be followed by its members. According to Buddhism the minimum code of ethics regulating the life of its adherents is the *pañcasīla,* the Five Precepts.[1] If one practices these virtues, one can have the satisfaction of leading a

1. Abstinence from killing, stealing, sexual misconduct, false speech and intoxicants.

righteous life to a great extent. Refraining from doing to others what one does not like others to do unto oneself is the basic principle underlying these virtues. Buddhism speaks of *hiri* and *ottappa,* the sense of shame and the fear to do wrong, as *deva-dhamma* or celestial qualities. These are the basic qualities which separate man from the animal kingdom. Unlike the animals man has a conscience which makes him squeamish about doing wrong. Buddhism recognizes blameless mental activity as well. Mental activities which spring from greed, hatred and delusion are unwholesome and blameworthy. Let us see how such mental behavior is a source of unhappiness. Take for instance the case of a person who is angry. What are the symptoms of anger? Hard breathing, accelerated heart beat, faster circulation of blood, feeling hot, sweating, trepidation, restlessness, etc.—these are the physical manifestations of anger. These are certainly not comfortable physical experiences. Each time the cause of anger is remembered, even though the physical manifestations of anger may not be that marked, one feels quite restless and mentally ill at ease. We use expressions such as "boiling with anger," "I got the devil on to me," etc. to mean getting angry and these sayings are literally expressive of the situation. It is just not possible for one to be angry and happy at the same time. An irritable person is truly a very sad person, and what is worse he infects others around him too with the same sadness. The cultivation of sublime modes of behavior such as loving kindness, compassion, sympathetic joy and equanimity are truly conducive to happy living. Those who live with such attitudes habitually are pleasant and amicable people who can be happy alone as well as in company.

If we truly understand the significance of the four kinds of happiness elucidated in our sutta, and translate them into action, life will be much more pleasant and happy even in this modern age.

The Mechanics of Bondage and Suffering

The Buddhist texts repeatedly describe man as being bound and fettered to suffering. Many Pali words are used to describe this pathetic situation, such as *saṃyojana*, *bandha* and *pāsa*, meaning bond, fetter, and snare, respectively. One sutta employs a simple simile to illustrate the manner in which man is fettered to *saṃsāric* life. According to this simile a black bull and a white bull are tied together with a rope. In this situation it cannot be said that the black bull is a fetter to the white bull, or that the white bull is a fetter to the black bull. Actually it is the rope with which the two are tied together that constitutes the fetter. Similarly the external world is not a fetter to man, nor is man a fetter to the external world. It is the desire for pleasure with which man is bound to the external world that forms the fetter. Desire is a very strong fetter which chains man to the external world and thereby to the ever recurring cycle of births and deaths. This strong fetter has six strands emerging from the six sense faculties, namely, the eye, ear, nose, tongue, body, and the mental faculty. The last mentioned faculty is called *mano* in Pali and is regarded as the sense that unifies all the other faculties.

The Pali word for sense faculty is *indriya*, a very interesting word which reveals much about our human situation. *Indra* means lord or king, and the sense faculties are called *indriyas* because they dominate us so much. They act as our lords or masters and we slavishly obey them. The eye wishes to see pleasant forms, the ear wishes to hear pleasant sounds, the nose to smell pleasant smells, the tongue to enjoy pleasant tastes, and the body to feel pleasant tactile objects. The mental faculty which unifies all other sense faculties, gets terribly disturbed as it is dragged in different directions by the different sense stimuli, while it has to deal with its own share of agitations in the form of hopes, memories, and imaginations. The *Chappāṇaka Sutta* of the Saṃyutta Nikāya beautifully illustrates the struggle of the six senses with an eloquent simile. According to this simile, six animals having different habits and diverse fields of action are tied together in one knot by a strong rope. The six animals are a crocodile who tries to run to the water, a bird who tries to fly in the air, a dog who tries to run to a village, a fox who tries to flee to a cemetery, a monkey who tries to go to the forest, and a snake who tries to creep into an anthill. These six animals are constantly struggling to reach their respective habitats. Similarly, the six senses are constantly seeking gratification in their own spheres, and the man who has no control over his sense faculties becomes terribly confused.

Through our senses we are chained to sense stimuli. We are chained to pleasant sense stimuli by the way of greed. We love to see pleasant objects and we spend a great deal of time, energy, and money in our endeavor to procure as many pleasant objects as possible. We love to hear pleasant words; if someone speaks in praise of us once we will often recall it with pleasure and be attached to that pleasure. We love to eat tasty food. This is a great weakness in most of us. Even when rich food is detrimental to our health, the desire to please the tongue is so great that we indulge in food even at the risk of our precious lives. This is how we sometimes go to the extent of beheading ourselves with our tongues. Man's desire to gratify his sex desire is also so intense that he runs the gravest risk of suffering great pain and debility with social diseases. AIDS (Acquired Immunity Deficiency Syndrome), the present dreaded disease which is taking a very heavy toll of human life in the West, is the latest severe penalty man is paying for his unrestrained greed for sensuality. The plight of modern man can be illustrated by the traditional simile of the ant fallen in the pot of honey, bogged down and drowning in the very pleasures he is trying to enjoy.

Just as much as we can become fettered by greed, so we can also get trapped by dislike or hatred. Our aversion is aroused by unpleasant sense stimuli. The stronger the aversion, the more tenaciously we become fettered to the unpleasant object. Let us take an example. Suppose we have seen a disgusting object just before or during a meal. Our aversion may grow so strong that we will reject even the most delicious food. If we see a worm in a bean curry, our aversion to it may even make us give up eating beans altogether, for each time we see beans we would be reminded of the unpleasant experience. Let us take another example from auditory experience. If somebody abuses us in front of a gathering, we would indeed get very angry with the abuser. This incident would come to our mind often and each time it came up we would experience anger. When we recall the abuse over and over and inject negative emotions of anger and hatred into this memory, we should know that a fetter has been formed.

By these obsessions of greed and hatred generated through the instrumentality of the senses, man's freedom of activity is limited and demarcated. He becomes like an animal tethered to a post by a rope, with its range of activity limited by the length of the rope. Here egoism is like the post, as we are all tied to the idea of self or "I". The rope stands for desire or aversion, for the stronger the idea of self, the more selfish we become, and the more selfish we become, the stronger grow our desires, likes, and dislikes. So it goes on in a vicious circle. Let us work out the simile in greater detail: when the rope of desire is strong, the rope itself becomes short, restricting man's freedom of activity proportionally. The man with a very strong sense of ego is like the animal who is smothered by the tightness and the shortness of the rope. The nature of this desire-rope is such that when negative emotions of likes and dislikes are weak, the rope itself is not only weakened but also lengthened, giving the human animal greater freedom of activity. When negative emotions become weak, positive emotions such as love and compassion emerge, expanding man's scope of freedom. The entire message of the Dhamma can be summarized as a method of rescuing human beings from the trammels of egocentricity, negative emotions, and ignorance, and granting them complete and unlimited freedom. In the language of our simile, it is like cutting the rope and uprooting the post to which the animal is tied.

The suttas also speak of another human tendency with regard to sense pleasures: dwelling on past sensual pleasures while even neglecting to enjoy present pleasures. The past sense objects have already passed away and changed, but we become attached to our memories of them and thus experience anguish. Another trap we fall into because of our enjoyment of sense objects is the generation of the three types of conceit. When we think that we have a greater share of sensual pleasures than others, we develop a superiority complex (*seyyamāna);* by considering ourselves equal to others, we develop the equality complex (*sadisamāna);* and by thinking of ourselves as being less fortunate than others in the enjoyment of sense pleasures, we develop the inferiority complex (*hīnamāna*). Thus, by using the measuring rod of sense pleasures to quantify status, we become more and more self-centered and suffer the consequences of all possible complexes. Therefore the Buddha calls sense pleasures the "snare of Māra," the Evil One.

A sutta in the Saḷāyatana Saṃyutta explains the situation from a different angle. When the sense faculties are unrestrained, the mind gets corrupted, wallowing in the enjoyment of sense objects. Such a corrupt mind does not find *pāmojja,* delight in those higher noble pursuits which elevate the mind.

When this *pāmojja,* or spiritual delight is absent, pious joy (*pīti*) is also absent. When pious joy is missing there is no *passaddhi,* physical and mental relaxation. He who is not relaxed, lives in tension, frustration, and misery. This is what is called in Pali *dukkha,* "suffering." Thus suffering is traced to non-restraint in the sense faculties.

Looking at the problem from another perspective, the Saḷāyatana Saṃyutta traces the origin of the world to sense experience. Depending on the sense faculties and sense objects there arises sense consciousness. The convergence of these three factors—sense faculties, sense objects and sense consciousness—is called contact (*phassa*). Contact generates feelings (*phassapaccayā vedanā*). In other words, if the object is delightful we experience pleasure in making contact with it. Feelings give rise to craving (*vedanāpaccayā taṇhā*) as we tend to desire more and more of the pleasant feelings. Craving generates clinging (*taṇhāpaccaya upādānaṃ*), when we try to possess the objects we crave for. Clinging nurtures the growth of personal factors (*upādānapaccayā bhavo*), which in turn causes birth (*jāti*). Birth brings in its wake all the ills of old age, death, grief, lamentation, etc. This is called the arising of the world. Thus we construct our own private worlds through the instrumentality of our sense faculties.

All this material goes to show that we are trapped to *saṃsāra* through the domination of our senses. If we allow them free rein, we allow them to control us. Bondage and suffering are proportionate to the extent that we allow our sense faculties to dominate us. If we desire freedom and happiness for ourselves we have to subjugate the senses and make them our servants.

Understanding and Managing Stress

Stress is a term adopted from engineering science by psychology and medicine. Simply defined, stress in engineering means force upon an area. As so many forces are working upon us in the modern age, and we find it extremely difficult to cope under so much pressure, stress is called the "disease of civilization." Philip Zimbardo in his *Psychology and Life* traces four interrelated levels at which we react to the pressures exerted upon us from our environment. The four are: the emotional level, the behavioral level, the physiological level, and the cognitive level. The emotional responses to stress are sadness, depression, anger, irritation, and frustration. The behavioral responses are poor concentration, forgetfulness, poor interpersonal relations, and lowered productivity. The physiological responses consist of bodily tensions, which may lead to headaches, backaches, stomach ulcers, high blood pressure, and even killer diseases. At the cognitive level one may lose self-esteem and self-confidence, which leads to feelings of helplessness and hopelessness. At worst such a person may even end up committing suicide.

In order to understand stress let us consider the various environmental factors which exert pressure on modern man. In this atomic age the very survival of the species is threatened. Nuclear war threatens every single human being on earth, irrespective of whether one lives in a country with nuclear weapons or not. Population explosion threatens man with severe food shortages; at present even a large segment of human population is undernourished while still others are dying of starvation and malnutrition. Environmental pollution causes severe health hazards and mental and physical retardation. Unemployment among the skilled is a growing global problem. The pace of life has become so hectic that man is simply rushing from one task to another without any relaxation. This is really paradoxical in an age when labor-saving devices are freely available and are in use to an unprecedented degree. Competition for educational and employment opportunities is so severe that it has contributed to a fair share to increase the rate of suicide. Enjoyment of sense pleasures has grown so obsessive that it has become like drinking salt water to quench thirst. Constant stimulation of the senses is today considered a necessity, and thus pocket radios with earphones, chewing gum, and cosmetics are marketed everywhere. Sense stimulation goes on unrestrained but satiation is far from achieved. It is no wonder that man, caught up in all this, is terribly confused and frustrated, and his life is intolerably stressful. This is the situation Buddhism describes as "tangles within and tangles without, people are enmeshed in tangles."

While the above observations were made from the point of view of modern studies and contemporary conditions, Buddhism makes similar observations from a psychological perspective. Man experiences stress and suffering because of five psychological states which envelop his whole personality. They are called *nivaraṇa* in the Pali language, meaning hindrances. They hinder happiness and overcloud man's vision of himself, his environment and the interaction between the two. The thicker and more opaque these hindrances, the greater the stress and suffering man experiences. The thinner and more sparse these hindrances, the less his suffering with a corresponding increase in happiness. These five hindrances are the desire for sensual pleasures, anger, indolence, worry and doubt. The Pali Canon illustrates the effect of these hindrances with the help of five eloquent similes. The mind overpowered by the desire for sense pleasures is compared to colored water which prevents a true reflection of a thing on the water. Thus a man obsessed with the desire for sense pleasures is unable to get a true perspective of either himself or other people or his environment. The mind oppressed by anger is compared to boiling water which cannot give an accurate reflection. A man overpowered by anger is unable to discern an issue properly. When the mind is in the grip of indolence it is like moss covered water: light cannot even reach the water and a reflection is impossible. The lazy man does not even make an effort at correct understanding. When worried the mind is like wind-tossed turbulent water, which also fails to give a true reflection. The worried man, forever restless, is unable to make a proper assessment of an issue. When the mind is in doubt it is compared to muddy water placed in darkness which cannot reflect an image well. Thus all the five hindrances deprive the mind of understanding and happiness and cause much stress and suffering.

Buddhism puts forward a methodical plan of action for the gradual elimination of stress and the increase of happiness and understanding. The first step recommended in this plan is the observance of the Five Precepts comprising the abstention from killing, stealing, illicit sex, falsehood and intoxicants. Stress is greatly enhanced by guilt, and these precepts help man to free his conscience of the sense of guilt. The *Dhammapada* says the evil-doer suffers here and hereafter; on the other hand, the man who does good deeds rejoices here and hereafter.

Buddhism firmly believes that evil increases stress while good increases happiness. In addition to the observance of the Five Precepts throughout life, Buddhism advocates the periodical observance of the Eight Precepts by laymen. These additional precepts attempt to train man for leading a simple life catering to one's needs rather than one's greeds. A frugal mode of life where wants are few and are easily satisfied is highly extolled in Buddhism. It is the avaricious and the acquisitive mentality that is responsible for so much stress that we experience.

The next step in the process of training is the control of the sense faculties. When our sense faculties are uncontrolled we experience severe strain. We have to first understand what is meant by being uncontrolled in the sense faculties. When a person sees a beautiful form with his eyes, he gets attracted to it; when he sees an unpleasant object, he gets repelled by it. Similarly with the other senses too. Thus the person who has no control over his senses is constantly attracted and repelled by sense data, as during waking life sense data keep on impinging on his sense faculties constantly. When pulled in different directions by sense stimuli, we become confused and distressed.

Our sense faculties have different spheres of activity and different objects, and as each sense faculty is a lord in its own sphere, and as they can severally and collectively dominate man, they are called in Pali *indriyas,* meaning "lords" or "masters." If we allow the sense faculties to dominate us, we get terribly confused. If we assert ourselves and control our sense faculties, we can have unalloyed pleasure (*avyāsekasukha*), so called because this pleasure is uncontaminated by defilements. It is also called *adhicittasukha,* meaning spiritual pleasure. Whereas sense pleasures increase stress, this type of spiritual pleasure reduces stressfulness and increases peace of mind and contentment.

The third step in the management of stress is the cultivation of wholesome mental habits through meditation (*bhāvanā*). Just as we look after and nurture our body with proper food and cleanliness, the mind too needs proper nourishment and cleansing. The mind is most volatile in its untrained state, but when it is tamed and made more stable it brings great happiness. Buddhism prescribes two fundamental meditative methods of mind-training called *samatha* and *vipassanā*, calm and insight. The former is the method of calming the volatile mind, while the latter is the method of comprehending the true nature of bodily and mental phenomena. Both methods are extremely helpful for overcoming stress. The *Sāmaññaphala Sutta* explains with the help of five appropriate similes how meditation reduces the psychological stress caused by the five hindrances. The man who practices meditation gains a great sense of relief and it is this sense of unburdening oneself that the similes illustrate. They are as follows: A man who has raised capital for a business by taking a loan, prospers in business, pays off the loan and manages his day-to-day affairs with financial ease. Such a man experiences a great sense of relief. The second simile portrays a man who has suffered a great deal with a prolonged chronic illness. He gets well at long last, food becomes palatable to him and he gains physical strength. Great is the relief such a man experiences. The third simile speaks of the relief a prisoner enjoys after being released from a long term in jail. The fourth is the slave who gains freedom from slavery. The fifth simile speaks of a well-to-do man who gets lost in a fearful desert without food. On coming to a place of safety he experiences great relief. When the stress caused by the five hindrances is eliminated from the mind, great joy and delight arise similar to the relief enjoyed by the men described in the similes. The best and most effective way of overcoming stress is the practice of meditation or mental culture. But as a prelude to that at least the Five Precepts must be observed.

The cultivation of positive emotions such as loving-kindness (*mettā*), compassion (*karuṇā*), sympathetic joy (*mudita*), and equanimity (*upekkhā*) is another means of conquering stress. Strained interpersonal relations is one of the common causes of stress in household life and in the workplace. *Loving kindness* is the positive wholesome attitude one can cultivate with benefit for oneself and others in all interpersonal relationships. *Compassion* is the emotion with which one should regard and help those in distress. *Sympathetic joy* is the ability to rejoice in the joy of another. It is difficult for a man of mean character to entertain this attitude as the joy of another brings jealousy to the mind of such a person. Where there is jealousy there is no unity, and where there is no unity there is no progress. The cultivation of these positive emotions stands for both material and spiritual progress. *Equanimity* is the attitude to be adopted in the face of the vicissitudes of life. There are eight natural ways of the world that we have to face in life. They are gain and loss, fame and lack of fame, praise and blame, happiness and sorrow. If one trains oneself to maintain an equanimous temperament without being either elated or dejected in the face of these vicissitudes, one can avoid much stress and lead a simple life with peace and contentment. We cannot change the world so that it will give us happiness. But we can change our attitude towards the world so as to remain unaffected by the stresses exerted by events around us. Buddhism teaches the way to bring about this wholesome change of attitude.

The Buddhist Attitude to Gain and Honor

The world today has evolved various means of bestowing honor on individuals whom society recognizes as worthy of being honored. The Nobel Prize is considered one of the most prestigious, and there are various other prizes and honorific titles that are bestowed annually or from time to time on distinguished persons. In the scholarly world the publication of felicitation and commemoration volumes and the conferment of honorary degrees are the usual methods of honoring academic celebrities. In society at large we indulge in various devices in the public display of honor and appreciation. Often we resort to overtly ego-boosting methods. As the public display of honor and esteem has become such an important phenomena in our social life, given much publicity over all the media—the press, radio and television—it is timely to pause to understand the Buddhist attitude towards the display and acceptance of such public honor. The Pali Canon uses terms such as *lābha, sakkāra, siloka, pūjā* and *vandana* to mean various expressions of honor, esteem and reverence.

According to Buddhism the presence of ethical and spiritual qualities is the primary criterion for eligibility for honor. The Buddha, the Paccekabuddha, the Arahant and the universal monarch rank as the highest personages who are worthy of honor and respect. Honor paid to those worthy of honor is listed as a great blessing in the *Mahā-maṅgala Sutta* (*pūjā ca pūjanīyānaṃ etaṃ maṅgalam-uttamaṃ*). The *Dhammapada* (vv. 105–6) declares that honor paid to a perfected saint is far better than a century spent in the performance of sacrifice. The same text reiterates that the merit of one who reverences those worthy of honor cannot be measured (v. 195). In the domestic sphere parents are greatly honored and esteemed. As they have done so much for the children, toiling through a whole lifetime, they deserve to be appreciated, honored and looked after by the children. There should be mutual honor and respect between husband and wife. This quality helps to weave a cohesive relationship to build a happy home for the rearing of progeny. It is also a healthy age-old custom to honor and welcome guests as is, for instance, maintained in the *Caṅkī Sutta* (M II 167). Respect shown to elders is also highly commended as is well illustrated by the parable of the *Tittira Jātaka* (J I 218). Thus noble spiritual qualities, parentage and seniority are recognized as some of the main criteria deserving the display of honor and respect.

Now let us turn our attention to the attitude to gain and honor by those who receive them. Since the Buddha's immediate disciples were monks, who by reason of their religious status regularly received gains and honor from the laity, it is to be expected that his statements on this subject are addressed primarily to the monks and their concerns. Moreover, as the monks have committed themselves fully to the quest for deliverance, the Buddha's advice to them naturally takes their special vocation into account. However, while recognizing the differences in their position, lay people can take the Buddha's counsel to the monks as guidelines for their own attitudes towards gain and honor.

The Pali texts show that it is possible to adopt one of the following three attitudes: (a) One could eagerly appreciate and enjoy the honor one receives, even actively seek it. (b) One could turn away and refuse to accept the honor bestowed. (c) One could be indifferent and entertain an attitude of equanimity towards such honors. We shall take these one by one for discussion.

(a) The *Mahāsāropama Sutta* (M I 192) elucidates the appreciative attitude to gain and honor with the help of a simile. If a monk who has entered the Order enjoys the gain and honor he receives and is satisfied therewith, he is like a man who, being in search of timber, is satisfied with the end trimmings of a huge tree. What he looked for is timber, but what he is satisfied with is just twigs and foliage. Devadatta (J I 186) is the classic example of one who fell into utter ruin by enjoying gain and honor. He had developed psychic powers, and he utilized these powers for convincing laymen of his spiritual development. The most influential layman who was thus convinced was Ajātasattu. The unconcealed display of superhuman powers gave rise to much gain and honor for Devadatta, so much so that in his utter stupidity he wished to kill the Buddha and usurp Buddhahood, and he enticed Ajātasattu to kill his father and usurp the kingship. The Buddha pronounced that it is for Devadatta's utter ruin and downfall that he was endowed with so much gain and honor, just as the plantain tree bears fruit for its own ruin. (S II 241). The *Dhammapada* maintains that gain and honor is one thing and the path to the realization of Nibbāna is another. Knowing this clearly a monk should not take delight in gain and honor (Dh. 75). According to the *Milindapañhā* (p. 377), just as a ship has to withstand various forces such as the force of strong currents, thunder and whirlpools, even so a monk has to withstand the forces of gain, honor, fame and homage. If a monk relishes these and gets a bloated ego, he flounders and sinks just like a wrecked ship. The *Milindapañhā* (p. 377) takes another simile from naval experience. A ship's anchor is able to hold a ship fast without letting it drift along, even in very deep waters, even so a monk must remain anchored to his purpose with great strength of character without letting the gain and honor that comes in the wake of virtue carry him adrift. It is no doubt the duty of the layman to honor and respect a virtuous monk, and also to provide him with the requisites. It is the responsibility of the monk to maintain a sane balanced attitude, without becoming elated. Buddhism maintains that it is difficult for a man of mean spiritual development to resist the enjoyment of gain and honor (*sakkāro kapurisena dujjaho,* Th 1053). There is the great danger of spiritual erosion when a man indulges and basks in the glory of fame and honor. One develops a bloated ego and boastfulness creeps into his character in the most surreptitious ways. Such men also develop contemptuous attitudes towards others who do not get so much honor. The *Lābhasakkāra Saṃyutta* sarcastically compares him to the dung beetle who entertains contempt towards other dung beetles for having less dung. The *Anaṅgaṇa Sutta* (M I 29–30) shows the abhorrence and disgust towards a monk who undertakes the religious life and difficult ascetic practices for the sake of public generosity and popularity. Such a monk is compared to one who places the carcass of a snake or a dog in a beautifully polished brand new metal bowl. The bowl of higher life (*brahmacariya*) is not meant for storing carcass-like immoral intentions.

Monks are advised in the most emphatic terms to guard against taking delight in gain and honor. The *Lābhasakkāra Saṃyutta* works out a number of similes in great detail to illustrate the point (S II 226–7). A young tortoise who defied the elders' advice is shot with a splinter to which a string is attached and he is bound to be caught by the hunter in no time. The hunter in the simile is none other than Māra himself. The splinter is gain, honor and fame. The string attached to the splinter is the monk's attachment to gain and honor. Again, gain and honor are compared to a bait which greedy monks might swallow to be utterly ruined in the hands of the trapper Māra.

(b) Now let us turn to the attitude of the monk who refuses gain and honor. Mahākassapa was an eminent monk who eschewed gain and honor, and found delight in helping the poor to earn merit by going to them for alms. Once the Buddha saw him begging his alms in a locality where poverty-stricken weavers lived, in spite of gods trying to procure for him a fine meal. On this occasion the Buddha gave expression to an inspired utterance (*Udāna,* p. 11) in appreciation of Mahākassapa's simplicity. Once a famous householder named Citta was impressed by the explanation of a knotty doctrinal point by a monk named Isidatta in a great assembly. Citta invited Isidatta to reside in the locality and promised him hospitality with all requisites. Isidatta seized the first opportunity to quietly leave the locality without informing Citta (S IV 286–8). Such was the scrupulous reticent behavior of those who understood the pernicious nature of gain and honor.

(c) Generally the Buddha and Arahants do not fight shy of gain and honor. They face it with the same equanimity as they face loss and blame. The *Mahā-Govinda Sutta* (D II 223) records that gods rejoice in the Buddha because of his attitude to gain and honor. The Buddha has received gain and fame which a king would long to have, but with no trace of elation whatsoever he fares along partaking of only the basic requisites. The gods declare that there was never a teacher of such calibre before. The lotus, though born in the water, remains unsullied above the water. Similarly the Buddha and Arahants rise uncontaminated above the mundane conditions of family, prestige, gain, fame, and reverence (*Milinda*, p. 375). "The Unique Ones (*asamasama*) are worshipped by gods and men. But they relish no honor. This is the norm of Buddhas" (*Milindapañhā*, p. 95). Cullasabhadda, an *upāsikā*, observes that while the world is elated and depressed by gain and loss respectively, the true monks maintain an equanimous attitude in the face of both.

The Buddha declares that he has personally known, seen and understood (*samaṃ ñātaṃ samaṃ diṭṭhaṃ samaṃ viditaṃ*, It 74) that beings who have been overwhelmed (*pariyādinnacitta*) by gain and honor, and also those who are obsessed by the lack of gain and honor, at the disintegration of the body are born in states of woe. The desire for honor and recognition is so insinuative that even normally upright individuals can succumb to it. The Buddha says that through his telepathic knowledge he knows that there are some who would not stoop so low as to tell a deliberate lie for the sake of silver and gold, a beauty queen, parents, children or even life, but who would do so to gain honor and prestige. So vicious and pernicious are the snares of gain and honor (S II 234, 243). Except Arahants, those of the highest order who have reached the state of *akuppa cetovimutti* (S II 239) or unshakable mental emancipation, all those of lesser spiritual development are said to be vulnerable in this respect. It is no wonder that gain and honor is a powerful member of the army of Māra (Sn 438–9). It should be recognized by all those who value spiritual progress as a disaster come in the guise of a blessing.

Livelihood and Development

Right livelihood (*sammā ājīva*) is the fifth factor in the Noble Eightfold Path. As a method of earning one's living is important to every human being, whether a member of the clergy or a layman, the correct understanding of right livelihood is crucial. For a monk, complete dedication to the higher life constitutes right livelihood. He then is rightly entitled to be supported by public generosity. In this essay we shall confine ourselves to an inquiry into the concept of right livelihood for the layman.

Right livelihood implies that one has to avoid a wrong means of earning a living, known as *micchā ājīva* in Pali. This includes trades which are directly or indirectly injurious to others, be they animal or human, such as trade in meat, liquor, poison, weapons and slaves. These are contrary to the basic five precepts which all lay Buddhists are expected to abide by. In the world today these trades, except perhaps the slave trade, are flourishing industries, and much of the revenue to governments comes from these industries. This shows to what an extent wrong livelihood is prevalent in the world today.

Even a blameless means of living can become blameworthy if practiced with inordinate greed and dishonesty. If a doctor in private practice makes mints of money exploiting his patients, he is guilty of wrong livelihood even though medicine itself is a noble profession. A vegetable dealer who cheats in weights and measures is similarly guilty of wrong livelihood. Honest scrupulous service rendered without exploiting the public is considered an essential feature of right livelihood.

Buddhism upholds the quality of having few wants (*appicchatā*) and the ability to be satisfied with little (*santuṭṭhi*) as great virtues. One has to practice these virtues not only in consumerism but in production too; in the modern world, however, these virtues have been totally lost sight of in both these spheres. Therefore governments as well as the private sector aim at ever increasing development. Such development, however, has no limit. Each time a target has been reached, the limit to possible growth recedes further like a mirage. More and more is produced, more and more is consumed. There is no satiation with development, nor with consumerism. This is a limitless race in a limited world with limited resources. Therefore mankind has to learn that the concept of development as it is understood today cannot go on forever, it is logically and practically impossible.

Nature seems to set its own limits to this process of escalated growth. It appears that there are biological, psychological, social and ecological limits to growth. The physical constitution of man seems to revolt against this limitless growth. There is an array of diseases man readily succumbs to today related to overconsumption and overindulgence. There are pressure-related diseases too, which affect both the human body and the human mind. Present-day development taxes man's endurance enormously and he becomes a psychological wreck due to the pressures of work, competition and maintaining standards. Interpersonal relationships have become superficial, brittle and sour, and this seems to be a sign that society cannot withstand the weight of its material development. In the external world too there are unequivocal signs which portend impending catastrophe unless man changes his course of action. There is air, water and land pollution everywhere, and this is extremely injurious not only to human life but to all forms of life on this planet. These are nature's ways of expressing her disapproval of the methods and rate of production and consumption man has chosen today.

Agriculture is recognized in Buddhism as a noble means of making a living, but what has happened in this sphere? Prompted by population pressures, and encouraged by the ever-expanding vistas of scientific knowledge, traditional methods of tilling the land have given way to mechanized industrial agriculture. Vast acres are plowed by machines; chemical fertilizers are applied freely; weedicides, insecticides and pesticides are used indiscriminately; and large harvests are gathered. More and more research is going on in agricultural engineering to produce better seeds which promise higher yields. Though production has increased, prices remain at a constant high level. In some countries when the price level threatens to go down due to overproduction, the products are methodically destroyed or dumped into the sea despite the fact that large masses of people in the world today are undernourished and some are actually starving to death. It is blatantly clear that the whole industrialized agricultural policy is prompted by inordinate greed and it is far from right livelihood.

From the Buddhist point of view this whole system is wrong. On the one hand it has resulted in the erosion of moral and human values. It has deprived man of sympathy for his fellow sentient beings as is evident from the large-scale use of insecticides. Economic gain seems to be the only criterion by which man is prompted to action. Blinded by short-term economic gain, man seems to turn a blind eye to the long-term repercussions of his aggressive policies on this planet. In the wake of the avaricious and aggressive industrialization, the crime rate has risen to an unprecedented degree, and this is a clear index to man's moral degeneration. On the other hand, the natural ecological balance of the earth has been disturbed to an alarming degree. Chemical pollution of land and water has affected bacteria, insects and fish. While some of these forms of life useful to man have died or are dying, others, especially insects dangerous to man, have become resistant to insecticides. As more and more effective chemicals are produced, these creatures become immune to them and the vicious circle goes on without any practical solution in sight. The natural fertility and the organic balance of the soil also diminish as more and more chemical fertilizers are applied throughout the years and thus a vicious circle gets formed there too.

All this evidence clearly shows that man cannot dominate and subjugate nature. In the long run nature emerges triumphant and man becomes the loser. Instead man must learn to co-operate with nature. Here we are reminded of an admonition given by the Buddha that in amassing wealth man must exploit nature as a bee collects pollen. The bee harms neither the beauty of the flower nor its fragrance, similarly man must not pollute or rob nature of its richness, beauty and its rejuvenating and replenishing capacity. This is the real implication of right livelihood when it comes to the utilization of natural resources.

It should be reiterated that the whole modern concept of development, which seems to have nothing short of the sky itself as the limit, is severely antithetical to Buddhist values. Buddhism sets the limit at the other end: it advocates that we feed our needs and not our greeds. Man needs the basic comforts of food, clothing, shelter and medicine. It is the responsibility of the rulers to provide avenues of employment so that the average man can afford to have these needs satisfied with a fair degree of comfort. As man is naturally prone to greed, Buddhism emphasizes the value of having few wants (*appicchatā*). Contentment (*santuṭṭhi*) is also a much valued virtue in Buddhism. Care is taken to see that these virtues do not degenerate into apathy and cause social stagnation. Buddhism encourages the layman to be industrious, to forge ahead in his chosen blameless occupation (*uṭṭhānasampadā*). Wealth earned by sheer perseverance, by the sweat of one's brow, is as highly praised as well gotten righteous wealth. It is even recommended that a layman should invest half of his earnings for improvement of his industry. Laymen are also exhorted to save (*ārakkhasampadā*) their hard earned money, and to lead a comfortable life consonant with earning capacity, avoiding both extremes of miserliness and extravagance/over-indulgence. Thus the tension between having few wants (*appicchatā*) and contentment (*santuṭṭhi*) on the one hand, and industriousness (*uṭṭhānasampadā*) and the saving habit (*ārakkhasampadā*) on the other, helps to keep society at a practically comfortable level of development which can be sustained for a long time. When these economic ideas are reinforced with the other moral values inculcated by Buddhism, a stable society with harmonious interpersonal relations can be expected.

The modern concept of large-scale industries and factories also does not agree with the Buddhist concept of right livelihood. These large industries and mechanized labor have made a few people enormously rich and thrown millions of employable people out of employment. Thus wealth gets concentrated among a few factory owners and businessmen while millions can barely eke out an existence. Misdistribution of wealth is regarded in Buddhism as a social evil which paves the way to crime and revolution. Moreover machines have robbed man of his creativity and left him terribly frustrated. This may be one of the reasons why the youth of today have turned to drugs to find an easy escape route.

The concept of right livelihood works with the notion that man is the central concern in economy as producer as well as consumer, not the profit made in the process of products changing hands. The skills and talents of the producer should be enhanced in the process of production and he should have the satisfaction derived from his output. The producer, not an employer above him or a middleman, should get a fair return commensurate with his labor and sufficient to afford him a decent living. The consumer, on the other hand, should get quality and quantity for what he pays. In sharp contrast to this ideology, the profit made by the employer is the central concern today: both the producer and the consumer are subservient to the profit motive. Therefore right livelihood would opt for small-scale industries which would satisfy the creative instinct of man and the basic needs of many more people, and would also ensure a more equitable distribution of wealth in society. It is better to have a large number of skilled cobblers than a well equipped mechanized shoe factory.

As right livelihood is a part and parcel of the Noble Eightfold Path, when it is rightly practiced it leads to the elimination of greed, hatred and delusion (S V 5). Just as the river Ganges is inclined towards the east, he who practices the Noble Eightfold Path is inclined towards Nibbāna. Thus the correct understanding of right livelihood is essential for the Buddhist layman who is bent on his spiritual welfare.

Facing Death Without Fear

Death is the only certain thing in life. It is also the thing for which we are least prepared. We plan and prepare for various other things—examinations, weddings, business transactions, building houses—but we can never be certain whether our plans will materialize according to our wish. Death, on the other hand, can come any minute, sooner or later; it is the most certain event in life. Just as the mushroom raises itself from the ground carrying a bit of earth on its hood, so every living being brings with himself the certainty of death from the moment of his birth.

The Aṅguttara Nikāya (A IV 136) illustrates the uncertainty and the evanescent nature of life with the help of a few evocative similes. Life is compared to a dew drop at the tip of a blade of grass: it can drop off any moment and even if it does not fall off, it evaporates as soon as the sun comes up. Life is also as fleeting as a bubble of water formed by the falling rain or a line drawn on the water. The text points out that life rushes towards death incessantly like a mountain stream rushing down without stopping. The Dhammapada compares the fragility of the body to foam (v. 46) and to a clay water pot (v. 40). Thus with various similes the uncertainty of life and the certainty of death are emphasized over and over again in the Buddhist texts.

It is accepted as a general truth that everybody fears death (*sabbe bhayanti maccuno*—Dhp 129). We fear death because we crave for life with all our might. It is also a fact that we fear the unknown. We know least about death, therefore we fear death for a duality of reasons. It seems reasonable to conjecture that the fear of death, or the fear of harm to life, lurks at the root of all fear. Therefore each time we become frightened we either run away from the source of fear or fight against it, thus making every effort to preserve life. But we can do so only so long as our body is capable of either fighting or running away from danger. But when at last we are on the deathbed face to face with approaching death, and the body is no longer strong enough for any protest, it is very unlikely that we will accept death with a mental attitude of resignation. We will mentally try hard to survive. As our yearning for life (*taṇhā*) is so strong, we will mentally grasp (*upādāna*) another viable place, as our body can no longer support life. Once such a place, for example the fertilized ovum in a mother's womb, has been grasped, the psychological process of life (*bhava*) will continue with the newly found place as its basis. Birth (*jāti*) will take place in due course. This seems to be the process that is explained in the chain of causation as: craving conditions grasping, grasping conditions becoming or the process of growth, which in turn conditions birth. Thus the average man who fears death will necessarily take another birth as his ardent desire is to survive.

Let us probe a little further into the process of death, going from the known to the unknown. We know that in normal life, when we are awake, sense data keep on impinging on our sense faculties. We are kept busy attending to these sense data, rejecting some, selecting some for greater attention, and getting obsessed with still other things. This is an ongoing process so long as we are awake. In the modern age man is reaching out and seeking more and more sense stimulation. The popularity of the portable radio with or without earphones, chewing gum, cosmetics and television is a clear indication of the present trend for more and more sense stimulation. By all this we have become alienated from ourselves; we do not know our own real nature, or the real nature of our mind to be more precise. Moreover, we go about our business in social life wearing masks appropriate for each occasion. We often do not show our true feelings of jealousy, greed, hatred, pride, or selfishness. We hide them in socially accepted ways of formalized verbal expressions such as congratulations, thank you, deepest sympathies. But there are times when our negative emotions are so acute that they come into the open in the form of killing, stealing, quarreling, backbiting, and so forth. But generally we try to keep these venomous snakes of negative emotions inhibited.

Now let us see what happens at the moment of death. We believe that death is a process and not just a sudden instantaneous event. When the senses lose their vitality one by one and they stop providing stimulation, the inhibitions too fall away. The masks we have been wearing in our various roles get cast off. We are at last face to face with ourselves in all our nakedness. At that moment if what we see are the venomous snakes of negative emotions of hatred, jealousy, etc., we would be laden with guilt, remorse and grief. It is very likely that our memories too will become quite sharp, as all the sensory disturbances and inhibitions which kept them suppressed have fallen off. We may remember our own actions committed and omitted during our lifetime with unpretentious clarity. If they are morally unwholesome we would be guilty and grief stricken (S V 386), but if they are morally wholesome we would be contented and happy. The *Abhidhammatthasaṅgaha* speaks of the presentation of *kamma* or *kammanimitta* at the mind door on the advent of death. This seems to be the revival in memory of an actual action or action veiled in symbols at the onset of death. It is said that rebirth will be determined by the quality of thoughts that surface in this manner.

Death is as natural an event as nightfall; it is but one of the manifestations of the law of impermanence. Though we dislike it immensely we have to orient ourselves to accept its inevitability, as there is no escape therefrom. The Buddhist texts advocate the cultivation of the mindfulness of death often so that we are not taken unawares when the event does take place. To face death peacefully one has to learn the art of living peacefully with one's own self as well as with those around. One method of doing so is to remember the inevitability of death, which will deter one from unwholesome behavior. The practice of meditation is the best technique which will enable one to live peacefully with oneself and others.

The practice of loving-kindness (*mettābhāvanā*) is an effective method of meditation. One of its special advantages is the ability to face death undeluded (*asammūḷho kālaṃ karoti*).

In one sutta (A III 293) the Buddha explains how to prepare for a peaceful death. One has to organize one's life and cultivate an appropriate attitude for this purpose. The instructions given there are as follows:

(1) One should not be fond of a busy life involved in various activities.
(2) One should not be fond of being talkative.
(3) One should not be fond of sleeping.
(4) One should not be fond of having too many companions.
(5) One should not be fond of too much social intercourse.
(6) One should not be fond of daydreaming.

Another sutta (A I 57–8) explains that if one avoids unwholesome wicked activities through body, speech and mind, one need not fear death. The *Mahā-parinibbāna Sutta* (D. II, 85–6) categorically states that those who are evil in character face death with delusion while the virtuous face death free from delusion. Thus if one leads a simple virtuous life one need not fear death.

Once Mahānāma Sakka (S V 369) disclosed to the Buddha that he was worried where he would be reborn if he were to meet with a violent death in a road accident. The Buddha explained that those who have cultivated the qualities of faith, virtue, learning, generosity and wisdom for a long time need not entertain such fears. To illustrate the position further the Buddha employs a simile. If a pot of oil or ghee is broken in deep water the potsherds will sink to the riverbed and the oil or ghee will rise to the surface of the water. Similarly in such a tragic situation the body would be discarded and may be devoured by vultures and jackals, but the mind will rise and progress upwards.

The account of the illness of Nakula's father (A III 295) is another interesting episode regarding the Buddhist attitude to death. Once Nakula's father was seriously ill and his wife noticed that he was fretful and anxious. She advised him that death with anxiety is painful and is denounced by the Buddha. Therefore he must compose himself. Comforting him, she said that he might be worried about the family income and the task of bringing up the children after his death. She assured him that she was capable of spinning and weaving and thus she could provide for the family and bring up the children. He may be anxious that she would remarry after his death. She said that he knows just as well as she that she has never been unfaithful to him ever since they were married at the age of sixteen, and she pledged that she would remain loyal to him even after his death. Perhaps he may worry about her spiritual development and she assured him that she would continue to be earnest in her spiritual welfare. Therefore he must face death, if need there be, with no anxiety. Such was her advice to her husband who was fatally ill. It is said that he regained self-composure and thereby good health too. The matter was later reported to the Buddha, who commended Nakula's wife for her wisdom and composure.

The suttas also discuss the advantages of the regular contemplation of death (A IV 46–48; S V 344, 408). The mind gets divested from the love of life, and being intoxicated with the zest of life, men commit various atrocities. That can be prevented by the habit of practicing mindfulness of death. If we only remember that we have not come to this world to stay forever, we would take care to lead much better lives. If, when we take stock, we find wicked negative emotions such as lust, hatred and jealousy in us, we should immediately take steps to eradicate them as we would try to put out the flames if our head were to catch fire (A IV 320).

Thus the Buddhist texts tirelessly reiterate the positive benefits of the regular contemplation of the inevitability of death. It helps one to lead a more wholesome life and also to face death, the one and only certain event in life, with calm composure and fearless confidence.

The Human Body

When alive the human body is the most precious and the most mysterious object in the whole world. We regard it as beautiful and spend much time, energy, and money to make it more beautiful. We regard it as an instrument for pleasure and spend nearly all our lives in procuring objects of pleasure. We assume it is a vital part of our self. It would be useful to discuss the validity of these attitudes and assumptions from the Buddhist point of view.

The human body is the most intricate machine in the world. Each human body is unique not only in appearance but also in its biochemical structure, sensitivity of sense faculties, disease resistance, disease susceptibility, etc., and hereditary laws alone are incapable of offering a satisfactory explanation. Buddhism holds that the body and its sense faculties have been so structured as the effect of former *kamma*. From the dawn of civilization man has tried to understand the mystery of the human personality and he has given rise to various sciences and religions. In one sutta the Buddha says that within this fathom-long sentient human body is found the whole world, its origin, its cessation and the path leading to its cessation. In a way this means that the world of experience is within the human body. In another sense it means that if one were to understand the mystery of the human body, that would amount to understanding the mystery of the world. In fact the external world is nothing but what we get to know through the instrumentality of our sense faculties. If we understand the sense faculties and sense data, we have understood everything.

The relationship of the body and the mind is most elusive. According to the *Sāmaññaphala Sutta* this relationship can be understood only after the attainment of the fourth *jhāna*. The adept can then see consciousness established in the physical constitution just as one can see a colored thread running through the aperture of a transparent gem. Another sutta explains the interdependency of body and mind through the simile of two bundles of reeds placed against one another supporting each other. Emotional changes in the mind affect body chemistry, and fluctuations in body chemistry affect the mind. As a gross example we can take the negative emotion of anger. Anger triggers off glandular secretions which alter body chemistry considerably to bring about changes such as trepidation, sweating, feeling hot, etc. On the other hand, changes in body chemistry produced, for instance, by the intake of alcohol or drugs affect the mind to bring about appropriate mood changes, euphoria and hallucinations. According to a sutta in the Aṅguttara Nikāya (A IV 385 f.) all thoughts are translated into sensations (*sabbe dhammā vedanāsamosaraṇā*). This shows the extent to which the body is influenced by the mind. Buddhism has clearly recognized this interdependency and utilized that knowledge in its path to liberation. The body is disciplined through morality (*sīla*) and is thus maintained at a reasonably healthy biochemical level. The mind is disciplined with meditation (*bhāvanā*) to produce healthy psychological changes and thereby reinforce a healthier biochemical composition of the body. This process goes on until the attainment of Arahantship, when the biochemical composition has undergone such a radical, irreversible change that an Arahant is said to be incapable of certain physiological functions which are antithetical to spiritual development but normal in average human beings.

Though the sentient human body is most precious, no precious material goes into its composition. It is precious because, through its instrumentality, man is able to probe into the deepest mysteries of the universe and of himself, into the meaning of life and the enigma of death. When we stand by the ocean in the evening twilight and gaze at the vast ocean as far as the horizon, or at the star-studded firmament receding into infinity as far as the eye can see, we are awe-struck by the magnitude of the universe. Compared to that man is but an infinitesimal speck of dust in size. But when we pay attention to the potentialities of man, it is he who can even conceive of this mighty universe, it is he who can unravel its mysteries. Though part and parcel of the universe, though subject to natural cosmic laws, man has the capacity to transcend the natural material world and can even reach Buddhahood. Therefore man is supreme and the sentient human frame is precious.

It is true that we generally look at the human body as a thing of beauty. We speak of beautiful eyes, teeth, face, hair, and figure. But Buddhism looks at the human body from a realistic point of view. The body is a bag of filth, it is full of impurities. The Buddhist texts dealing with the thirty-two parts of the body spell out in detail its foul material constituents. If we only pause a moment to consider attentively the state of the face prior to a wash in the morning, we can gain a fair idea of the body's repulsive nature. It exudes so much dirt from its major nine apertures and numerous pores that it needs constant cleaning. Just imagine how intolerable the body would be if we neglect to clean what it discharges from the outlets even for a single day, let alone for a long period. Great care has to be taken to keep the body clean, so that it is not offensive to oneself and others. If no regular cleaning is done, it can be the home of various parasites, and thus a public nuisance. We have to understand the real nature and the composition of the body in order to reduce and eliminate our infatuation with it.

We have to feed the body very carefully throughout life. However well the body is fed, it grows hungry over and over again. Hunger is the worst disease says the *Dhammapada.* There is no end to feeding the body until death. The stomach is like an open sore which needs careful periodical dressing. Gross food is but one of the nutriments the body needs according to Buddhism; contact with the environment (*phassa*), volition (*manosañcetanā*), and consciousness (*viññāṇa*) are the other three nutriments. All these four forms of nutriment are essential for the continuance of the body in health. The body also needs to be protected from heat, cold, rain, injurious germs and external harm. We have to be ever alert to protect the body from these various sources of external danger. For these reasons Buddhism says that the body is a source of great anxiety—*bāhudukkho ayaṃ kāyo.* Great is the hardship man has to undergo just to keep the body viable, clean and healthy.

The body is endowed with sense faculties and they are ever in search of pleasure. The eye is in search of pleasant forms, the ear of pleasant sounds, the nose of pleasant smells, the tongue of pleasant tastes and the body of pleasant tactile. Most of our life is spent in the pursuit of these pleasures. But it remains a fact that the body texture is such that it does not tolerate excessive pleasure. However desirable pleasures may be, the body falls ill when overloaded with them. For instance, however palatable rich food may be, when it is taken in excess, the body becomes a victim of killer diseases. Similarly, excessive indulgence in sex causes social diseases, of which the most dreaded today is AIDS, Acquired Immunity Deficiency Syndrome, for which a cure has not yet been found. Therefore restraint in the enjoyment of sense pleasures is the best course of conduct for those desirous of health and long life.

When we look at the body in its various postures of standing, sitting, walking and lying down, we realize that the body can tolerate these postures only for a very short time. Even if we are sitting in the most comfortable seat, we continue to remain in the same position without moving around only for a short time. Automatically we move about adjusting our limbs to more comfortable positions in a constant search for pleasure. But pleasure is short-lived; pain raises its head and we move and adjust ourselves again to eke out a little pleasure. Thus the search for pleasure goes on and we delude ourselves saying that we enjoy life. The basic truth is that the body is a source of misery, but we prefer to turn a blind eye to this fact and cling desperately to fleeting pleasures. The Buddha says that there is no doubt an iota of pleasure *appassāda,* but the misery is far in excess of this pleasure, *bāhudukkha.*

The body in its various stages of growth also brings much pain. Birth causes excruciating pain both to mother and baby. The infant is completely at the mercy of others around it. If its needs are not duly attended to, it experiences much misery, which it expresses by pitiful cries. Teething is a significant landmark in the series of growing pains. All attempts to master the various physical postures contribute their own quota of hardships to infancy. Puberty and adolescence are also harassed by the growing pains appropriate to those ages. Old age is particularly notorious for aches and pains. The sense faculties are on the decline, sight fails, hearing becomes short and other senses too diminish in their acuity. Various joint pains and body aches become more constant and the body-strength ebbs away. Even the Buddha in his old age said that his body was like an old worn-out cart which could be kept going only with much repair. He added that he enjoyed physical comfort only when he spent time in *jhānic* ecstasy. Such is the nature of the body in old age. We cannot forget that the body is prone to various diseases during all stages of its growth.

Though the body is thus a source of great misery we cannot afford to hate it. To have a healthy attitude towards the body we should avoid both extremes of being infatuated with the body and hating it. We should have *mettā,* a friendly attitude towards the body. Realistically understanding its nature, we should avoid misusing it as an instrument only for pleasure. We should be very careful not to form habits which are injurious to the body, such as smoking, drinking, and the excessive indulgence in sensual pleasures. The body becomes a prey to self-inflicted diseases if we fail to cultivate an attitude of friendliness towards it. If we want to enjoy a reasonably healthy body, we have to cultivate morally wholesome moderate habits.

We have the habit of regarding the body as a vital part of our self. When we say: "I am tall, I am fat, I am fair, I am beautiful or ugly," we really mean that the body has these attributes. But as we keep on using the pronoun "I" we get caught in the grammatical subject and assume the existence of an ontological subject such as the soul or the ego. Therefore we establish a relationship of identity and possession with the body. Thus the body becomes a vital part of the self. The Buddha argues that if the body is really ours as we assume it is, it should behave according to our wishes. It should remain young, healthy, beautiful and strong as we always wish it to be. But the body hardly behaves according to our wishes and we come to grief when it goes against our wishes and expectations. The Buddha points out that the body really does not belong to us, nor is it really our self or a part of our self. We should therefore give up craving for it, we should cease to identify ourselves with it. Giving up craving for the body results in much happiness and peace. In order to wean ourselves from our habitual identification and ownership we have to impress the repulsive and alien nature of our bodies into our minds with deep sensitivity, so that an attitudinal change takes place in us with regard to the body. Observation of the repulsive and misery-producing nature of our bodies repeatedly, over and over again, is one sure way of gaining the realistic perspective. This is the path leading out of misery.

Sensualistic Social Trends and Buddhism in Modern Times[2]

Causes for Sensualistic Social Trends[3]

Scientific and technological advancement has brought about widespread changes in the lifestyle of modern man. Changes have been so rapid and overwhelming during the 20th century, that this century seems to far outweigh all other centuries put together in this respect. Man's attitudes, values, goals and ideals too have undergone radical change. Scientific knowledge regarding the nature and evolution of the universe, man, society, culture and civilization has unsettled many of the old certitudes and undermined the very basis and authority of the Western theistic religious traditions. With the loss of respect for authority and tradition, the validity of moral values too came to be questioned. Ever renewing scientific knowledge, which exposed traditional beliefs one after another as superstitious or mythical, gave a halo of superiority to modernity. Nurtured in such an environment, the younger generation became alienated from the lifestyle of their parents and the age-old generation gap assumed unprecedented proportions.

While scientific knowledge rendered man a skeptic alienated from his cultural heritage, technology robbed him of his creative ability. The machine with its vast powers of production reduced man to a button pusher and threw millions of workers out of employment. Their muscular and creative powers were left unharnessed, thwarted and frustrated. As a result the indigenous folk arts and crafts of all nations, which were in fact expressions of sublimated emotions, became almost extinct. Man in his admiration for creativity and feeble struggle for self-expression has now become an antique collector.

---

2. Paper read at the Conference on Buddhism and the Modern World, Dongguk University, Seoul, Korea, 1976.

3. Works consulted are: Vance Packard, *The Sexual Wilderness* (London, 1968); Lord Annan *The Disintegration of an Old Culture* (Oxford, 1966).

The next force which completely overwhelmed modern man was the tyranny of commercialization and advertising. When production exceeded consumption man had to be persuaded into consuming more, lest trade suffer with a backlog of unconsumed stockpiles. Deliberate and calculated attempts were made to change traditional frugality into an ethic of consumption. Mass media were utilized to convince the people of the virtues and necessity of increasing consumption to maintain the newly acquired standard of affluent living. Research into motivational and behavioral psychology betrayed the susceptibilities of man, and advertising agents made capital by playing upon these weaknesses, namely, man's innate greed for sensual pleasure, personal property and social prestige. Unleashed as he was from his cultural moorings, and frustrated as he was in his creative urge, modern man succumbed to the attractive appeals of mass media and plunged into a life of self-indulgence.

Harmful Effects on Individual and Society

Having thus briefly outlined the main causes responsible for modern sensualistic social trends, it is useful to glance at the effects they have produced on the individual and society of today. Venereal diseases have become rampant; it is reported that there was an increase of 300% within one decade in the United States. The ever widening field of psychiatry shows that mental health is rapidly deteriorating. Alcoholism and drug addiction are major health problems. The crime rate is ever mounting. Bonds of wedlock have become sadly brittle and the divorce rate is alarmingly high. The family as a viable institution is threatened, according to some sociologists, with extinction in the not too distant future. Disruption of family life has affected child life most pathetically. A British report of Health Economics published in January 1976 informs us that babies are the most common homicide victims in Britain since the early 1960's. They are battered to death at times of family stress. Teenage drug addictions and juvenile delinquency have become alarming problems of the day. These social phenomena are directly related to man's attitude towards sense pleasure and serious rethinking seems most urgent today if man is to be saved from the imminent danger of self-destruction through sensuality.

Can Buddhism Help?

Buddhism has been a great civilizing force and a guiding principle for millions of people during the last twenty-five centuries. It would be useful to see what light Buddhism sheds on the present chaotic situation, and what wisdom it offers for self-adjustment under modern conditions and for healthy family and interpersonal relations. Though criticism is often leveled that Buddhism is a life-denying ascetic ideal, and that it is antisocial and antipolitical, it should be remembered that Buddhism embraces in its dispensation not only monks (*bhikkhu*) and nuns (*bhikkhunī*), but also male and female lay followers (*upāsaka, upāsikā*). The intellectual and disciplinary training of the laity is as important a concern in Buddhism as that of the monks. Therefore Buddhism offers a social and a political philosophy, the goal of which is the creation of a society where human rights are safeguarded, human enterprise is the key to success, resources are well distributed and justice reigns supreme. As Trevor Ling too maintains, Buddhism is not just a religion or a philosophy, it is in fact a whole civilization, a full fledged multi-faceted philosophy of life designed to meet the secular and spiritual needs of man.[4]

Sensuality and Human Ambitions

According to Buddhism, ambitions of man center on the acquisition of wealth, pleasure, fame, longevity and happiness after death. (A II 66–68). Accepting these as human aspirations and goals of human endeavor, Buddhism advocates a way of life to help man realize these aims. For the danger is ever present that man in his pursuit of pleasure will in the long run defeat those very aims. Wealth and sex are two important means of acquiring pleasure. A prudent attitude towards them would go a long way for the realization of the other three human ambitions as well. As most of the social ills of today are attributable to the mishandling of these two, a correct understanding of the Buddhist attitude towards them would be most profitable.

4. Trevor Ling, *The Buddha* (London, 1973), pp. 17, 24 f.

Wealth

The Buddhist attitude towards wealth is such that it has never prescribed a ceiling on income. What it has prescribed is that wealth should be acquired through righteous means and expended also in a righteous manner. Wealth earned by the sweat of one's brow without harming, deceiving or exploiting others is highly commended. It is always emphasized that wealth has only instrumental value. It should be utilized for (a) living in comfort making one's family, parents, dependents and friends happy, (b) insuring oneself against possible calamities through fire, water, etc., (c) performing one's duties to relatives, guests and state, and for religio-cultural activities, and (d) patronizing those engaged in spiritual advancement. According to one's means, on a large or very small scale, one should try to make the best use of one's resources in the most righteous manner.

What is deplored in Buddhism is the excessive acquisitive greed and the hoarding habit. While niggardliness is held in contempt, frugality is extolled as a virtue. Wastefulness is a deplorable habit and it is even regarded as anti-social. Once Ānanda explained to a king how the monks put the gifts offered to them to maximum use. When new robes are offered the old ones are taken as coverlets, the old coverlets are utilized as mattress covers, the former mattress covers are used as rugs, the old rugs are taken as dusters, the old tattered dusters are kneaded with clay and used to repair cracked floors and walls (Vin II 291). Such was the Buddhist monks' conscientious use of resources. The same frugality has influenced the laity too and the famous episode of a wealthy merchant, who bade a servant to collect a drop of ghee off the floor, lest it be wasted, is a very fine example. The same merchant was so generous that his largesse surprised the recipients (Vin I 271). Though frugality and generosity appear to be incompatible, they are recognized as commendable virtues in their own right to be cultivated by one and all. When these simple virtues are compared with the information revealed to us, for instance, by Vance Packard's epoch-making eye-opener *The Waste Makers*, one begins to wonder whether sanity and common sense have left the knowledgeable man of science today. Some investigators estimate that American consumption of the world's resources within forty years is equal to what mankind has consumed during the last 4000 years. As the earth's resources are not unlimited, it is high time that modern man did some rethinking and cultivated some economical Buddhist habits at least out of sympathy for posterity. It is true that oceanography opens unexploited resources to man, but it must be remembered that the ocean too is not unlimited, whereas man's greed knows no limit nor satiation.

Sex

Buddhism recognizes the sex attraction as a universal reality. Among animals the sex impulse is regulated by nature and thus their mating and breeding are seasonal. Among humans there is no such natural mechanism, and man has by a long process of experiment and adjustment arrived at certain taboos, rules and regulations to handle his sex drive in a manner appropriate to himself and his fellow beings. Though these rules differ according to time and place, on the whole they have helped man to emerge from savagery to civilization. The family is the social institution which was thus born.

According to Buddhism monogamy is the ideal form of marriage, while chastity and fidelity form ideal behavior before and after marriage. This alone is not sufficient for success in married life. Mutual confidence (*saddhā*), morality (*sīla*), self-denial (*cāga*) and prudence (*pañña*) are emphasized as virtues which ensure conjugal happiness and success. In other words, mutual confidence means dependability, morality implies strength of character, self-denial or the joy of selfless service to the beloved denotes emotional maturity, and prudence shows intellectual maturity. These qualities bring the spouses so close to one another, it is said, that the relationship could persist even after death in a future existence. Nakula's parents are portrayed in Buddhist literature as an ideal couple who, in their old age, expressed the wish that their love should survive death. The Buddha replied that the wish would materialize if the above qualities are equally shared by both partners (A II 61–62).

Marital bonds of modern man are so brittle and fragile because these cohesive emotional forces are lost in sensuality. Much emphasis is laid on carnal pleasure while personality adjustments and emotional involvement, which call for sacrifices and selflessness respectively, are ignored or neglected. Though sex is an important basic requirement in marriage, it is certainly not the be-all and end-all of family life. Indulgence in sex for its own sake never brings satisfaction, whence fulfillment? The insatiability of lust is disdainfully illustrated in Buddhist literature by the traditional simile of a dog licking a bone to satisfy hunger. But sex as an expression of conjugal love is a satisfying emotional experience. If sex was the only concern, man need not have evolved an institution like the family. Animals too satisfy their sex instinct, but nothing compared to the human family has evolved in the animal kingdom. The important function of family life seems to be to teach man a great moral lesson to overcome his egocentric nature. Man starts life in his mother's womb as the most selfish parasite. He then passes through the emotional stages of self-love, conjugal love and parental love. As a mature man and a parent he completely loses himself in the service of his offspring. His self-denial is such he even relinquishes his personal possessions, acquired through the toil of a lifetime, in favor of them. Finally he makes an emotional self-sacrifice when he gets a partner for his child to love and cherish. In his old age he regards his offspring with equanimity and contentment. This emotional maturity and fulfillment is utterly impossible if sensuality is regarded as the goal of married life.

Fame and Longevity

These two ambitions of man depend to a very large extent, as mentioned earlier, on the manner he handles his wealth and pleasure. Special mention should be made that liquor, like sensuality, is a great betrayer of all human ambitions. It has been aptly remarked that a man's conscience is soluble in alcohol. According to Buddhism both liquor and sensuality destroy man's physical and mental health, drain his resources, spoil his public image and distort his intellectual capacities (D III 182–184).

Happiness After Death

In this age of material pleasure, man is not much concerned with a life after death. The Buddhist axiom is that a man reaps what he sows. If one has led a useful moral life and reached old age with a sense of fulfillment, contentment and equanimity, one has no regrets. A well-spent blameless life has, according to Buddhism, happiness beyond the grave. Such a person is said to progress from light to brighter light (*joti joti parāyaṇo*, A II 86).

Sensuality and Intellectual Maturity

Another noteworthy ill effect of self-indulgence is the inhibition of intellectual capacities. Buddhism emphasizes that obsession with sensuality prevents clear thinking, distorts vision, clouds issues, inhibits wisdom and destroys peace of mind. While these observations were made twenty-five centuries ago by the Buddha, the inhibitory effect of sex on brain activity seems to be indicated quite independently by medical research on the pineal gland.

In man, the pineal gland is a pear-shaped midline structure located at the back of the base of the brain. This gland synthesizes a hormone called melatonin which affects behavior, sleep, brain activity, and sexual activity such as puberty, ovulation and sexual maturation. While melatonin stimulates brain activity, it inhibits sexual activity. Again it has been recognized that light, dark, olfaction, cold, stress and other neural inputs affect the pineal function. Exposure to light reduces the synthesis of melatonin and depresses pineal weight. On the other hand light accelerates sexual maturation and activity.[5]

It will be useful to compare this medical information with Buddhist ideology. Buddhism maintains that sense stimuli disturb mental activity. If the sense doors are well guarded (*indriyesu guttadvāro hoti*), i.e., if visual, auditory, olfactory, gustatory and tactile inputs are controlled, a corresponding degree of concentrated mental activity becomes possible. *Cittassa ekaggatā* or the ability to fix the mind on one point is greatly determined by the control of the sense faculties. In terms of physiology it seems to mean that such sense control helps the synthesis of melatonin in the pineal gland, which stimulates brain activity and retards sexual activity. Thus, with the help of medical research it seems

5. See G.E.W. Wolstenholme and Julie Knight, eds., *The Pineal Gland* (London, 1971).

possible to confirm the Buddhist point of view that sensuality inhibits intellectual maturity.

Sensuality and Culture

According to the *Aggañña Sutta,* which gives an account of the evolution of the world and society, the earliest inhabitants of the earth were mind-made and self-luminous beings who subsisted on joy and moved about in the sky. After a long time they tasted something extremely flavorsome and were delighted with this new gustatory sense experience. Craving entered into them and they went on tasting food in this manner. Consequently their bodies became coarser and coarser; they lost their radiance and the ability to subsist on joy and to traverse in the sky (D III 84–86).

Now what is important for us here is not the authenticity of this evolutionary process, but the point that sensual desire has caused the loss of higher mental and physical capacities which man is supposed to have once possessed.

The *Cakkavattisīhanāda Sutta* (D III 69–74) deals with the problem of social change. As a result of the unequal distribution of wealth, poverty becomes widespread and moral standards deteriorate rapidly. With moral degeneration there is a corresponding decrease in physical beauty and length of life. As time goes on and immorality settles down, society comes under the grip of three derogatory phenomena, namely, perverted lust (*adhammarāga*), wanton greed (*visamalobha*) and a wrong sense of values (*micchādhamma*). Disrespect for family, religious and cultural traditions becomes an accepted social phenomenon. When moral degradation continues thus a time will come when the life-span is reduced to ten years and the marriageable age goes down to five. By that time food will undergo so much change that delicacies such as ghee, butter, honey, etc. will vanish, and what is considered coarse today will be a delicacy of that time. All concepts of morality will disappear and language will have no word to denote morality. Immorality will reign supreme with social sanction. There will be no marriage laws nor kinship, and society will fall into a state of utter promiscuity, as among animals. Among such humans keen mutual enmity will become the rule, and they will be overcome by passionate thoughts of killing one another. A world war will break out and large-scale massacre would be the result. After this mass blood bath, the few destitute who are left behind will find solace in each other's company and they will begin to regard one another with kindly thoughts. With this change of heart there will be a gradual re-evolution of moral values. Step by step the good life will be restored, physical beauty will reappear and the life-span will increase. Mental potentialities too will gradually develop. Such are the Buddhist ideas of social change. Society stands or falls with the rise or fall of moral values.

It is noteworthy that some present-day sociological studies too have revealed that morality and culture are causally connected. William Stephens observes that primitive tribes have great sexual freedom, premarital as well as extramarital, when compared with civilized communities which have tight sex restrictions.[6] Dean Robert Fitch has connected the decline of the Roman civilization with the deterioration of their sexual morality.[7] The most important contribution in this respect is made by J.D. Unwin in a study called *Sex and Culture.*[8] He has conducted a survey of the sexual behavior and the level of culture of eighty uncivilized tribes and also those of six known civilizations. He concludes that there is a definite relationship between permissiveness and primitiveness, and sex restrictions and civilization. Sexual freedom gives rise to what he calls a zoistic (dead level of conception) culture where people are born, they satisfy their desire, they die and are forgotten after the remains are disposed of. They are not able to rationally find out the causal connection between events. When afflicted by illness, for instance, they resort to witchcraft and nothing more. When a certain degree of sex restriction, occasional, premarital, or post-nuptial, is present, the result is a shamanistic culture where ancestors are worshipped at times of crisis, but without a definite place of worship. Strict sex regulations as in monogamy produce a deistic culture with definite places of worship. Culture in the sense of the external expression of internal human energy resulting from the use of human powers of reason, creation and self knowledge becomes possible only with strictly enforced monogamous sex mores. The mechanism of this

6. *The Family in Cross-Cultural Perspective* (New York, 1963), pp. 256–259.
7. Quoted by Packard, *The Sexual Wilderness,* p. 417.
8. London: Oxford University Press, 1934.

operation is not known, just as it is not known how carbon placed under different settings turns to coal or diamond.[9] All that can be said is that there is a definite causal link between sexual behavior and the culture pattern. As Unwin comes to this conclusion after conducting exhaustive methodical investigations, it is possible to maintain that scientific inquiries too have confirmed the Buddhist point of view regarding the relationship between morality and culture.

Sensuality and Environment

The Aṅguttara Nikāya (A I 160) maintains that rainfall decreases when society comes under the sway of perverted lust, wanton greed and wrong values. Drought causes famine as a result of which the mortality rate goes up. Though it is difficult to establish a direct connection between immorality and lack of rain, an interpretation of the five natural laws mentioned in the commentaries might offer a plausible explanation.

In the cosmos there are five natural laws or forces, namely *utuniyāma* (lit. "season law"), *bijaniyāma* (lit. "seed law") *cittaniyāma*, *kammaniyāma*, and *dhammaniyāma*.[10] These can be translated as physical laws, biological laws, psychological laws, moral laws, and causal laws. While the first four laws operate within their respective spheres, the last law of causality operates within them as well as among them. Thus the physical environment or ecology affects living organisms, i.e., biology; this influences psychology, which determines the moral force. The opposite process also operates with harmful or beneficial results depending on the nature or the forces at work. Perhaps the operation can be illustrated with a concrete example. Man's greed for luxury, wealth and power has caused the setting up of vast factories. They created the problems of air, water and noise pollution, which have adversely affected both fauna and flora.[11] The inadvertent modifications of atmospheric properties and processes caused by human activities are intensively studied by scientific bodies today. It is complained that although the effects of pollutants and smog upon people, plants and economic activities

9. Ibid., pp. 424, 417, 412, etc.
10. *Atthasālinī*, PTS ed., p. 272.
11. Mitchell Gordon, *Sick Cities* (New York, 1963), pp. 92, 80.

have been extensively studied, relatively little attention has been paid to the effects of pollution and smog upon climatic patterns. It is well known that many climatic elements such as radiation, cloudiness, fog, visibility and the atmospheric electric field are affected by pollution. Temperature and humidity are influenced indirectly and effects on precipitation are also suspected.[12] Science will reveal in the course of time whether pollution is definitely responsible for weather and climatic change, but it remains a fact that the world is already confronted with an acute shortage of water.

It is no secret that man uses his inherent powers of reason, intelligence and creativity to change his environment for his advantage. But man is not aware that the moral force he himself creates brings about corresponding changes in his environment to his weal or woe whether he likes it or not.

Conclusion

Concluding this essay, it should be emphasized that there is a Cosmic Moral Force which profoundly influences man. According to Buddhism it is this Cosmic Moral Law or Force which makes the world and mankind go on: *kammanā vattati loko, kammanā vattati pajā* (Sn 654). This Cosmic Moral Force is generated by none other than man himself, for the Buddha maintains that human thoughts are a moral force (*cetanāhaṃ bhikkhave kammaṃ vadāmi,* A III 410). It is also more directly said that thoughts (or ideologies) make the world go on (*cittena ni yato loko,* S I 39). Therefore man has to discover his own inherent powers which are, at present, mostly dissipated on alcohol and sensuality. The discovery of the potentialities of *The World Within* is the most urgent need of today as modern man living in *Sick Cities,* lost in a *Sexual Wilderness,* unaware of *The Hidden Persuaders,* is being slowly but surely reduced to a *Naked Ape.*[13]

---

12. *Weather and Climate Modification: Problems and Prospects,* Vol. II (National Academy of Sciences, Washington, 1966) pp. 82–108.

13. References are to the titles of works by Gina Cerminara (New York, 1957), Mitchell Gordon, Vance Packard (op. cit. and London, 1957), and Desmond Morris (New York, 1967).

The Tragic, the Comic and the Personal

Selected Letters of
Ñāṇavīra Thera

Edited, with Foreword and Notes, by
Sāmaṇera Bodhesako

WHEEL PUBLICATION NO. 339/340/341

Foreword

When Osbert Moore and Harold Musson arrived on the shores of Sri Lanka (then Ceylon) in 1949, they brought with them a shared attitude of open-minded thoughtfulness and a firm determination to devote the remainder of their lives to seeking understanding by means of the Buddha's Teaching; and this they proceeded to do. Since they had first met during World War II, when they were British officers, they had found a commonality of view about the futility of life, and when Musson happened upon an Italian book on Buddhism and (in order to brush up on his Italian he was an interrogator in Intelligence) decided to translate it,[1] they discovered a mutual attraction towards and sympathy for that Teaching.

Moore, who at his ordination was given the name the Venerable Ñāṇamoli Bhikkhu, is well-known to readers of the Wheel series and other BPS publications as an essayist and skillful translator of the Pali Suttas and commentaries. Musson, who became known as the Venerable Ñāṇavīra Bhikkhu, was more solitary. Apart from a few early essays, he has shared his learning and wisdom with a general audience only in his small book, *Notes on Dhamma*, published privately in 1983. But until his death in 1965 (five years after the Ven. Ñāṇamoli's) he also carried on a correspondence with a few laypeople who wished to benefit from his learning.

Now these letters have been collected and edited and, together with the final text of *Notes on Dhamma* (revised somewhat in the last two years of the author's life), they are being issued in a single volume.[2] It is from this volume that the present selection has been made, except for the first two letters, which appear here for the first time.[3] The recipients of the letters include his doctor

---

1. *The Doctrine of Awakening*, by J. Evola (Luzane, 1951).
2. *Clearing the Path: Writings of Ñāṇavīra Thera* (Colombo: Path Press, 1987).
3. The essay "Mindfulness and Awareness"—also originally a letter and included in *Clearing the Path*—was first Published by the BPS as a *Bodhi Leaf* (BL 60).

(with whom the Ven. Ñāṇavīra also discussed the ailments that eventually led to his death), a judge (who became the publisher of *Notes on Dhamma*), a provincial businessman, a barrister, and two British citizens.

Having been born in England in 1920 and educated at Cambridge University, the Ven. Ñāṇavīra Thera[4] naturally sought an approach to the Buddha's Teaching via Western thought (see letter 23). After acquainting themselves thoroughly with the Pali Suttas the two friends explored many modes of Western thought—even quantum mechanics!—through reading and discussion. When the Ven. Ñāṇavīra moved to a remote section of Ceylon, where he lived alone for the rest of his life, their discussions continued through voluminous correspondence which lasted until 1960, the year of the Ven. Ñāṇamoli's death. Increasingly they found that the Western thinkers most relevant to their interests were those belonging to the closely allied schools of phenomenology and existentialism, to whom they found themselves indebted for clearing away a lot of mistaken notions with which they had burdened themselves. These letters make clear the nature of that debt; they also make clear the limitations which the Ven. Ñāṇavīra saw in those thinkers. He is insistent that although for certain individuals their value may be great, yet eventually one must go beyond them if one is to arrive at the essence of the Buddha's Teaching. Existentialism, then, is in his view an approach to the Buddha's Teaching and not a substitute for it.

These letters are concerned in part with an approach to the Teaching; but the approach is not the Teaching, and other letters discuss the Teaching itself. Here wherever possible the Ven. Ñāṇavīra offers Sutta references to support his statements; and the careful reader of these letters will easily perceive that their author had a profound veneration for those texts. It is this veneration for the Suttas, and for their profound message, that he tries to communicate.

In this presentation the letters are arranged in a purely chronological order. To indicate the subject matter of each letter they are preceded by a title provided by the editor. Following the

4. *Thera* (elder) is a monastic honorific appended to one's name upon completion of ten years as a bhikkhu (monk).

editorial notes is a Pali-English Glossary, provided for the benefit of those who may not be familiar with some of the Pali words used in the text. The English equivalents given are those preferred by the Ven. Ñāṇavīra Thera.

Sāmaṇera Bodhesako

Selected Letters of Ñāṇavīra Thera

1. Good action (6 August 1956)

It is difficult to live a good life, and the benefits may not be apparent here and now; but if we believe what the Buddha has told us then it is very well worth the effort that it costs *even if it kills us*. Not for the sake of life will a *sotāpanna* break the five precepts. The depressing effects of bad *kamma* done in the past may last for many lives, not just for one; but do not forget that good *kamma* also has its effect for a long time—sometimes for longer than bad *kamma*. And this is important: if we do good *kamma* now we shall be reborn in a position to go on doing good *kamma*, for a man who is rich because of past good *kamma* has the opportunity of doing more good *kamma* now than a poor man who has not done good *kamma* in the *past*. And remember also that, although your past *kamma* is not good enough to make you rich and successful now, it is none the less very good *kamma* indeed, for you have been born a human being during the time of a Buddha's Sāsana. The next time you see a sick dog or a cow dying of thirst, think, "I might have been born as *that*; and if I do wrong now it is probable that I *shall* be born as that." It is always better to bear up when misfortune assails us, but *there is nothing else we can do*: we inherit our past deeds.

2. Mettā in meditation and in life (10 October 1958)

I have just received your letter. It may be said, perhaps, that *mettā* is recommended by the Buddha for getting rid of anger, and that anger normally arises in our dealings with other people, and that it is therefore in our dealings with other people that *mettā* is best practised. It is most certainly true that we have need of *mettā* in our dealings with other people; but the trouble is this: before we can be in a position to have *mettā* we have first to know what *mettā* is, and second to have it at our command. Now, just as it is possible to practise *ānāpānasati* in the presence of other people when one has already become skilled in it by oneself, so it is possible to practise *mettā* in the presence of others only when one has practised it a great deal when alone. And just as the worst conditions for practising *ānāpānasati* are the noise and bustle of other people, so it is with *mettā*. Until you are able to practise either *ānāpānasati* or *mettā* in solitude you will never succeed in company—the obstacles are far too great.

For example, suppose there is someone you dislike, and in whose presence you become angry: unless you are already able to prevent anger from arising when you think of him in his absence (which needs much practice), you will have no chance at all of getting rid of the anger that arises when you actually meet him. Once anger takes possession of you there is very little you can do except to stop it from finding expression in words or deeds, and to allow it to subside; it is far too late to start practising *mettā*. But if you thoroughly practise *mettā before* you meet such a person, then it is possible that anger will not arise when you do meet him. Having *mettā* in your dealings with other people consists in having *mettā before* you deal with them, that is, in solitude—once you start dealing with them you will have little opportunity of attending to *mettā* (or if you do attend to *mettā* it will interfere in your dealings just as attending to your in-and-out breaths takes your mind away from the matter in hand).

You might, however, be thinking that, whereas *ānāpānasati* concerns only myself since it is a matter of watching my own breaths and not somebody else's, *mettā* on the contrary concerns other people, since it is a question of my relationship with other people and of my attitude towards them. And you might think that it follows from this that the presence of other people is either an advantage or even absolutely necessary for the practice of *mettā*. In a certain sense this is true: you cannot practise *mettā* towards other people unless they are in some way present—but the presence of other people does not imply that their *bodies* must be present. I do not mean that their "spirit" is present while their body is absent (which is a mystical confusion of thought), but simply that "other people" is a fundamental structure of our conscious constitution.

Let me give an illustration. It happens to all of us that upon some occasion when we are doing something perhaps rather shameful (it might be simply when we are urinating or excreting, or it might be when we are peeping through a keyhole or something like that) and we believe we are alone and unobserved, we suddenly hear a slight sound behind us and we immediately have the unpleasant idea "I am being watched." We turn round and look and find nobody there at all. It was only our own guilty conscience. Now this is an indication that in order to have a relationship with other people we do not need other peoples' bodies: we are conscious of other people (at least implicitly) all the time, and it is this consciousness that we have to attend to when we practice *mettā*.

When we practise *mettā* we are developing and gradually changing our attitude towards other people; and we always have an attitude towards other people whether their bodies are present or not. The only thing a (living) body does when we meet one is to be the occasion for the consciousness, "This is another person." And if we have already been practising *mettā* and have acquired an un-angry attitude towards other people, then when we actually meet another person our attitude towards him will be correct right at the beginning, and no anger will arise. It is only when we are already disposed to anger that we get angry when we meet someone; and if we are disposed to *mettā* (through long practise in solitude, on our consciousness of other people whose actual bodies are absent) we have *mettā* in our dealings with them.

3. Addiction (25 May 1962)

I have finished the Beverley Nichols.[5] I think that one question is raised that calls for a detailed reply. B. N. describes how a certain morphine addict became "changed" and, as a result, lost all interest in the drug; and he points out that to give up a drug addiction is one of the hardest things in the world (with which we may agree). The question, then, is this: What has the Buddha's Teaching to offer a drug addict?

5. Nichols is prolific. The book discussing opium addiction has not been identified; but in a later book, *Father Figure,* he discusses the instant cure of his father from lifelong alcoholism, albeit not by "faith in God" but rather through "loss of faith in inheritance."

In the first place the Buddha requires intelligence of a man, else nothing can be done. In the second place the Buddha tells us that the taking of intoxicants (which of course will include morphine and so on) leads to the decline of intelligence. Putting two and two together, we find that to give up drugs a man must understand that unless he gives them up he will not be able to give them up, or in other words, to give up drugs one must understand the way to give up drugs, which is to give them up. At first glance this does not seem to be very helpful—"A glimpse of the obvious," perhaps you will say; "of course the addict understands that the way to give up drugs is to give them up: the whole trouble is that he *can't* give them up." But is this just a glimpse of the obvious?

Let me recall my own experience when I gave up cigarettes. I had been smoking forty or more a day for several years when I decided to give them up. Not being able to do things in half-measures I stopped smoking all at once. I remember walking in the park not long after I had finished my last cigarette, and feeling pleased with myself that I had actually taken the decision. (I also felt rather light-headed, which was no doubt a deprivation symptom—this continued for some days.) But the principal thought that assailed me was this: though I had no doubt that I could stick to my resolution, there was one thing that I really needed to confirm it and to fortify me in my determination not to have another cigarette, and that one thing was ... a cigarette. Far from its being obvious to me that in order to give up cigarettes I should give up cigarettes, I had the greatest of trouble to resist the pressing suggestion that in order to give up cigarettes I should take a cigarette.

Let me also tell you of the researches of Dr. Klar[6] when he was in Persia shortly after the war. Dr. Klar, besides being a physician, is also interested in psychology; and he had with him in Persia an ingenious device for reading a person's character and state of mind. (This consists of a number of cards each with about eight pairs of coloured squares pasted on them. The subject is simply required to indicate which colour in each pair he prefers. He "read" us all

6. Dr. Helmut Klar is a well-known German Buddhist. The test described here sounds like the Lüscher Color Test, popularized in the 1970's by a paperback book of that title.

at the Hermitage,[7] with devastatingly accurate results that did not really please all of us. But this is a digression.) He told us that eighty percent of all Persians over the age of thirty-five (I think he said) take opium (and also that all Persians tell lies on principle—but this is another digression), and with such a wealth of material to hand[8] he was able to do some research. He would give each addict two readings, one before taking opium and one after. The readings all said the same thing: *before* the opium the mental state of the addict was abnormal and disorganized; *after* the opium the mental state was normal and organized. The effect of the opium on the addict was not, as one might think, to disintegrate the personality; on the contrary, the effect was to integrate a disintegrated personality. The opium was necessary to restore the addict to normal. (I have heard similar observations from another doctor who was for many years a medical missionary in China: if you want to do business with an opium addict, drive your bargain when the effect of his last dose is wearing off.)

What can we conclude from all this? We conclude that, unlike a "normal" person who may take a drug once in a while for the novelty or pleasure of the effect, and who at that time becomes "abnormal," the confirmed addict is "normal" only when he has taken the drug, and becomes "abnormal" when he is deprived of it. The addict reverses the usual situation and is dependent upon the drug to keep him in his normal integrated state. (This does not mean, of course, that the addict derives *pleasure* from occasional deprivation as the abstainer does from occasional intoxication; quite the contrary: in both cases the drugged state is more pleasant, but for the one it is normal and for the other it is abnormal.) The addict can only do his work efficiently and perform his normal functions if he takes the drug, and it is in this condition that he will make plans for the future. (If he cannot take the drug the only plan he makes is to obtain another dose as quickly as possible.) If he decides that he must give up his addiction to the drug (it is too expensive; it is ruining his reputation or his career; it is undermining his health; and so on) he will make the decision

7. The Hermitage is the Island Hermitage, Dodanduwa, Sri Lanka, where both the Ven. Ñāṇamoli and the Ven. Ñāṇavīra lived for many years.

8. In Persia, evidently, opium is the religion of the masses.

only when he is in a fit state to consider the matter, that is to say when *he is drugged;* and it is from this (for him, *normal*) point of view that he will envisage the future. (Thus, it was *as a smoker* that I, decided to give up smoking.) But as soon as the addict puts his decisions into effect and stops taking the drug he ceases to be normal, and decisions taken when he was normal now appear in quite a different light—and this will include his decision to stop taking the drug. *Either,* then, he abandons the decision as invalid ("How could I possibly have decided to do such a thing? I must have been off my head") and returns to his drug-taking, *or* (though he approves the decision) he feels it urgently necessary to return to the state in which he originally took the decision (which was when he was drugged) *in order to make the decision seem valid* again. (And so it was that I felt the urgent need of a cigarette to confirm my decision to give them up.) In both cases the result is the same—a return to the drug. And so long as the addict takes his "normal" drugged state for granted at its face value—i.e. as normal—the same thing will happen whenever he tries to give up his addiction.

Not only is the drug addict in a vicious circle—the more he takes the more he wants, the more he wants the more he takes—but, until he learns to take an outside view of his situation and is able to see the nature of drug addiction, he will find that all his attempts to force a way out of the vicious circle simply lead him back in again. (A vicious circle is thus a closed system in stable equilibrium.) It is only when the addict *understands* addiction, and holds fast to the right view that—in spite of all appearances, in spite of all temptations to think otherwise—his "normal" drugged state is not normal, that he will be able to put up with the temporary discomfort of deprivation and eventually get free from his addiction. In brief, then, an addict decides to give up drugs, and he supposes that in order to do so all that is necessary is to give them up (which would certainly be a glimpse of the obvious were it not that he is profoundly deceiving himself, as he very soon finds out). No sooner does he start giving them up than he discovers (if he is very unintelligent) that he is mistaken and has made the wrong decision, or (if he is less unintelligent) that, though the decision is right, he is wrong about the method, and that in *order to give up drugs it is necessary to take them.* It is only the intelligent man who understands (against all appearances) that both the decision and the method are right; and it is only he that succeeds. For the intelligent man, then, the instruction "to give up drugs it is necessary to give them up," far from being a glimpse of the obvious, is a profound truth revealing the nature of addiction and leading to escape from it.

I would ask you to pause before dismissing this account as fanciful; this same theme—the vicious circle and the escape from it by way of understanding and in spite of appearances—is the very essence of the Buddha's Teaching. The example discussed above—drug addiction—is on a coarse level, but you will find the theme repeated again and again right down to the finest level, that of the four noble truths. It will, I think, be worthwhile to illustrate this from the Suttas.

In the 75th Sutta of the Majjhima Nikāya (M I 506-8) the Buddha shows the vicious circle of sensual desire and its gratification in the simile of a man with a skin disease (*kuṭṭhi*—a leper?). Imagine a man with a fiercely itching skin disease who, to relieve the itching, scratches himself with his nails and roasts himself near a brazier. The more he does this the worse becomes his condition, but this scratching and roasting give him a certain satisfaction. In the same way, a man with finely itching sensual desire seeks relief from it in sensual gratification. The more he gratifies it the stronger becomes his desire, but in the gratification of his desire he finds a certain pleasure. Suppose, now, that the skin disease were cured; would that man continue to find satisfaction in scratching and roasting himself? By no means. So, too, a man who is cured of sensual desire (an *arahat*) will find no more pleasure in sensual gratification.

Let us extend the simile a little. You, as a doctor, know very well that to cure an itching skin disease the first thing to do is to prevent the patient from scratching and making it worse. Unless this can be done there is no hope of successfully treating the condition. But the patient will not forego the satisfaction of scratching unless he is made to understand that scratching aggravates the condition, and that there can be no cure unless he voluntarily restrains his desire to scratch, and puts up with the temporarily increased discomfort of unrelieved itching. And similarly, a person who desires a permanent cure from the torment of sensual desire must first be made to understand that he must put up with the temporarily increased discomfort of celibacy (as a bhikkhu) if the Buddha's treatment is to be successful. Here, again, the way out of the vicious circle is through an understanding of it and through disregard of the apparent worsening of the condition consequent upon self-restraint.

Consider, now, the four noble truths. The fourth of these truths is, "This is the way leading to the cessation of suffering, that is to say, the noble eight-factored path"; and the first factor of this path is right view, which is defined as knowledge of the four noble truths. But, as before, the fourth truth is the way leading to cessation of suffering. So we come to the proposition, "The way leading to cessation of suffering is knowledge of the way leading to the cessation of suffering," or "To put an end to suffering one must understand the way to put an end to suffering." And what is this but a repetition, at the most fundamental level, of our original theme, "To give up drugs one must understand the way to give up drugs?"[9]

Not everybody is addicted to morphine, but most people are addicted to sensual gratification, and all except the *ariyasāvakas* are addicted to their own personality (*sakkāyadiṭṭhi*)[10] and even the *ariyasāvakas,* with the exception of the *arahat*, still have a subtle addiction, the conceit "I am" (*asmimāna*). The *arahat* has put an end to all addiction whatsoever. There is thus no form of addiction that the Buddha's Teaching will not cure, provided the addict is intelligent and willing to make the necessary effort.

4. Love and death (4 January 1963)

It is curious, is it not, that whereas, since Freud, the most extravagant fancies in the realm of love are considered to be

9. The rationalist, who would not for a moment dream of practising the Buddha's Teaching, can *never* understand that this is anything else than a glimpse of the obvious. Arthur Koestler, on first meeting the Buddha's Teaching, exclaimed "But it's all tautologous, for Heaven's sake!"

10. Below this point, though the essential structure of addiction remains the same, it is no longer possible to get an outside view of it by voluntary effort. In other words, one cannot give up *sakkāyadiṭṭhi* (and become a *sotāpanna*) as simply as one can give up tobacco, merely by deciding to do so and sticking to the decision. Indeed, it is so difficult that it takes a Buddha to find out about it and tell others.

perfectly normal (a person without them is regarded as a case for treatment), in the realm of death (the other great pole of human life) any strange fancies are still classed as "morbid." The Suttas reverse the situation: sensual thoughts are the thoughts of a sick man (sick with ignorance and craving), and the way to health is through thoughts of foulness and the diseases of the body, and of its death and decomposition. And not in an abstract scientific fashion either—one sees or imagines a rotting corpse, for example, and then pictures one's very own body in such a state. Our contemporaries are more squeamish.

5. Positives and negatives (15 January 1963)

Once one recognizes that one is totally responsible for all one's decisions and actions, one can no longer hide behind convenient ready-made excuses; and this, though it makes life rather less comfortable by removing one's habitual blinkers, endows one with unexpected self-reliance and resilience in difficult situations. And once it becomes habitual to think in this way, the task of living is discovered to be a full-time job and not merely a drudge to be got through by killing time as best one can. In other words, it abolishes boredom. And, as I mentioned some time ago, it is only in this authentic or responsible attitude that the Buddha's Teaching becomes intelligible.

But people, for the most part, are totally absorbed in and identified with positive worldly interests and projects, of which there is an unending variety. That is to say, although they differ from one another in their individual natures, the contents of their respective positivities, they are all alike in being positive. Thus, although the fundamental relation between positives is conflict (on account of their individual differences), they apprehend one another as all being in the same boat of positively, and they think of men generally in terms of human solidarity, and say "we."

But the person who lives in the subjective-reflexive mode is absorbed in and identified with, not the positive world, but himself. The world, of course, remains "there" but he regards it as accidental (Husserl[11] says that he "puts it in parenthesis, between brackets"),

11. Edmund Husserl was the founder of the phenomenological school in

and this means that he dismisses whatever positive identification he may have as irrelevant. He is no longer "a politician" or "a fisherman," but "a self." But what we call a "self," unless it receives positive identification from outside, remains a void, in other words, a negative. A "self," however, is positive in this respect—it seeks identification. So a person who identifies himself with himself finds that his positively consists in negativity—not the confident "I am this" or "I am that" of the positive, but a puzzled, perplexed, or even anguished, "What am I?" Eternal repetition of this eternally unanswerable question is the beginning of wisdom (it is the beginning of philosophy); but the temptation to provide oneself with a definite answer is usually too strong, and one falls into a wrong view of one kind or another. (It takes a Buddha to show the way out of this impossible situation. For the *sotāpanna*, who has understood the Buddha's essential Teaching, the question still arises, but he sees that it is unanswerable and is not worried; for the *arahat* the question no longer arises at all, and this is final peace.) This person, then, who has his centre of gravity in himself instead of in the world (a situation that, though usually found as a congenital feature, can be acquired by practice), far from seeing himself with the clear solid objective definition with which other people can be seen, hardly sees himself as anything definite at all: for himself he is, at best, a "What, if anything?"

It is precisely this lack of assured self-identity that is the secret strength of his position—for him the question-mark is the essential and his positive identity in the world is accidental, and whatever happens to him in a positive sense the question-mark still remains, which is all he really cares about. He is distressed, certainly, when his familiar world begins to break up, as it inevitably does, but unlike the positive he is able to fall back on himself and avoid total despair. It is also this feature that worries the positives; for

---

the early years of this century. This school has been very influential on the European continent, though less well-known in English-speaking countries. Husserl's article "Phenomenology" in the 14th edition of the *Encyclopaedia Britannica* was praised by Ven. Ñāṇavīra as a lucid summary of its methodology. Among Husserl's well-known disciples were Maurice Merleau-Ponty, Martin Heidegger, and Jean-Paul Sartre; hence phenomenology and existentialism are frequently linked.

they naturally assume that everybody else is a positive and they are accustomed to grasp others by their positive content, and when they happen to meet a negative they find nothing to take hold of. It quite often happens that a positive attributes to a negative various strange secret motives, supposing that he has failed to understand him (in a positive sense); but what he has failed to understand is that there is actually nothing there to be understood. But a negative, being a rare bird himself, is accustomed to positives, by whom he is surrounded, and he does not mistake them for fellow negatives. He understands (or at least senses) that the common factor of positivity that welds them together in the "we" of human solidarity does not extend to him, and mankind for him is "they." When a negative meets another negative they tend to coalesce with a kind of easy mutual indifference. Unlike two positives, who have the differences in their respective positivities to keep them apart, two negatives have nothing to separate them, and one negative recognizes another by his peculiar transparency—whereas a positive is opaque.

It happens that, for Heidegger,[12] contemplation of one's death throughout one's life is the key to authenticity. As Sartre has observed, Heidegger has not properly understood the nature of death, regarding it as *my* possibility, whereas in fact it is always accidental, even in suicide (I cannot kill myself directly, I can only cut my throat and *wait* for death to come). But death of one's body (which is always seen from outside, like other people's bodies) can be imagined and the implications envisaged. And this is really all that is necessary (though it must be added that there are other ways than contemplation of death of becoming authentic).

6. Towards realization of the Dhamma (7 March 1963)

What we call the "self" is a certain characteristic of all experience that seems to be eternal. It is quite obvious that for all men the reality

12. Heidegger's major work is translated into English as *Being and Time;* Sartre's is *Being and Nothingness.* Because the Ven. Ñāṇavīra read French but not German the latter book had a greater influence upon him; but when the former book was eventually translated and a copy reached him, he remarked that where the two disagreed, it was generally Heidegger who was in the right.

and permanence of their selves, "I," is taken absolutely for granted; and the eternal "subject" strives to possess the temporal "object," and the situation is at once both comic and tragic-comic, because something temporal cannot be possessed eternally, and tragic, because the eternal cannot desist from making the futile attempt to possess the temporal eternally. This tragicomedy is suffering (*dukkha*) in its profoundest sense. And it is release from this that the Buddha teaches. How? By pointing out that, contrary to our natural assumption (which supposes that the *subject* "I" would still continue to exist even if there were no *objects* at all), the existence of the subject depends upon the existence of the object; and since the object is manifestly impermanent, the subject must be no less so. And once the presumed-eternal subject is seen to be no less temporal than the object, the discrepancy between the eternal and the temporal disappears (in four stages—*sotāpatti, sakadāgāmitā, anāgāmitā*, and *arahatta*); and with the disappearance of the discrepancy the two categories of "tragic" and "comic" also disappear. The *arahat* neither laughs nor weeps; and that is the end of suffering (except, of course, for bodily pain, which only ceases when the body finally breaks up).

In this way you may see the progressive advance from the thoughtlessness of immediacy (either childish amusement, which refuses to take the tragic seriously, or pompous earnestness, which refuses to take the comic humourously) to the awareness of reflexion (where the tragic and the comic are seen to be reciprocal, and each is given its due), and from the awareness of reflexion (which is the limit of the *puthujjana*'s philosophy) to full realization of the Noble Dhamma (where both tragic and comic finally vanish, never again to return).

7. The phenomenological method (15 May 1963)

About Huxley's strange creatures of the mind, though few such experiences have come my way, I have no doubt at all that these curious (and perhaps terrifying) things are to be met with in certain mental circumstances.[13] That weird and fantastic

13. The book being discussed is "*The Doors of Perceptions* & *Heaven and Hell*". Huxley had a strong influence on the Ven. Ñāṇavīra in his youth; later their views diverged considerably.

creatures do actually exist, though normally invisible to us, we may gather from the reports (in the Suttas, for example; see the Lakkhaṇa Saṃyutta/S II 254-62) of people who have practised meditation and developed the *dibbacakkhu* or "divine eye." (I am occasionally asked by visitors whether in my meditations I have "had any experiences"—quite an improper question to put to a bhikkhu—and by this they usually mean, "have I seen any devas or other unusual objects?" Fortunately, I am able to assure them that I have not seen any at all, not a single one.) But all these various creatures, whether they exist in their own right—i.e. are independently conscious—or not (and this distinction is not always easy to make simply by looking at them), are of interest only to the lover of variety, to the collector of strange objects. To suppose, as Huxley does (and it is this fidelity of his to the scientific method that condemns him never to be more than a second-rate thinker), that by collecting and examining the various objects of the mind one can learn something essential about the nature of mind is much the same as supposing that one can learn something about the structure of the telescope by making a list of the great variety of objects one can see through it.

The phenomenological method (of existential thinkers) is not in the least concerned with the peculiarities (however peculiar they may be) of the individual specimen; what it is concerned with is the universal nature of experience as such. Thus, if a phenomenologist sees a duck-billed platypus, he does *not* exclaim with rapture, "What a strange creature! What a magnificent addition to the sum of human knowledge (and also to my collection of stuffed curiosities)!"; he says, instead, "This is an example of a living being," thus putting the platypus with all its duck-billed peculiarities "in brackets" and considering only the universal characteristics of his experience of the platypus. But a dog would have done just as well; for a dog, too, is "an example of a living being"; and besides, there is no need to go all the way to Australia to see one. The phenomenologist does not seek *variety*, he seeks *repetition*—repetition, that is to say, of experience (what it is experience *of* does not interest him in the least), so that he may eventually come to understand the *nature* of experience (for experience and existence are one and the same). And this is just as true of imaginary (mental) experience as of real experience. The Venerable Sāriputta Thera, for all his proficiency in the practice of *jhāna*, had not developed the *dibbacakkhu* (Th 996). And even so he was the leading disciple of the Buddha, and the foremost in *paññā*, or understanding. After the Buddha himself there was nobody who understood the Dhamma as well as he—and yet, on his own admission, he was unable to see "even a goblin" (Udāna IV.4/Ud 40). Evidently, then, the seeing of strange creatures, in normal or abnormal states of mind, does not advance one in wisdom.

8. Reflexive and immediate experience (19 May 1963)

Your question about *satisampajañña*. *Observing* the particular "doing" or "feeling" is *reflexive* experience. The "doing" or "feeling" itself (whether it is observed or not) is *immediate* experience. But since one obviously cannot observe a "doing" or a "feeling" unless that "doing" or "feeling" is *at the same time present*, there is no reflexive experience (at least in the strict sense used here) that does not contain or involve immediate experience. Reflexive experience is a complex structure of which immediate experience is a less complex part (it is possible that I use the term "reflexive consciousness" a little ambiguously—i.e. either to denote reflexive experience *as a whole* or to distinguish the purely reflexive part of reflexive experience from the immediate part).

Yes: observing the "general nature" of an experience is reflexion (though there are also other kinds of reflexion). No: in reflexively observing the "general nature" of an experience you have *not* "left out the immediate experience"; you have merely "put the immediate experience in brackets"—that is to say, by an effort of will you have *disregarded* the individual peculiarities of the experience and *paid attention* to the general characteristics (just as you might disregard a witness's stammer when he is giving evidence and pay attention to the words he is uttering). You simply consider the immediate experience as "an example of experience in general"; but this does not in any way abolish the immediate experience (any more than your disregarding the stammer of the witness stops his stammering).

9. Fear of death (7 September 1963)

Feelings of fear and helplessness at times of sickness or danger are very unpleasant, but they can also be very instructive. At such times one may get an almost pure view of *bhavataṇhā*, craving for existence. The fear is not fear of anything in particular (though there may *also* be that), but rather of *ceasing to exist*, and the helplessness is an *absolute* helplessness in the face of impending annihilation. I think that it is very probable that these feelings will put in an appearance at any time that one thinks one is going to die (whether one actually dies or not), and it is perhaps half the battle to be prepared for this sort of thing. Once one knows that such feelings are to be expected one can take the appropriate action quickly when they actually occur, instead of dying in a state of bewilderment and terror. What is the appropriate action? The answer is, Mindfulness. One cannot *prevent* these feelings (except by becoming an *arahat*), but one can look them in the face instead of fleeing in panic. Let them come, and try to *watch* them: once they know themselves to be observed they tend to wither and fade away, and can only reassert themselves when you become heedless and off your guard. But continued mindfulness is not easy, and that is why it is best to try and practise it as much as possible while one is still living. Experiences such as yours are valuable reminders of what one has to expect and of the necessity for rehearsing one's death before one is faced with it.

10. The Laws of Thought and the problem of existence (15 December 1963)

Any proposed solution to the problem of existence that disregards the three Laws of Thought[14] is, in the profoundest sense, *frivolous*. For the *puthujjana* the problem is brought to light by persistent refusal to disregard these laws. It is the merit of the existentialist philosophers that they do in fact bring the problem to light in this way. What happens is this: the thinker examines and describes his own thinking in an act of reflexion, obstinately refusing to tolerate

14. Identity—"A is A;" Contradiction—"A is not both B and not B;" Excluded Middle—"A is either B or not B."

non-identities, contradictions, and excluded middles; at a certain point he comes up against a contradiction that he cannot resolve and that appears to be inherent in his very act of thinking. This contradiction is the existence of the thinker himself (as *subject*). This is concisely present in the later part of the Mahānidāna Suttanta (DN 15/D II 66-8), where the Buddha says that a man who identifies his "self" with feeling should be asked *which* kind of feeling, pleasant, unpleasant, or neutral, he regards as his "self." The man cannot identify his "self" with all three kinds of feeling at once, since only one of the three kinds is present at a time: if he does make this identification, therefore, he must do it with the three different kinds of feeling in *succession*. His "self," of course, he takes for granted—as self-identical—"A is A"—that is to say as the *same* "self" on each occasion. This he proceeds to identify in turn with the three *different* feelings: B, C, and D. A is therefore both B and C (not to mention D); and C, being different from B, is not B: so A is both B and not B—a violation of the Law of Contradiction. But whether or not it is with feeling that the *puthujjana* is identifying his "self," he is always identifying it with *something*—and it is a *different* something on each occasion. The *puthujjana* takes his existence for granted—*cogito ergo sum*—(which, as Sartre says, is apodictic reflexive evidence of the thinker's existence)—and is in a perpetual state of contradiction.

So we have the following situation. Assuming the validity of the Laws of Thought, the thinker discovers that the whole of his thinking depends upon an irreducible violation of the Laws of Thought, namely the contradictory existence of the thinker. And this itself is a contradiction. If he tolerates this contradiction he denies the validity of the Laws of Thought whose validity he assumed when he established the contradiction in the first place; there is therefore no contradiction for him to tolerate, and consequently he is not denying the Laws of Thought; the contradiction therefore exists and he tolerates it ... Or he may refuse to tolerate the contradiction; but if he does so, it is in the name of the Law of Contradiction that he does so, and refusal to tolerate the contradiction requires him to deny the validity of the Laws of Thought by which the contradiction was originally established; he has therefore no reason to refuse to tolerate the contradiction, which, if the Laws of Thought are invalid, is inoffensive; he therefore does not deny the validity of the Laws of Thought, and the contradiction is offensive and he refuses to tolerate it ... Or perhaps he neither tolerates the contradiction nor refuses to tolerate it, in which case he violates the Law of Excluded Middle ... Most certainly the problem exists!

How is it dealt with? (i) The *rationalist*, by remaining on the level of reason and refusing to look at his premises, asserts the validity of the Laws of Thought, and successfully blinds himself to the standing violation of the Laws of Thought—his own existence. (ii) The *mystic* endorses the standing violation of the Laws of Thought by asserting their invalidity on principle. This obliges him to attribute their apparent validity to blindness or ignorance and to assert a Reality behind appearances that is to be reached by developing a mode of thinking based on the three laws: "A is not A"; "A is both B and not B"; "A is neither B nor not B." (iii) The *existentialist* says: "Contradiction is the truth, which is a contradiction, and therefore the truth. This is the situation, and I don't like it; but I can see no way out of it." To maintain this equivocal attitude for a long time is exhausting, and existentialists tend to seek relief in either rationalism or mysticism; but since they find it easier to endorse their personal existence than to ignore it they are more inclined to be mystical than rational.

Obviously, of these three attitudes, the first two evade the problem either by arbitrarily denying its existence or by arbitrarily denying the Laws of Thought upon which it depends. Only the third attitude asserts the Laws of Thought and asserts the existence of the problem. Though the *puthujjana* does not see the solution of the problem, he ought at least to see that to *evade* the problem (either by denying its existence or by denying the Laws of Thought on which it depends) is not to *solve* it. He will therefore choose to endure the discomfort of the third attitude until help comes from outside in the form of the Buddha's Teaching, or he himself finds the way out by becoming a Buddha.

11. Conceptual thought and reflexion (1 January 1964)

Thank you for Huxley's article.[15] Generally speaking, a concept, an idea, and a thought, are much the same thing, and can be described as an imaginary picture representing some real state of affairs. But this "representation" is not simply a photographic reproduction (in the mind) of the real state of affairs in question. In a very simple case, if I now imagine or think of some absent object, the image that I have bears some sort of resemblance to the absent object. But suppose I want to think about something like "the British Constitution." I cannot simply produce an imaginary picture "looking like" the British Constitution, because the B. C. does not "look like" anything. What happens is that, over the years, I have built up a complex image, partly visual, partly verbal, and perhaps also with elements from other senses; and this complex image has an internal structure that corresponds to that of the B. C., at least in so far as I have correctly understood it. If, in my studies of the British Constitution, I have consulted faulty authorities, or omitted part of it, these faults or omissions will be represented in this complex image. Whenever I wish to think about the B. C. (or even whenever anybody mentions it) this complex image comes to my mind, and it is with reference to it that I (for example) answer questions about the B. C. This complex image is a concept—it is my concept of the B. C. With luck, it may correspond fairly closely with the original thing, but most probably it is a very misleading representation. (Note that, since the essence of the concept is in the structure of the complex image, and not in the individual images that make up the complex image, it is quite possible to have a number of different complex images, but all with the same structure, to represent the real state of affairs in question. Here, the concept remains the same, though the image is different. Thus, in the world of art, it is possible to express the same idea either in music or in painting.)

Now all conceptual thinking is abstract; that is to say, the thought or concept is entirely divorced from reality, it is removed

15. The Huxley article was a newspaper clipping the correspondent had passed on to the Ven. author.

from existence and is (in Kierkegaard's phrase) *sub specie aeterni*. *Concrete* thinking, on the other hand, thinks the object *while the object is present*, and this, in the strict sense of the words, is *reflection* or *mindfulness*. One is mindful of what one is doing, of what one is seeing, while one is actually doing (or seeing) it. This, naturally, is very much more difficult than abstract thinking; but it has a very obvious advantage: if one is thinking (or being mindful) of something while it is actually present, no mistake is possible, and one is directly in touch with reality; but in abstract thinking there is every chance of a mistake, since the concepts with which we think are composite affairs, built up of an arbitrary lot of individual experiences (books, conversations, past observations, and so on).

What Huxley is getting at, then, is simply this. As a result of our education, our books, radios, cinemas, televisions, and so on, we tend to build up artificial concepts of what life is, and these concepts are grossly misleading and are no satisfactory guide at all to real life. (How many people, especially in the West, derive all their ideas about love from the cinema or T.V.—no wonder they run into difficulties when they begin to meet it as it is in reality!) Huxley is advocating a training in mindfulness (or awareness), *satisampajañña*—in thinking about life as it is actually taking place—instead of (or, at least, as well as) the present training in purely abstract thinking. In this way, so he maintains—and of course he is quite right—people will be better fitted for dealing with life as it really is.

12. Revolt with intelligence (4 March 1964)

The attitude you speak of, that of cursing the world and oneself, is, in a sense, the beginning of wisdom. Revolt is the first reaction of an intelligent man when he begins to understand the desperate nature of his situation in the world; and it is probably true to say that nothing great has ever been achieved except by a man in revolt against his situation. But revolt alone is not enough—it eventually contradicts itself. A man in blind revolt is like someone in a railway compartment trying to stop the train by pushing against the opposite seat with his feet: he may be strong enough to damage the compartment, but the damaged compartment will nevertheless continue to move with the train. Except for the *arahat*, we are all in this train of saṃsāra, and the problem is to stop the train whilst still travelling in it. Direct action, direct revolt won't do; but something, certainly, must be done. That it *is*, in fact, possible to stop the train from within we know from the Buddha, who has himself done it:

> I, monks, being myself subject to birth, decay, and death, having seen the misery of subjection to birth, decay, and death, went in search of the unborn, undecaying, undying, uttermost quietus of extinction (*nibbāna*), *and I reached the unborn, undecaying, undying, uttermost quietus of extinction.* (MN 26/M I 167)

Revolt by all means, but let the weapons be intelligence and patience, not disorder and violence; and the first thing to do is to find out exactly what it is that you are revolting against. Perhaps you will come to see that what you are revolting against is ignorance (*avijjā*).

13. Western thought; impermanence (15 March 1964)

The passage on Western philosophy that you quote from Lin Yutang is partly justified, but it must be remarked that it refers only to speculative (or abstract) philosophy, in other words the classical Western philosophies. Existential philosophy, as its name implies, is concerned with *existence*, and Lin Yutang could hardly complain that Kierkegaard, Nietzsche, and Marcel—to name only three—did (or do) not live in accordance with their philosophies (even though he would scarcely agree with them—they do not regard life as a "poem"). Certainly it is futile to look to speculative philosophy for guidance on how to live; and to follow such a philosophy is to be like one of the blind men of the Sutta in the Udāna (V I,4: 68-9) who were shown an elephant and told to describe it—one grasps a small fragment of the truth abstracted from the whole, and fondly imagines that one knows all. On the other hand, a study of such philosophies, in certain circumstances, may not be a waste of time. Shortly before his Parinibbāna, the Buddha told Māra that he would not pass away before there were disciples who were capable of correctly refuting any outside views that might spring up, and this argues that for those who had themselves reached right view a study of wrong view would be an advantage rather than a disadvantage—that is, when dealing with people who did not accept the Buddha's Teaching. But here, it will be understood, these various speculative philosophies would be studied against a background of right view, with the effect that they would be fitted into their proper place—just as the king, who could see the whole of the elephant, was able to reconcile the widely divergent descriptions of the blind men and put them in the proper perspective. It may also not be a disadvantage to have a fairly wide knowledge of various philosophies when one is in the position of having to understand the Suttas when no trustworthy (i.e. non-*puthujjana*) living teacher is available. If one has to find out for oneself what the texts mean, such a background may—at least for certain people—be a help rather than a hindrance. And finally the development of a lucid understanding of these philosophies—of their virtues and their limitations—may become a real pleasure to the mind.

As a solution to impermanence you suggest that we might forego "an impermanent use of what is impermanent." Impossible! We are making impermanent use of what is impermanent all the time—and this is as true for the *arahat* as it is for the *puthujjana*. So long as there is consciousness at all there is the passage of time, and the passage of time consists in the *use* of things, whether we like it or not. The eating of food, the breathing of breaths, the thinking of thoughts, the dreaming of dreams—all are impermanent use of what is impermanent. Only in *nirodhasamāpatti* does this lapse for any living being. In the last Sutta of the Majjhima Nikāya (MN 152/M III 298-9) the desperate expedient is suggested of "not seeing forms with the eye, not hearing sounds with the ear," but the Buddha ridicules this, saying that this is already achieved by a blind and deaf man. He goes on to indicate *upekkhā*, indifference, as the proper way. The fault does not lie in the impermanence (which is inevitable), but in *attachment to* (and *repulsion from*) the impermanent. Get rid of attachment (and repulsion) and you get rid of the suffering of impermanence. The *arahat* makes impermanent use of the impermanent, but with indifference, and the only suffering he has is bodily pain or discomfort when it arises (and that, too, finally ceases when his body breaks up).

14. Three kinds of trainees (4 April 1964)

Bradley makes a distinction that seems to have a certain (limited) application to the Dhamma. He speaks of the metaphysicians, on the one hand, who speculate on first principles and the ultimate nature of things; and on the other, of those who are not prepared for metaphysical enquiry, who feel no call towards thankless hours of fruitless labour, who do not care to risk a waste of their lives on what the world for the most part regards as lunacy, and they themselves but half believe in.

(*Principles of Logic*, p. 340)

(What a cry from Bradley's heart!) This second category contains those who take principles as working hypotheses to explain the facts, without enquiry into the ultimate validity of those principles (this is the normal practice with those who study special subjects—physics, chemistry, biology, psychology, and so on—and who are metaphysicians, if at all, in their own conceit). In brief: those who look for first principles, and those who take things on trust because they work in practice. In the Suttas, too, we find something of this distinction between those *sekhas* who are *diṭṭhipatta* ("attained-through-view") and those who are *saddhāvimutta* ("released-through-faith"). The former have heard the Buddha's Teaching, reflected on it, and accepted it after considering the ultimate principles on which it is based. The latter have heard the Teaching and reflected on it (as before), but instead of seeking its first principles, have accepted it because it inspires them with trust and confidence. Both of them have practised the Teaching, and both have attained to *sotāpatti* or beyond, but one puts *paññā* foremost, and the other *saddhā*. But there is also a third kind of *sekha*, the *kāyasakkhi* ("body-witness"), who is quite without any corresponding, category in Western philosophy: he is one who puts *samādhi* foremost—he develops mental concentration and gets all the *jhānas*, and needs not so much *paññā* or *saddhā*. In AN 3:21/A I 118-20 the Buddha is asked which of these three is the best, but he declines to discriminate between them, saying that any one of them may outdistance the other two and arrive first at the final goal.

It is actually on this question of *samādhi* that Eastern thought is at its greatest distance from Western; and the latter can certainly be charged with sterility on this score (and this will include the existentialists). The trouble seems to be this. Western thought has a Christian background (its individual thinkers can almost all be classed as pro or anti-Christian, and rarely, if ever, as neutral), and, since the practice of meditation is normally connected with religious beliefs (in a wide sense), all states attained through such practices are automatically classed as Christian (or at least as Theist or Deist), and therefore as essentially *mystical*. Now, no philosopher who respects the Laws of Thought can possibly find a place for the mystical in his scheme of things, since mysticism is an act of faith in the principle of non-contradiction (i.e. that the Law of Contradiction does not hold)—in other words, God (who is, one might say, self-contradiction personified, and, being the Ultimate Truth, is therefore no contradiction).[16] So *samatha* practice (*ānāpānasati*, for example), even were it known in the West (which it is not), would first be misunderstood as mystical, and then, on the strength of this, would be banished from the philosopher's system (except, of course, on Sundays).

15. The Suttas and outside philosophies (12 April 1964)

I am always pleased when I find a connection between the Suttas and outside philosophies: it is not, to be sure, that the former can be reduced to the latter—the Dhamma is not just *one* way of thinking amongst others—but rather that the Buddha has seen all that these philosophers have seen, and he has *also* seen what they could not see; and to discover this is extraordinarily exhilarating. Nobody can say to the Buddha, "There is this or that that you have not taken into account"[17]: it is all taken into account, and still more. The Suttas give not the slightest pretext for the famous "sacrifice of the intellect"—Ignatius Loyola and Bodhidharma are strange bedfellows, indeed. Certainly there is more to the Dhamma than intellect (and this is

16. Some philosophers take advantage of this situation: they develop their system as far as possible, carefully avoiding self-contradictions; but when they encounter one that they cannot explain, instead of confessing defeat they proudly declare that they have proved the existence of God.
17. Cf. AN 7 55/A IV 83.

sometimes hard for Europeans to understand), but there is nothing to justify the wilful abandonment of the Principle of Identity.

16. The Law of Identity (14 July 1964)

The Principle (or Law) of Identity is usually stated as "A is A" which can be understood as "Everything is what it is." Bradley (*Principles of Logic*, p. 141) remarks that, in this form, it is a tautology and says nothing at all:

> It does not even assert identity. For identity without difference is nothing at all. It takes two to make the same, and the least we can have is some change of event in a self-same thing, or the return to that thing from some suggested difference. For, otherwise, to say "It is the same as itself" would be quite unmeaning.

In referring to Loyola and Bodhidharma in my last letter, I had in mind two "wilful abandonments of the Principle of Identity." (i) Loyola: "In order never to go astray, we must always be ready to believe that what I, personally, see as *white* is *black*, if the hierarchical Church defines it so." (ii) Bodhidharma (or, rather, a modern disciple of his, in an article in *The Middle Way*[18]): "The basic principle of Zen is 'A is not A'." A great deal of modern thinking, including mathematics, is based on a deliberate rejection of one or another of the Laws of Thought, of which Identity is the first. This may be all very well in poetry or physics, but it won't do in philosophy—I mean as a fundamental principle. Every ambiguity, for a philosopher, should be a sign that he has further to go.

17. Mindfulness; Huxley's Island (6 August 1964)

Sati, in a loose sense, can certainly be translated as "memory" but memory is normally memory of the *past*, whereas in the eight-factored path *sati* is more particularly concerned with the *present*. In so far as one can speak of memory of the present, this

18. The *Middle Way* is the journal of the Buddhist Society of Great Britain.

translation will do, but memory of the present—i.e. calling to mind the present—is less confusingly translated as "mindfulness." Here are two Sutta passages illustrating these two meanings of *sati*: in the first passage *sati* is "memory," and in the second it is "mindfulness." The passages can be translated as follows:

(i) The noble disciple is mindful, he is endowed with the highest mindfulness (memory) and prudence, he remembers and recalls what was done and what was said long ago. (SN 48:50/S V 275)

(ii) Here, monks, a monk dwells contemplating the body in the body ... feelings in feelings ... the mind in the mind ... ideas in ideas, ardent, aware, mindful, having put away worldly covetousness and grief. Thus, monks, is a monk mindful. (SN 36:7/S IV 211)

I have been sent Huxley's last novel—*Island*. It is a most unsatisfactory book. Since Huxley had visited Ceylon shortly before writing the book, and since the inhabitants of the Island are Buddhists, it has been thought that the Island is Ceylon. But this is clearly a mistake. The Island is undoubtedly Bali (Huxley calls it Pala), from its geographical and political environment. Besides, the people are Mahāyāna Buddhists (Tantric to boot) with a strong admixture of Shiva worship. The book is a kind of *Brave New World* turned inside out—it describes a Utopia of which he approves. It is based almost entirely on *maithuna* (sex) and mescalin (one of the characters quotes a Tantric Buddhist saying that Buddhahood is in the *yoni*—a very convenient doctrine!), which in combination (so it seems) are capable of producing the Earthly Paradise. The awkward fact of rebirth is eliminated with the statement that the Buddha discouraged speculation on such questions (whereas, in fact, the Buddha said quite bluntly throughout the Suttas that there *is* rebirth: the speculation that the Buddha discouraged was whether the Tathāgata [or *arahat*] exists after death, which is quite another question). And precisely the worst feature of the book is the persistent misinterpretation (or even perversion) of the Buddha's Teaching.

It is probable that Huxley picked up a certain amount of information on the Dhamma while he was in Ceylon but, being antipathetic to Theravāda (this is evident in his earlier books), he has not scrupled to interpret his information to suit his own ideas. We find, for example, that according to Freudian doctrine Mucalinda Nāgarāja (Udāna II 10) is a phallic symbol, being a serpent. So "meditating under the Mucalinda tree" means sexual intercourse. And this in complete defiance of the verses at the end of the Sutta:

> Dispassion for worldly pleasure,
> getting beyond sensuality,
> putting away the conceit "I am,"
> —this indeed is the highest pleasure.

In short, the book is a complete misrepresentation of the Buddha's Teaching in a popular form that is likely to be widely read. Huxley, of course, is sincere in his views and no doubt means well; but that does not make the book any the less unfortunate.

18. Meditations: a non-mystical practice (18 May 1964)

R. C. Zaehner (in his *Mysticism: Sacred and Profane*) admits he doesn't know much about Pali Buddhism, but what he does say is wrong in two respects. (i) In the first place, he more or less identifies the *anattā* ("not-self") doctrine with Advaita Vedānta, and he does this with more than a suspicion that neither Buddhists nor even the Buddha himself would allow this.[19] Though this identification is quite gratuitous,[20] there is some excuse for it in view of certain books published in Europe which hold this view (Coomaraswamy in England, Georg Grimm in Germany). No doubt you will gather that I certainly do not hold the view that the object of the exercise is to get rid of my temporal "self" in order to attain the permanent "Self" behind it. (ii) In the second place, Zaehner appears to assume that all experience attained in

19. "... the Buddha saw something that did not change, over against *prakriti* he saw *purusha* though he would not have formulated it thus." And again, "Moreover the Hindus, overwhelmingly, and the Buddhists when they are off their guard, speak of this eternal being as the 'self' ..."

20. There is one text (at least) that directly opposes the idea that *nibbāna* (extinction) is *attā* (self).

the practice of meditation (I use the word here in the widest sense) is of the mescalin/manic-depressive type, or at least that one has to pass through this state to reach the "Beatific Vision."

Now, whatever the case may be with the Christian mystics, or with the Mohammedan Sufis, or with the Hindus—or even with Mahāyāna and Zen Buddhists—about none of whom am I well informed (and, still less, practised in their disciplines), I can quite definitely assert that (to speak only of the practice of concentration—*samādhi*) the effect of practice according to the Theravāda tradition (details in the *Visuddhimagga—Path of Purification*) is quite different from anything Zaehner has described. I am quite familiar with the low-level results of this practice. There is a gradual and increasing experience of calm and tranquillity as the object of meditation (in my case, the in-and out-breaths) becomes clearer and more definite, and at the same time distracting thoughts about other matters become less. If one *does* turn one's attention to such matters, they are seen much more clearly and steadily than at normal times.) As one proceeds, one's capacity for practice increases, and one may be able to continue (with interruptions for meals, etc.) for many hours;[21] and also one positively dislikes any outside interruption, and necessary breaks are most unwelcome. In all this there is, right from the start, no sign at all of elation and depression (or expansion and contraction—Zaehner, pp. 85 ff.), and no experience of "oneness" (with nature, with Self, with God, or with anything else). There is nothing one could possibly call "ecstatic" about it—it is pleasurable, and the more so the more one does it, but that is all. To begin with, certainly, one may be attacked either by sleepiness or by mental agitation (i.e. about other matters), but with persistence, and particularly when the object of meditation begins to appear clearly, these things no longer arise; but sleepiness is not depression and mental distraction is not manic exultation. About the higher states (called *jhānas*), in the descriptions of these attainments in the Suttas there is, once again, nothing that corresponds to what Zaehner describes; and, in particular, these practices *alone* do not lead to "liberation" in the highest sense—*nibbāna*—though Zaehner seems to assume that they do (pp. 155-6). Moreover, it is by no

21. In the Suttas, the Buddha and others continue for a week at a time "without changing their sitting position," and this is, to me, perfectly credible.

means necessary to reach the highest stages of concentration in order to attain *nibbāna*—first *jhāna* (minimum) is sufficient.

I have wearied you with all this only because it seems possible that, in denying that there was anything "mystical" about the Buddhism of the Pali Texts, I might have given you the impression that there was (in my opinion, at least) no *practice of meditation*. This, however, would be a mistake. In denying that Pali Buddhism was mystical, all I intended to convey was that (i) the practice of meditation (or, more specifically, concentration—*samādhi*) that it teaches cannot in any way be described as *mystical* (though certainly its effects are, to begin with, *unusual*—because few people practise—and eventually, *supernormal*—they can lead to mastery of *iddhi* powers: levitation, clairvoyance, memory of past lives, and so on); and (ii) that eventual liberation—*nibbāna*, extinction—is not a mystical union with the Deity, nor even absorption in a Higher Self (both of which cover up and intensify the fundamental ambiguity of the subject ["I", "myself", etc.), but rather the attainment of the clear understanding and comprehension (*paññā, aññā*) about the nature of this ambiguity (which, when combined with suitable *samādhi* actually causes—or, rather, *allows*—the ambiguity to subside once for all).

There are many world-views against which as a background the Buddha's Teaching is wholly incomprehensible—indeed, the Buddha himself, upon occasion, when asked about his teaching, would answer, "It is hard for you, having (as you do) other teachers, other persuasions, other views, to understand these matters." Zaehner's *Weltanschauung*, for example, is hopeless.

19. Ignorance and reality (2 August 1964)

The world's relativity (or variety) stubbornly resists all our efforts to reduce it to a single Whole. "The primitive hostility of the world rises up to face us across millennia" (Camus, in *The Myth of Sisyphus*, p. 11). Three quotations will perhaps illustrate this. Here, first, is Jean Grenier (*Absolu et Choix*)[22] on the Hindu *māyā*:

22. *Absolu et Choix* was published by Presses Universitaires de France in 1961. The quotation was sent in French. The translation used here is provided by the editor, from pp. 53–55 of Grenier's book. The Prajñāpāramitā quotation

> The world may be the product of a sort of dream, not the dream of a spirit but the dream of a power inherent in the world. That would be the case of this illusion that the Vedantists call *māyā*. For Indians; *māyā* is *shakti*, which is to say a power from (and of) Brahma, through which the latter takes a perceptible appearance ... The Vedic hypothesis of *māyā*, a hypothesis that would better be called a postulate, because of its generality and indemonstrability, consists in supposing that the world is the product of a cosmic illusion, a modification of Brahma. This modification would be apparent only, like the rope one thinks to be a snake but which nevertheless remains a rope. The absolute would not be more easily reached through it than the desert through the mirage.

Second, here is a passage from the Prajñāpāramitā on the Mahāyānist *avidyā*:

> Objects exist only insofar as they do not exist in reality. Insofar as they do not exist they are called *avidyā*, which means "non-knowledge." Common and ignorant people are attached to these things because they do not receive guidance (teaching) on this subject. They picture to themselves all these objects as existing, whereas in reality no one (no thing) exists.

Finally, a verse from the Pali Suttas:

> Thought and lust are a man's sensuality,
> Not the various things in the world;
> Thought and lust are a man's sensuality,
> The various things just stand there in the world;
> But the wise get rid of desire therein.[23]

(AN 6:63/A III 411)

---

was also sent in French, and would seem to be quoted from an essay, "Le Bouddhisme d'après les Textes pālis," by Solange Bernard-Thierry on p. 608 of *Presence du Bouddhisme*, the Feb.–June 1959 issue of the journal *France-Asie*, published in Saigon. The quotation seems to be from one of the more recent strata of the Prajñāpāramitā Sūtra. The English translation is by the editor.

23. *Saṅkapparāgo purisassa kāmo*
Na te kāmā yāni citrāni loke
Saṅkapparāgo purisassa kāmo

For the Hindu, then, the variety of the world is *illusion*, and for the Mahāyānist it is *ignorance*; and in both cases the aim is to overcome the world, either by union with Brahma or by attainment of knowledge. Unlike the Hindus and the Mahāyānists, the Pali Suttas teach that the variety of the world is neither illusion (*māyā*) nor delusion (*avidyā*) but perfectly real. The attainment of *nibbāna* is certainly cessation of *avijjā*, but this leaves the variety of the world intact, except that affectively the variety is now uniformly indifferent. *Avidyā*, clearly enough, does not mean to the Mahāyānist what *avijjā* does in the Pali Suttas.

20. Desire to end desire (31 August 1964)

As to that Sutta you mention (AN 4:159/A II 144-7): a bhikkhunī sends for the Ven. Ānanda Thera, being infatuated with him and hoping perhaps for sexual intercourse. The Ven. Ānanda understands the situation and gives her a suitable Dhamma-talk. He tells her (i) that this body is a product of food and that, depending on food, food is to be given up (a bhikkhu's body is made of food, but he must go on taking food to keep alive and practise the Dhamma if he wishes to give up food in the future by not being reborn); (ii) that this body is a product of craving and that, depending on craving, craving is to be given up (a bhikkhu, having been born on account of craving in his previous life, hears that so-and-so has become an *arahat* and, craving that for himself, sets to work to get it; and in course of time he succeeds, his success being, precisely, the giving up of all craving); (iii) the same with *māna* or conceit (the bhikkhu, hearing that so-and-so has become an arahat, thinks "I'm as good as he is, and if he can do it, so can I," and sets to work; and in due course, prompted by conceit, he puts an end to conceit); (iv) that this body is a product of copulation, and that the Buddha has said that (for monks) copulation is absolutely not to be practiced. In (ii), the bhikkhu *craves* for arahatship since he thinks in terms of "I" or "self" ("When shall *I* attain that?"), and all such thoughts contain *bhavataṇhā*, though of course here there is no *sensual* craving (*kāmataṇhā*). But anyone who thinks "When

---

Tiṭṭhanti citrāni tath'eva loke
Ath'ettha dhīrā vinayanti chandaṃ.

shall *I* become an *arahat*?" is *ipso facto* failing to understand what it means to be an *arahat* (since being an *arahat* means *not* thinking in terms of "I"). So, on account of his craving for arahatship, he sets out to get it. But, since he does not understand what arahatship is, he does not know what it is that he is seeking; and when, in due course, he *does* come to know what it is he is seeking, he has *ipso facto* found it (or at least the first instalment of it). It is by making use of *bhavataṇhā* that he gives up *bhavataṇhā* (and *a fortiori* all other kinds of *taṇhā*). It is *because* of *bhavataṇhā* that, *with the Buddha's help*, we make an attempt to recognize *bhavataṇhā* and succeed in doing so, thereby bringing *bhavataṇhā* to an end.

21. Sending good wishes (20 September 1964)

Your question about the propriety of sending good wishes ("Is not wishing desire, and so to be shunned?") can be answered, though not in one word. There is desire and desire, and there is also desire to end desire. There is desire that involves self-assertion (love, hate) and desire that does not (the *arahat*'s desire to eat when hungry, for example), and the former can be either self-perpetuating (unrestrained passion) or self-destructive (restrained passion). Self-destructive desire is bad in so far as it is passionate, and therefore good in so far as, translated into action, it brings itself to an end. (By "translated into action" I mean that the desire for restraint does not remain abstractly in evidence only when one is not giving way to passion, but is concretely operative when there is actually occasion for it, when one is actually in a rage. To begin with, of course, it is not easy to bring them together, but with practice desire for restraint arises at the same time as the passion, and the combination is self-destructive. The Suttas say clearly that craving is to be eliminated by means of craving; and you yourself are already quite well aware that nothing can be done in this world, either good or bad, without passion—and the achievement of dispassion is no exception. But passion must be intelligently directed.) Since an *arahat* is capable of desiring the welfare of others, good wishes are evidently not essentially connected with self-assertion, and so are quite *comme il faut*.

I hope that your leave is passing pleasantly for you—that is, I do not hope that it is *passing*, but that it is *pleasant* in its passing:

whether I hope or do not hope, it will pass, alas! like all good things, save one. But that one thing—again alas!—is not to be had simply by wishing.

> In creatures subject to birth, ageing, and death, friends, there arises such a wish as "O that we were not subject to birth, ageing, and death! O that birth, ageing, and death might not come nigh us!" But that is not to be attained by wishing; and in this, too, not to get what one wishes is to suffer (DN 22/D II 307).

With all best wishes, including this (that is, if you would wish it for yourself).

22. Dhamma and socialism (23 November 1964)

I enclose a press cutting about Sartre.[24] The view that he is expounding here ("A writer has to take sides ...") finds no justification at all in his philosophy. If, therefore, he holds this view, he does so simply because he finds it emotionally satisfactory. This view, of course, is quite familiar to us—it is the socialist argument we sometimes hear, that since one cannot practise the Dhamma if one is starving, therefore food comes first; and therefore food is more important than the Dhamma; and therefore it is more important to produce food than it is to behave well; and therefore any of violence or deceit is justified if it helps to increase food production.

As Sartre puts it, it seems plausible—it is better to feed the poor than to entertain the rich. But when we look at it more closely we see that certain difficulties arise. To begin with, it assumes (as all socialists, Sartre included, do assume) that this life is the only one, that we did not exist before we were born, and shall not exist after we die. On this assumption it is fairly easy to divide mankind into two groups: the rich oppressors, and the poor oppressed, and the choice which to support seems easy. But if this is not the only life, how can we be sure that a man who is now poor and oppressed is not suffering the unpleasant effects of having been a rich oppressor in his past life? And, if we take the principle to its logical conclusion, should we not

24. The article was entitled "Bread Before Books."

choose to be on the side of the "oppressed" inhabitants of the hells, suffering retribution for their evil ways, and to condemn the fortunate ones in the heavens, a privileged class enjoying the reward of virtue, as the "idle rich"? And then this view ignores the fact that our destiny at death depends on how we behave in this life. If bad behaviour in this life leads to poverty and hunger in the next, can we be sure that bread is more important than books? What use is it providing the hungry with bread if you don't tell them the difference between right and wrong? Is metaphysics so unimportant if it leads men—rich and poor, no matter—to adopt right view and to behave accordingly?

Of course, the very fact that Sartre's philosophy does not have anything to say about the hungry and oppressed is a blemish on his philosophy; and it might be argued that Sartre is therefore better occupied standing up for the hungry and oppressed than in propagating his metaphysical views; but that still does not justify the principle. And, in the last analysis, the Buddha's Teaching is for a privileged class—those who are fortunate enough to have the intelligence to grasp it (the Dhamma is *paccattaṃ veditabbo viññūhi* (MN 38/M I 265)—"to be known by the wise, each for himself"), and they are most certainly not the majority! But Sartre's attitude is symptomatic of a general inadequacy in modern European thought: the growing view that the majority must be right, that truth is to be decided by appeal to the ballot-box. (I read somewhere that, in one of the Western Communist countries, it was decided by a show of hands that angels do not exist.)

23. Interpreting the Canon (29 November 1964)

Mr. X remarks that I explain too inductively, that I tend to look for my ideas in the Canon instead of *deducing* from the passages what *they* mean. This criticism, however, supposes that we are, in fact, able to approach the Canon with a perfectly virgin mind, equipped only with a knowledge of Pali and a sound training in logic. But this is precisely what we cannot do. Each of us, at every moment, has the whole of his past behind him; and it is in the light of his past (or his background or his presuppositions) that he interprets what is now presented to him and gives it its meaning. Without such a background nothing would ever appear to us with any meaning at all—a spoken or written word would remain a pure presentation, a bare sound or mark without significance. But, unfortunately, each of us has a different past; and, in consequence, each of us approaches the Canon with a set of presuppositions that is different in various ways from everybody else's. And the further consequence is that each of us understands the Canon in a different sense. We try to discover our personal ideas in the Canon because there is nothing else we can do. It is the only way we have, in the first place, of *understanding* the Canon. Later, of course, our understanding of the Canon comes to modify our ideas; and thus, by a circular process, our later understanding of the Canon is better than, or at least different from, our earlier understanding, and there is the possibility of eventually arriving at the right understanding of the *ariyapuggala.* Certainly we can, to some extent, deduce from the Canon its meaning; but unless we first introduced our own ideas we should never find that the Canon had any meaning to be deduced.

For each person, then, the Canon means something different according to his different background. And this applies not only to our understanding of particular passages, but also to what we understand by the Buddhadhamma as a whole. (i) We may all agree that certain passages were spoken by the Buddha himself and that they represent the true Teaching. But when we come to ask one another what we understand by these passages and by the words they contain we often find a profound disagreement that is by no means settled simply by reference to other Sutta passages. (ii) Since everybody already has his own ideas (vague or precise) of what constitutes happiness, he will naturally look to the Buddha (that is, if he has placed his *saddhā* in the Buddha) to supply that happiness, and he will interpret the Dhamma as a whole in just that sense. Later, of course, he may find that the Dhamma cannot be taken in the sense that he wishes, and he will then either change his ideas or else abandon the Dhamma for some other teaching. But, in any case, there is no reason at all for supposing that two people (unless they have both ceased to be *puthujjanas*) will be agreed on what it is, precisely, that the Buddha teaches.

So, in the present case, I do not find that Mr. X's view of the Dhamma—so far as I can grasp it—has any very great resemblance to mine; and that difference evidently reflects the difference in our respective backgrounds against which we interpret the Dhamma. He may (perhaps) say that he reads and understands the Suttas without any reference to a background, and (if so) I have no wish to argue the point; but I know that, for my part, I never come without a background (in a sense I *am* my background) when I consider the texts, even though that background is now very different from what it was when I first looked at a Sutta. And if he disagrees with what I am saying, that disagreement will itself be reflected in the way each of us understands the nature of the Dhamma.

24. Numinous experience (8 December 1964)

You speak of "feeling the incarnating of God in ourselves so that we realize that we are of the very stuff of God," and then you go on to say, "Oh, I know how you will react to any such statement ..." Well, how do I react? I say that to take what we call "experience of God" as evidence of the existence of God is a mistake: But there are mistakes and mistakes, and it is perhaps worth looking a little more closely.

Observe, to begin with, that I do not *deny* that we may have "experience of God." Numinous experience is just as real as romantic love or aesthetic experience; and the question that must be answered is whether these things are to be taken at their face value as evidence of some kind of transcendent reality or whether the eternity they point to is a delusion.

Certainly in sexual love we do seem to experience eternity; and this is often taken as religiously significant (by the Hindus, for example, with their Shivalingam, not to mention their temple eroticism). But what a derisory eternity it is that lasts for a few seconds or minutes and then leaves us wondering what all the fuss was about! As an advertisement for eternity, sex is a joke. In romantic love, true, we manage to live in a kind of eternity for months and perhaps years: every love-affair lasts forever—while it lasts. Our past loves can be absolutely dead, even when we meet the loved one again. And so with aesthetic enjoyment, the transcendental sense of Mozart's G Minor Quintet, his Adagio and Fugue, the late Beethoven, Bartok's quartets, Stravinsky's Octet for Wind Instruments, so evident to me before I joined the army—where was it when I got back home after the war?

When we come to more specifically numinous experience the situation is more delicate. In its grosser forms, certainly—awe in a cathedral, panic fear in a thunderstorm—it can come and go, and we oscillate between eternity and transience; and even if transience can be eternal, eternity cannot possibly be transient. But a more subtle approach is possible. For Karl Jaspers the world has a threefold aspect. There is "being-there," "being-oneself," and "being-in-itself." The first is everything that can be an object for me, thoughts as well as things. The second is personal existence, or *myself.* This transcends the first, and can be apprehended, though not wholly, in an act of self reflexion. The third transcends the second as the second transcends the first, and is Transcendental Being. This is the ultimate sense or meaning of the other two, but it can never be directly apprehended. All we can do is to approach it. And Jaspers here develops his doctrine of "ciphers": a cipher (which is quite unintelligible to abstract reason) is an experience that is apprehended as incomplete—but only as pointing to a reality that is "present but hidden."

Although Jaspers distinguishes various kinds of ciphers, the important point is that *anything* can be read as a cipher if we care to make the effort of "existential contemplation." Since anything can indicate Transcendental Being, there is at least the theoretical possibility that one might pass the whole of one's life reading one's every experience as a cipher, and in such a case we should perpetually be approaching Eternity. This attitude is less easy to dismiss, and Jaspers has taken care to tie up all the loose ends with an ultimate cipher. Although we can perpetually approach Being, we can never actually reach it, and this inevitable failure and frustration of our efforts may be a temptation to despair. This temptation to despair, says Jaspers, should spur us on to "assume" the cipher of frustration. But it must be emphasized that the assumption of this cipher is an act of faith in Transcendence and without such faith we can never make the necessary jump—indeed, they are really one and the same thing.

So, then, Jaspers leads us to the point where everything indicates Transcendence and nothing reveals it, and thence to despair; and despair is an invitation to jump to the conclusion that Transcendence (or Eternity, or God) exists. But different attitudes are possible in the face of this invitation. The theists, of course, accept the invitation with many thanks. Jaspers himself is inclined to accept it in spite of the difficulties involved. Sartre explains away the invitation, too easily dismissing what is a real problem. Camus accepts the invitation to Transcendence in a contrary sense—as evidence of the non-existence of God.

And what, then, about the Buddha's Teaching—how does it tell us to deal with the question whether or not God exists? The first thing is to refuse to be bullied into giving a categorical answer, yes or no, to such a treacherous question. The second thing is to see that the answer to this question will depend on the answer to a more immediate question: "Do I myself exist? Is my self in fact eternal, or is it something that perishes with the body?" And it is here that the difficulties begin. The Buddha says that the world is divided, for the most part, between the Yeas and the Nays, between the eternalists and the annihilationists, and that they are forever at each other's throats. But these are two extremes, and the Buddha's Teaching goes in between. So long as we have experience of our selves, the question "Does my self exist?" will thrust itself upon us: if we answer in the affirmative we shall tend to affirm the existence of God, and if we answer in the negative we shall deny the existence of God. But what if we have ceased to have experience of ourselves? (I do not mean reflexive experience as such, but experience of our selves as an ego or a person.) If this were to happen—and it is the specific aim of the Buddha's Teaching (and of no other teaching) to arrange for it to happen—then not only should we stop questioning about our existence and the existence of God, but the whole of Jaspers' system, and with it the doctrine of ciphers, would collapse. And what room, then, for despair? For the *arahat* all sense of personality or selfhood has subsided, and with it has gone all possibility of numinous experience; and *a fortiori* the mystical intuition of a transpersonal Spirit or Absolute Self—of a Purpose or an Essence or a Oneness or what have you—can no longer arise.

25. A good life and a good death (30 December 1964)

I myself started thinking about the unpleasant business of dying, perhaps three or four years ago. Up to then, like most people, I had not given it much thought. But I was struck by the statements of two doctors on the subject. The first said that if we overeat we tend to die earlier than if we take less; and that since death is more painful when one is still young (because the body has stronger resistance) than when one is old and decrepit, it is advisable to eat less and live as long as possible. The other doctor was commenting (in a medical journal) on a proposal to institute voluntary euthanasia for people who had reached the age of sixty. He was in favour of the proposal because, he said, as a doctor he was well aware of the horrible diseases that are liable to attack us in the seventh and eighth decades of our lives. So there you are you die young you probably have a difficult death because your body is strong and if you keep alive into old age you run the risk of dying unpleasantly from some frightful affliction. And, after that, I was struck by the obsessive thought of death that runs right through Dr. Axel Munthe's book *The Story of San Michele.* In the Suttas, whenever the Buddha speaks of severe pain, it is always "pain like that of dying."

In Camus' long novel *La Peste* ("The Plague") a character declares, "The only concrete problem that I know of today is whether it is possible to be a saint without God." In the Christian tradition, of course, one is good, one becomes a saint, in order to please God or to fulfil his will. But when (as is largely the case in Europe today) people no longer believe in the existence of God, is there any reason (apart from the police) for continuing to behave well or for aspiring to sainthood? This character in *La Peste* has seen human suffering, and has seen that much of this suffering is due to the cruelty or thoughtlessness of human beings themselves; and the question that he asks himself is whether a belief in God is necessary before one can live a good life, or whether a concern for other people's welfare is enough, and whether this will give a man final peace. Actually, in one of the Suttas, the Buddha more or less answers this question by saying (in effect) that *so long as one believes in God it is not possible to become a saint.* And the reason is quite simple. If God exists, he is responsible—since he created us—for all our actions, good or bad; and so, if I believe in God, I shall not myself feel responsible for my actions, and so I shall have no motive for behaving well rather than badly. (The question of God's responsibility for evil is one that perpetually torments Christian theologians, and they have never found an adequate answer.)

One of the conclusions that this character of Camus arrives at is that if one is going to live well, one can never afford to be distracted. In other words, one must always be mindful. And one of the striking things in the book is the contrast between the deaths of the ordinary victims of the plague, who are indeed no more than, in Huxley's expression, "moaning animals," tossing about on their beds "with no more thoughts, but only pain and vomiting and stupor" between these and the death of this one character who aspires to sainthood and practises mindfulness. Like the others, he dies of plague; but the whole time he is dying (according to Camus' description) he gives the impression of being intelligent and retaining his lucidity right up to the last. He *knows* that he is dying, and he is determined to have "a good death." Naturally, this is only a death in a novel, and we can't take it as necessarily true of real life (did Camus, I wonder, ever see a man trying to die mindfully?); but I myself am rather of the opinion that, if one is *really* determined to make an effort, a great deal can be done towards remaining intelligent at the time of one's death. But I don't suppose that it is very easy unless one has already made a long habit of mindfulness.

26. The autonomous mood (1 January 1965)

A pleasant surprise to get your letter! But how hard it is to communicate! Kierkegaard held that direct communication was impossible, and said (with Dostoievsky) that the surest way of being silent is to talk. I have been reading your letter and trying to grasp its meaning (the words and sentences, of course, are quite clear)—trying, in other words, to get the feel of it, to seize upon its Archimidean point.

Your reference to the autonomous mood in the Irish grammar can perhaps be turned to account, particularly since you yourself go on to suggest that a linguistic approach to the deeper questions of life might be rewarding. There is, in fact, a Sutta in which all the five aggregates (the factors present in all experience) are defined in this very way.

Matter is what *matters*;[25] feeling is what *feels*; perception is what

25. I.e., is afflicted or breaks up—the phrase *ruppatī ti rūpaṃ* is untranslatable into English.

perceives; determinations (or intentions) are what *determine* (or intend); consciousness is what *cognizes* (SN 22:79/S III 86-7).

The ordinary person (the *puthujjana* or "commoner") thinks, "*I* feel; *I* perceive; *I* determine; *I* cognize," and he takes this "I" to refer to some kind of timeless and changeless ego or "self." But the *arahat* has completely got rid of the ego-illusion (the conceit or concept "I am"), and, when he reflects, thinks quite simply, "*feeling* feels; *perception* perceives; *determinations* determine; *consciousness* cognizes." Perhaps this may help you to see how it is that when desire (craving) ceases altogether "the various things just stand there in the world."[26] Obviously they cannot "just stand there in the world" unless they are felt, perceived, determined and cognized (Berkeley's *esse est percipi* is, in principle, quite correct); but for the living *arahat* the question "*Who* feels, perceives, determines, cognizes, the various things?" no longer arises—the various things are felt by feeling, perceived by perception, determined by determinations, and cognized by consciousness; in other words, they are "there in the world" *autonomously* (actually they always were, but the *puthujjana* does not see this since he takes himself for granted). With the breaking up of the *arahat*'s body (his death) all this ceases. (For other people, of course, these things continue unless and until they in their turn, having become arahats, arrive at the end of their final existence.)

A further point. When an *arahat* is *talking* to people he will normally follow linguistic usage and speak of "I" and "me" and "mine" and so on; but he no longer (mis)understands these words as does the *puthujjana*. There is a Sutta (in verse) which I translate (prosaically) as follows:

—A monk who is a worthy one (*arahat*), his task done,
His cankers destroyed, wearing his last body—
Is it because this monk has arrived at conceit
That he might say "*I* say,"
And that he might say "They say *to me*"?

—For one who is rid of conceit there are no ties,
All his ties of conceit are dissolved;

26. See letter 19.

This wise man, having got beyond conceiving,
Might say "*I* say,"
And he might say, "They say *to me*":
Skilled in worldly expressions, knowing about them,
He might use them within the limits of usage.

(SN 1:25/S I 14)

It would be unfair on my part to allow myself to suggest, even by implication, that the Buddha's Teaching is easier to understand than it is; and still more unfair to lead you to suppose that I consider myself capable of benefiting you in any decisive manner. All I can do is to plant a few signposts in your way, in the hope, perhaps, of giving a certain orientation to your thinking that might stand you in good stead later on.

27. Ulysses: a glimpse of futility (7 April 1965)

Your reaction to *Ulysses* (a feeling of sadness) is appropriate and shows that you have not misread the book; but surely the sympathy you feel for the ageing Molly Bloom should be extended to Mr. Bloom himself (and, in a lesser degree, to most of the other characters)? Actually, when I first read the book it was not so much the ageing of the characters that affected me as the ultimate meaninglessness and futility of all their actions and aspirations. They are busy, all of them, seeking their immediate satisfactions, and avoiding their immediate discomforts; and everything that they do—whether it is making money, making music, making love, or simply making water—is quite pointless—in terms, that is to say, of an ultimate purpose or meaning in life. At the time I read it—when I was about twenty—I had already suspected (from my reading of Huxley and others) that there *is* no point in life, but this was still all rather abstract and theoretical. But *Ulysses* gets down to details, and I found I recognized myself, *mutatis mutandis*, in the futile occupations that fill the days of Joyce's characters. And so I came to understand that all our actions, from the most deliberate to the most thoughtless, and without exception, are determined by *present* pleasure and present pain. Even what we pompously call our "duty" is included in this law—if we do our duty, that is only because we should feel uncomfortable if we neglected it, and we seek to avoid discomfort. Even the wise man, who renounces a present pleasure for the sake of a greater pleasure in the future, obeys this law—he enjoys the present pleasure of knowing (or believing) that he is providing for his future pleasure, whereas the foolish man, preferring the present pleasure to his future pleasure, is perpetually gnawed with apprehension about his future. And when I had understood this, the Buddha's statement, "Both now and formerly, monks, it is just suffering that I make known and the cessation of suffering," (MN 22/M I 140) came to seem (when eventually I heard it) the most obvious thing in the world—"What else," I exclaimed, "could the Buddha possibly teach?"

28. Humour (18 May 1965)

Yes, this existence of ours is no laughing matter, and yet we laugh. And the great laughers are not those who least see the grimness. Perhaps, then, laughter is something less simple than the sigh of pure innocent bliss. When do we laugh most spontaneously, with the least affectation? Is it not, possibly, when we have been threatened by some horrible menace and have just escaped by the skin of our teeth? The experience is familiar enough, and we may well take it as a starting point. It seems to suggest that laughter is in some way connected with fear. We are threatened; we fear; the threat passes; we laugh. Let us pursue this idea.

A few weeks ago, at the Hermitage, an unwanted young dog was dumped on the island from the mainland. I watched it, lying on its belly in front of one of the long-resident old curs there, whining and laughing (baring its teeth as dogs do when they are pleased) for all it was worth. Why? Because it actually was pleased? Because it was delighted to meet a new acquaintance? Far from it. There was every probability that it was extremely nervous and apprehensive about its reception by the other dogs, and was doing its utmost to placate them. But why should it laugh? In order, simply, to show the others and to persuade itself that *no danger was threatening*. Its laughter was a mode of conduct, a kind of charm, to keep danger at a distance. Since we laugh when danger passes, danger passes when we laugh—or that, at least, is the idea. The ingratiating grin that some people wear on their face (perhaps we all do at times) is simply to prove to themselves that they are not nervous—when, of course, they are shaking in their boots. So far, so good.

But why do we laugh at jokes? Let us ask, rather, why we tell one another jokes. Might it not be so that we can enjoy the pleasure of escaping from *imaginary* dangers? Most of our jokes, surely, are about somebody else's misfortune, are they not? So-and-so has some unfortunate, humiliating or ridiculous experience, an experience that *might* have happened to us but *actually* happened to somebody else; and the relief we feel that the discomfort was *his*, not *ours*, takes the form of laughter. (Compassion, of course, may inhibit laughter; but some of our jokes are pretty heartless.)

We laugh, then, when fear passes; we laugh as a charm to make fear pass; and we entertain imaginary fears to make ourselves laugh. Now, according to Kierkegaard we laugh when we apprehend a contradiction. Might it not be that a contradiction is something to be feared—that it is, in some way, a *threat*?

Heidegger tells us that we normally exist in a state of "fallenness." By this he means that most men hide from themselves by identifying themselves with the anonymous "one" or "they" or "the Others" and people in general. This kind of existence Heidegger calls "inauthenticity"; and it is what Sartre calls "serious-mindedness". It is the inauthentic, the serious-minded, the solemn, who are your non-laughers. Or rather, they do laugh—but only at what the "they" have decided is funny. (Look at a copy of *Punch* of a hundred, or even fifty, years ago; you will see how completely the fashion in humour has changed. The "sick joke" was quite unthinkable in Victoria's days—"one" simply did not laugh at that sort of thing, it was "not done.") The inauthentic, absorbed by the world like ink by a blotter,[27] accept their views and values ready made, and go about their daily business doing whatever "is done." And this includes their relaxations. To be "serious-minded" is to go to see comic films and laugh at whomever "one laughs at," and see tragedies and have one's emotions purged by the currently approved emotional purgative—the latest version, perhaps, of *Romeo and Juliet*.

---

27. Cf. the Khajjaniya Sutta (SN 22:79/S III 87–8) where it is said that we are normally "devoured" by matter, feeling, perception, determinations, and consciousness.

Now if we agree with Kierkegaard that both comedy and tragedy are ways of apprehending contradictions, and if we also consider how much importance people attach to these things, we shall perhaps suspect that contradiction is a factor to be reckoned with in everyday life. But all this is on the inauthentic level, and to get more light on the question we must consider what Heidegger means by "authenticity."

Our existence, says Heidegger, is *care*: we are concerned positively or negatively for ourselves and for others. This care can be described but it cannot be accounted for—it is primordial and we just have to accept it as it is. (Compare here the Buddha's statement [AN 10:62/A V 116] that there is no first point to *bhavataṇhā*, "craving for being." The difference is that whereas Heidegger sees no way of getting rid of it, the Buddha *does* see the way and has followed it.) Care, says Heidegger, can be "lived" in either of two modes: authentic or inauthentic. The authentic man faces himself reflexively and sees himself in his existential solitude—he sees that he is *alone* in the world—whereas the inauthentic man takes refuge from this disquieting reflexion of himself in the anonymous security of people-in-general, of the "they." The inauthentic man is fleeing from authenticity—from *angst*, that is to say, or "anxiety"; for anxiety is the state of the authentic man (remember that Heidegger is describing the *puthujjana*, and he sees no way out of anxiety, which, for him, is the mark of the lucid man facing up to himself). But the normally smooth surface of the public world of the "they" sometimes shows cracks, and the inauthentic man is pierced by pangs of anxiety, recalling him for a moment or two to the state of authenticity. Chief amongst these is the apprehension of the possibility of death, which the inauthentic man suddenly realizes is *his* possibility (death, of course, is certain: but this simply means that *at any moment it is possible*). He is torn from his complacent anonymity and brought up against the hard fact that he is an *individual*, that he himself is totally responsible for everything that he does, and that he is sure to die. The hitherto friendly and sheltering world suddenly becomes indifferent to him and meaningless in its totality. But this shattering experience is usually fleeting, and the habitually inauthentic man returns quickly enough to his anonymity.

At this point let us see what the Suttas have to say about *angst* or anxiety (*paritassanā*). In the Alagaddupama Sutta (MN 22/M I 136–7) a monk asks the Buddha, "Can there be anxiety, lord, about objective absence?" The Buddha says that there can be such anxiety, and describes a man grieving about the way his possessions slip away from him. Then the monk asks, "Can there be anxiety, lord, about subjective absence?," and again the Buddha says that there can. In this case we have a *sassatavādin*, holding himself and the world to be eternal, who hears about extinction (*nibbāna*) and apprehends it as annihilation. These two aspects, objective and subjective, are combined in the Uddesavibhaṅga Sutta (MN 138/M III 227–8), a passage from which I translate as follows:

> And how, friends, is there anxiety at not holding? Here, friends, an uninstructed commoner, unseeing of the nobles, ignorant of the noble Teaching, undisciplined in the noble Teaching, unseeing of good men, ignorant of the good men's Teaching, undisciplined in the good men's Teaching, regards matter (feeling, perception, determinations, consciousness) as self, or self as endowed with matter (... consciousness), or matter (... consciousness) as belonging to self, or self as in matter (... consciousness). That matter (... consciousness) of his changes and becomes otherwise; as that matter (... consciousness) changes and becomes otherwise, so his consciousness follows around (keeps track of) that change of matter (... consciousness); anxious ideas that arise born of following around that change of matter (... consciousness) seize upon his mind and become established; with that mental seizure, he is perturbed and disquieted and concerned, and from not holding he is anxious. Thus, friends, there is anxiety at not holding.

This, you will see, fairly well confirms Heidegger's view of anxiety; and the more so when he makes the distinction that, whereas fear is shrinking in the face of something, anxiety is shrinking in the face of—nothing. Precisely. We experience anxiety when we find that the solid foundation upon which our precious and familiar self rests—upon which it *must* rest—*is not there.* Anxiety is shrinking in the face of a contradiction—or rather, not *a* contradiction, but *the* contradiction. *This* is the contradiction that we fear; *this* is the contradiction that threatens us in our innermost being—the agonizing possibility that, after all, we have *no* being, and that we *are not*. And *now* we can see why all the seemingly little contradictions at which we laugh (or weep) in our everyday life are really veiled threats, sources of danger. These are the little cracks and fissures in our complacent serious-minded existence, and the reason why we laugh at them is to keep them at a distance, to charm them, to exorcise them, to neutralize them—just as the young dog at the Hermitage laughed at the older one to ward off danger.

Anxiety—shrinking before nothing—is the father of all particular fears—shrinking before this or that. (Heidegger emphasizes that the prior condition to all fear is anxiety. We *can* fear only because we are fleeing from anxiety.) And the contradiction between our *eternal* self and its *temporal* foundation is the father of all particular contradictions between this and that. Whether we laugh because we have just crawled out unscathed from a car smash, or wear a sheepish grin when the boss summons us to his office, or split our sides when we hear how Jones had his wife seduced by Smith, or smile when we see a benevolent tourist giving a few cents out of compassion to an ill-dressed but extremely wealthy *mudhalali*—it can all be traced back to our inherent desire to fly from anxiety, from the agonized recognition that our very being is perpetually in question. And when we laugh at a comedy or weep at a tragedy what we are *really* doing is busying ourselves repairing all the little crevices that have appeared in our familiar world in the course of the day or the week, which, if neglected, might become wider and deeper, and eventually bring our world crashing down in ruins about us. Of course, we don't actually admit to ourselves that this is what we are doing; and the reason is that inauthentic existence is a *degraded* mode of existence, where the true nature of things is concealed—or rather, *where we conceal the true nature of things from ourselves.* Obviously, the more serious-minded one is, the less one will be willing to admit the existence of these cracks and crevices in the surface of the world, and consequently one will take good care not to look too closely—and, of course, since laughter is already a tacit admission of the existence of such things, one will regard all kinds of levity as positively immoral.

Without leaving the sphere of the *puthujjana,* let us turn to the habitually authentic man—one who is anxious, and lucid in his anxiety, who keeps perpetually before him (though without being able to resolve it) the essential contradiction in human existence. Once one has accepted anxiety as one's normal and proper state, then one faces the contradiction, and this, *granted* the anxiety, neither as plain tragic nor as plain comic, but as tragicomic. This, of course, can be put in several ways (you can do it yourself). This is perhaps as good as any: it is tragic that we should take as meaningful a world that is actually meaningless, but comic that the world we take as meaningful should actually be meaningless.

Man is a discrepant combination of the *infinite* and the *finite.* Man, as he looks at himself, sees himself as pathetic ("pathos" in the sense of "passion," as in "so-and-so is passionately interested in his work") or as comic, according as he looks towards the eternal or towards the world. The tragicomedy of the human (*puthujjana*'s) situation as apprehended by the authentic man in his lucid anxiety is the source of all tragedy and comedy on the purely everyday level. And, whereas the inauthentic man laughs or weeps without knowing why he does so—in other words, *irresponsibly*—the authentic man, when he laughs or weeps, does so *responsibly*. The authentic man, when he laughs at something (it will very often be at the serious-minded man, who is both *very* comic and *very* tragic), will always have the other side of the picture present to mind, as the shadow of his comic apprehension. (And when he weeps, the comic aspect of the situation will be there outlined on the background.) He laughs (and weeps) *with understanding*, and this gives his humour a depth and an ambiguity that escapes the inauthentic man. In consequence of this, the authentic man is able to use his humour as a screen for his more *authentic* seriousness—seriousness, that is to say, about the human, or rather the existentialist paradox (he is looking for the solution and concluding, again and again, that the solution is that there is no solution; and this is the limit of the *puthujjana*'s field of vision.) This sort of thing allows the authentic man to indulge in a kind of humour that horrifies and outrages the inauthentic.

It is obvious enough that there can be no progress in the Dhamma for the inauthentic man. The inauthentic man does not even see the problem—all his effort is devoted to hiding from it. The Buddha's Teaching is not for the serious-minded. Before we deal with the problem we must see it, and that means becoming authentic. But now, when we consider your original question about the relation of humour to the Buddhadhamma, a certain distinction must be made. There is a cardinal difference between the solution to the problem offered by the Buddha and that (or those) offered by other teachings; and this is perhaps best illustrated in the case of Kierkegaard.

Kierkegaard sees that the problem—the essential contradiction, *attā hi attano n'atthi* ("He himself is not his own"), Dhp 62—is in the form of a paradox (or, as Marcel would say, a mystery: a problem that encroaches on its own data). And this is quite right as far as it goes. But he does not see how to resolve it. Further, he concludes (as I have suggested above) that, in this temporal life at least, the solution is that there is no solution. This itself is a reduplication of the original paradox, and only seems to make the problem more acute, to work up the tension, to drive man further back into himself. And, not content with this, he seizes upon the essential Christian paradox—that God became man, that the Eternal became temporal—which he himself calls "absurd," and thus postulates a solution which is, as it were, a kind of paradox cubed, as one might say—(paradox). But as we have seen, the original paradox is tragicomical; it contains within its structure, that is to say, a humorous aspect. And when the paradox is intensified, so is the humorous—and a joke raised to the third power is a very tortuous joke indeed. What I am getting at is this: that in every teaching where the paradox is not resolved (and *a fortiori* where it is intensified), *humour is an essential structural feature.* Perhaps the most striking case is Zen. Zen is above all the cult of the paradox. ("Burn the scriptures!", "Chop up the Buddha image for firewood!", "Go listen to the sound of one hand clapping.'"), and the old Zen masters are professional religious jokers, sometimes with an appalling sense of humour. And all very gay too—but the Buddha alone teaches the resolution of the original paradox, not by wrapping it up in bigger paradoxes, but by *unwrapping* it.

If humour is, as I have suggested, in some way a reaction to fear, then so long as there remains a trace of the contradiction, of the existential paradox, so long will there remain a trace of humour. But since, essentially, the Buddha's Teaching is the cessation of fear (or more strictly of anxiety, the condition of fear), so it leads to the subsidence of humour. Not, indeed, that the *arahat* is humourless in the sense of being serious-minded; far from it; no—it is simply that the *need* he formerly felt for humour has now ceased. And so we find in the Suttas (AN 3:105/A I 261) that whereas excessive laughter "showing the teeth" is called childishness, a smile when one is rightly pleased is not out of place. Perhaps you may like to see here a distinction between inauthentic and authentic humour.

You ask also about play: Sartre observes that in play—or at least in sport—we set ourselves the task of overcoming obstacles or obeying rules that we arbitrarily impose upon ourselves; and he suggests that this is a kind of anti-serious-mindedness. When we are serious-minded we accept the rules and values imposed upon us by the world, by the "they"; and when we have fulfilled these obligations we feel the satisfaction of having "done our duty." In sport it is we who impose the obligations upon ourselves, which enables us to enjoy the satisfaction of fulfilling them, without any of the disadvantages that go along with having to do what "they" expect us to do (for example, we can stop when we are tired—but you just try doing that when you are in the army!). In sport, we play at being *serious*; and this rather suggests that play (sport), like plays (the theatre), is really a way of making repairs in a world that threatens to come apart at the seams. So there probably is some fairly close connexion between play and humour. Certainly, we often laugh when we are at play, but I don't think this applies to such obviously serious-minded activities as Test Matches.

29. Laughter and fear (24 May 1965)

Reflecting on what I wrote a few days ago about humour, it occurs to me that I might have brought out certain aspects of what I had to say rather more clearly—in particular the actual relationship between laughter and fear. I think I merely said that laughter is "in some way a reaction to fear." But this can be defined more precisely. To be "authentic" is to face the existential paradox, the essential contradiction, in a state of lucid anxiety, whereas to be "inauthentic" is to take refuge from this anxiety in the serious

-mindedness of the anonymous "they." But the contradiction is tragicomic; and this (I suggested) is the source of all tragedy and comedy in the everyday world. It follows from this that the inauthentic man, in hiding in his serious-mindedness from the anxiety of contradiction, is actually hiding from the two aspects of existence, the comic and the tragic. From time to time he finds his complacent unseeing seriousness threatened with a contradiction of one kind or another and he *fears*. (The fearful is contradictory, and the contradictory is fearful.)

Pain, of course, is painful whether it is felt by the *puthujjana* or the *arahat*; but the *arahat*, though he may avoid it if he can, does not fear pain; so the *fear* of the inauthentic man in the face of physical danger is not simply the thought "there may be pain." No—he fears for his physical existence. And this is the tragic aspect of the contradiction showing itself. And when the threat passes, the contradiction shows its other face and he laughs. But he does not laugh because he *sees* the comic aspect (that may happen later), his laughter *is* the comic aspect (just as his fear is the tragic aspect): in other words, he is not *reacting to* a contradictory situation, he is *living* it. Tragedy and comedy, fear and laughter: the two sides of a contradiction. But he may be faced with other contradictions to which, because they are less urgent, he *is* able to react. He half-grasps the contradiction *as* a contradiction, and then, *according to the way he is oriented* in life, either laughs or weeps: if he finds the tragic aspect threatening he will laugh (to emphasize the comic and keep the tragic at a distance), and if he finds the comic aspect threatening he will weep. (A passionate woman, who finds life empty and meaningless when she is not emotionally engaged in love—or perhaps hate—and fearing the comic as destructive of her passion, may weep at the very contradiction that provokes laughter in a man who has, perhaps, discovered the ghastly boredom of being loved without loving in return and who regards the comic as his best defence against entanglements.) Laughter, then, is not a so much *reaction* to fear as its *counterpart*.

Another question is that of the *sekha* and anxiety. Granted that he is now fairly confidently authentic, by nature does he still experience anxiety? To some extent, yes; but he has that faculty in himself by means of which, when anxiety arises, he is able to extinguish it. He knows of another escape from anxiety than flight into inauthenticity. He is already leaving behind him both laughter and tears. Here is a passage from SN 22:43/S III 43:

> Having come to know, monks, the impermanence, changeability, absence of lust for and ceasing of matter (feeling, perception, determinations, consciousness), and if matter (... consciousness) formerly was as it is now, then all matter (... consciousness) is impermanent, unpleasurable, of a nature to change. Thus seeing as it actually is with right understanding, whatever is the arising of sorrow, lamentation, pain, grief, and despair, they are eliminated; these, eliminated, there is no anxiety; not having anxiety he dwells at ease; dwelling at ease, this monk is called extinguished.

30 (a). Investigation of laughter (2 June 1965)

Certainly, I quite agree that we often, and perhaps mostly, laugh when no fear is present. But then (though I may not have made myself clear) I did not really want to maintain that fear *is* always present—indeed, I would say, precisely, that we laugh when fear is *absent*. Whenever we laugh—I think you may agree—there is always some contradiction or absurdity lurking in the situation, though this is not usually *explicit*: we laugh in a carefree way, then we may pause and ask ourselves "Now, why did I laugh then?", and finally we see (if we have some reflexive or introspective facility) that what we laughed at was some incongruity—or more precisely, that our laughter was our mode of apprehending that incongruity. What I had in mind, when I associated laughter with fear, was rather this: that every contradiction is essentially a threat (in one way or another) to my existence (i.e. it shakes my complacency); and that fear and laughter are the two alternative modes in which we apprehend a threat. When the threat is advancing and may reach us, we *fear*; when the threat is receding or at a safe distance, we *laugh*. *We laugh when there is no need to fear.*

Children, as you rightly observe, laugh and laugh; and this—as I see it—is often because the child lives in a world where there are grown-up people, and the function of grown-up people—in a child's eyes—is to keep threats at a distance. The child is *protected* from threats; he knows that they will not reach him, that there is nothing to fear, and so he laughs. The sea can be a dangerous thing; but if it is calm, or there is a grown-up about the place, the child can splash about and *play* with this danger because it is merely potential. He pits his puny strength against the vast might of the ocean; and this is a contradiction (or incongruity), which he can apprehend in one of two ways, fear or laughter. If the ocean has the upper hand, he fears, but if he is getting the best of it (he plunges into the sea and emerges unharmed, he splashes, he kicks it, and the sea does not resent it) then he laughs: his laughter shows that "there is nothing to fear," that fear is absent. But it does *not* show that fear is non-existent; merely that it is not there *today*.

You ask, rhetorically, if superiority feelings, "self" feelings, are not at the root of all guilt complexes. Certainly they are. But with guilt goes anxiety (we are superior—or we just "are"—and we are unable, to justify our superiority, our existence, and so we are anxious. Pride goes before a fall—and this is true right back as far as *asmimāna,* the conceit "I am"). And anxiety is anxiety before the essential contradiction, which shows its unfunny aspect. So, as you say, our feeling of superiority inhibits laughter. But it does not necessarily follow that when we lose the superiority we shall laugh along with everybody else. A practised yogin, certainly, particularly if he has been doing *karuṇā* (compassion) is not in the least superior; but it may well be that, by his practice, he has put fear so far from him that he has lost the urge to laugh.

How far our investigation of humour tends to destroy it in the act of investigating it (like atomic physicists when they "observe" an electron), depends principally upon the method used. If we adopt the scientific attitude of "complete objectivity"—actually an impossibility—then we kill it dead, for there is nobody left to laugh. This leads to the idea that jokes are funny in themselves—that they have an intrinsic quality of funniness that can be analysed and written about in a deadly serious manner. The other way is to watch ourselves as we laugh, in a reflexive effort, and then to *describe* the experience. This is the phenomenological (or existential) method of "going direct to the things themselves." Of course, this needs practice; and also it *does* modify the original humour (for example, it tends to bring into view the tacit pathetic background, which is normally hidden when we laugh in the immediate, or inauthentic, mode). Nevertheless, the humour, though modified, is still there, and something useful *can* be said about it—though what is said will be very unlike what is said by the serious-minded university professor who writes his two scholarly volumes. Kierkegaard is insistent upon the principle, *Quidquid cognoscitur, per modum cognoscentis congoscitur,* "Whatever is known is known in the mode of the knower"; and he would say that a serious-minded person is inherently incapable of knowing anything of humour. If we are going to find out what is funny in this or that joke, we must allow ourselves to be amused by it and, while still amused, *describe* our amusement.

30 (b). Existentialist Idiom and Sutta idiom (2 June 1965) (contd.)

Yes, the existentialist idiom is difficult, until you get the feel of it. The difficulty arises from the phenomenological method that I have just been talking about. The scientist (or scholar) becomes "objective," puts himself right out of the picture (Kierkegaard is at his best when he describes this "absent-minded" operation), and concerns himself only with *abstract facts;* the existentialist remains "subjective" (not in the derogatory sense of being irresponsible), keeps himself in the picture, and describes *concrete things* (that is, things in relation to himself as he experiences them). This radical difference in method, naturally enough, is reflected in the kind of language used by the scientist on the one hand and the existentialist on the other—or rather, in the difference in the way they make use of language. I was struck, when I first read Sartre, by the strange sort of resemblance between certain of his expressions and some of the things said in the Suttas. Sartre, for example, has this:

> ... we defined the senses and the sense-organs in general as our being-in-the-world in so far as we have to be it in the form of being-in-the-midst-of-the-world.
>
> (*Being and Nothingness*, p. 325)

In the Suttas (e.g. SN 35:116/S IV 95) we find:

> The eye (ear, nose, tongue, body, mind) is that in the world by which one is a perceiver and conceiver of the world.

Now whatever the respective meanings of these two utterances[28] it is quite clear that despite the twenty-five hundred years that separate them, Sartre's sentence is closer in *manner* of expression (as well as in content) to the Sutta passage than it is to anything produced by a contemporary neuro-physiologist supposedly dealing with precisely the same subject—our sense organs and perception of the world. This remarkable similarity does not oblige us to conclude that Sartre has reached enlightenment, but simply that if we want to understand the Suttas the phenomenological approach is more promising than the objective scientific approach.

Although the existentialist philosophers may seem close to the Buddha's Teaching, I don't think it necessarily follows that they would accept it were they to study it. Some might, some might not. But what often happens is that after years of hard thinking, they come to feel that they have found the solution (even if the solution is that there is none), and they lie back resting on their reputation, or launch themselves into other activities (Marcel has become a Catholic, Sartre is politically active); and so they may feel disinclined to reopen an inquiry that they have already closed to their satisfaction (or dissatisfaction, as the case may be). Besides, it is not so easy to induce them to take up a study of the Dhamma. Even translations of the Suttas are not always adequate, and anyway, they don't practise *samatha bhāvanā*.

I don't want to be dogmatic about the value of a familiarity with the existential doctrines; that is, for an understanding of the Dhamma. Of course, if one has a living teacher who has himself attained (and ideally, of course, the Buddha himself), then the essence of the Teaching can sometimes be conveyed in a few words. But if, as will be the case today, one has no such teacher, then one has to work out for oneself what the Suttas are getting at. And here, an acquaintance with some of these doctrines can be—and, in my case, has been—very useful. But the danger is, that one may adhere to one or other of these philosophers and fail to go beyond to the Buddha. This, certainly, is a very real risk—but the question is, is it a justifiable risk?

---

28. Where the Sutta says "the eye is that in the world ...," Sartre says that we (as our sense-organs) are "amidst-the-world"; and where the Sutta says "one is a perceiver and conceiver of the world," Sartre speaks of "our being-in-the-world."

You say, "Questions that strike a Sartre or a Kierkegaard as obvious, urgent, and baffling may not have ever occurred to Bāhiya Dārucīriya." I am not so sure. I agree that a number of "uneducated" people appear, in the Suttas, to have reached extinction. But I am not so sure that I would call them "simple." You suggest that Bāhiya may not have been a very complex person and that a previous "Sartre" phase may not have been essential for him. Again I don't want to be dogmatic, but it seems to me that your portrait of him is oversimplified. Your quotation of the brief instruction that the Buddha gave Bāhiya is quite in order as far as it goes; but—inadvertently, no doubt—you have only given part of it. Here is the passage in full (Udāna 10: 8):

> Then, Bāhiya, you should train thus: "In the seen there shall be just the seen; in the heard there shall be just the heard; in the sensed there shall be just the sensed; in the cognized there shall be just the cognized"—thus, Bāhiya, should you train yourself. When, Bāhiya, for you, in the seen there shall be just the seen ... cognized, then, Bāhiya, you (will) not (be) that by which (*tvaṃ na tena*); when, Bāhiya, you (shall) not (be) that by which, then, Bāhiya, you (shall) not (be) in that place (*tvaṃ na tattha*); when, Bāhiya, you (shall) not (be) in that place, then, Bāhiya, you (will) neither (be) here nor yonder nor between the two: just this is the end of suffering.

This is a highly condensed statement, and for him simple. It is quite as tough a passage as anything you will find in Sartre. And, in fact, it is clearly enough connected with the passage that I have already quoted alongside a passage from Sartre: "The eye (etc.) is that *in the world by which* one is a perceiver and conceiver of the world."

Let us now try, with the help of Heidegger's indications, to tie up these two Sutta passages.[29]

---

29. Part of the letter not included among these selections includes a discussion of *Being and Time*,* pp. 169-172, particularly of a passage on page 171:

> The entity which is essentially constituted by Being-in-the-world is itself in every case its "there". According to the familiar signification of the word, the "there" points to a "here" and a "yonder". The "here" of an "I—here" is always understood in relation to a "yonder" ready-to-hand, in the sense

(i) To begin with, "I—here" is I as identical with my senses; "here," therefore refers to my sense organs (eye, ear, nose, tongue, body, and also mind). The counterpart of "here" is "yonder," which refers to the various things in the world as sense-objects. "Between the two" will then refer (though Heidegger makes no mention of this) to consciousness, contact, feeling, and so on, as being dependent upon sense organ and sense object—"Dependent upon eye and visible forms, eye-consciousness arises; the coming together of these three is contact; with contact as condition, feeling," etc. (SN 35:107/S IV 87).

(ii) In the second place, Heidegger says that "here" and "yonder" are possible only in a "there"; in other words, that sense-organs and sense-objects, which are "amidst-the-world," in Sartre's phrase, are possible only if there *is* a world for them to be "amidst." "There," then, refers to the world. So the "here and yonder" and the "there" of the Bāhiya Sutta correspond in the other Sutta to the "eye (and so on)" as "that in the world ..."

(iii) But Heidegger goes on to say that there is a "there" only if there is an entity that has made a disclosure of spatiality as the being of the "there"; and that being-there's existential spatiality is grounded in being-in-the-world. This simply means that, in the very act of *being*, I disclose a spatial world: my being is always in the form of a spatial being-there. (In spite of the Hindus and Hegel, there is no such thing as "pure being." All being is limited and particularized—if I *am* at all, I am in a spatial world.) In brief,

---

of a Being towards this "yonder"—a Being which is deseverant, directional, and concernful. Dasein's existential spatiality, which thus determines its "location", is itself grounded in Being-in-the-world. The "yonder" and belongs definitely to something encountered within-the-world. "Here" and "yonder" are possible only in a "there"—that is to say, only if there is an entity which has made a disclosure of spatiality as the Being of the "there." This entity carries in its ownmost Being the character of not being closed off. In the expression "there" we have in view this essential disclosedness. By reason of this disclosedness, this entity (Dasein), together with the Being-there of the world, is "there" for itself.

(* *Being and Time*, a translation by J. Macquarrie and E. S. Robinson of *Sein und Zeit*, by Martin Heidegger (London: SCM Press, 1982; New York: Harper and Row, 1962).)

there is only a "there," a spatial world (for senses and objects to be "amidst"), if *I am there.* Only so long as *I am there* shall I be "in the form of being-amidst-the-world"—i.e. as sense-organs ("here") surrounded by sense-objects ("yonder").

(iv) But on what does this "I am there" depend? "I am there" means "I am in the world"; and I am "in the world" in the form of senses (as eye ... mind). And Heidegger tells us that the "here" (i.e. the senses) is always understood in relation to a "yonder" ready-to-hand, i.e. something that is *for* some purpose (of mine). I, as my senses, "am towards" this "yonder"; I am "a being that is deseverant, directional, and concernful." I won't trouble you with details here, but what Heidegger means by this is *more or less* what the Venerable Ānanda Thera means when he said that "The eye (and so on) is that ... by which one is a perceiver and a conceiver of the world." In other words, not only am *I in the world*, but I am *also*, as my senses, that *by which* there is a world in which I am. "I am there" *because* "I am that by which there is an I-am-there"; and consequently, when "I shall not be that by which," then "I shall not be there." And when "I shall not be there," then "I shall neither be here nor yonder nor between the two."

(v) And *when* shall we "not be that by which?" This, Heidegger is not able to tell us. But the Buddha tells us: it is when, for us, in the seen there shall be just the seen, and so with the heard, the sensed, and the cognized. And when in the seen is there just the seen? When the seen is no longer seen as "mine" (*etaṃ mama*) or as "I" (*eso'ham asmi*) or as "my self" (*eso me atta*): in brief, when there is no longer, in connexion with the senses, the conceit "I am," *by which* "I am a conceiver of the world."

So, although it would certainly be going too far to suggest that Bāhiya had already undergone a course of existentialist philosophy, the fact remains that he was capable of understanding at once a statement that says more, and says it more briefly, than the nearest comparable statement either in Heidegger or Sartre. Bāhiya, I allow, may not have been a cultured or sophisticated man-of-the-world; but I see him as a very subtle thinker. Authenticity may be the answer, as you suggest; but an authentic man is not a *simple* person—he is *self-transparent* if you like, which is quite another matter.

31. Who judges? And with what as standard? (2 July 1965)

About your query—the "Q.E.D." at the end gives it rather a rhetorical air, and it looks as if it might have been aimed at me as a knockout punch. Let me see if there is anything left for me to say.

> **Query**: If all things are adjudged as characterized by *dukkha*, who does the judging? And with reference to what criterion or norm? A *subject* (immortal soul) with reference to an objective *sukha*, no? Q.E.D.

You ask "Who does the judging?" This question takes for granted that judging is done "by somebody." But this is by no means a foregone conclusion: we are quite able to give an account of judgement (or knowing) without finding ourselves obliged to set it up as "a relation between subject and object." Knowledge is essentially an *act of reflexion*, in which the "thing" to be known presents itself (is presented) *explicitly* as standing out against a background (or in a context) that was already there implicitly. In reflexion, a (limited) totality is given, consisting of a centre and a periphery—a particular cow appears surrounded by a number of cattle, and there is the judgement, "The cow is in the herd." Certainly, there is an *intention* to judge, and this consists in the deliberate withdrawal of attention from the immediate level of experience to the reflexive; but the question is not whether judgement is an intentional action (which it is), but whether there can be intention (even reflexive intention) without a subject ("I", "myself") who intends. This, however, is not so much a matter of argument as something that has to be seen for oneself.

Of course, since knowledge is very commonly (Heidegger adds "and superficially") defined in terms of "a relation between subject and object," the question of the subject cannot simply be brushed aside—no smoke without fire—and we have to see (at least briefly) why it is so defined. Both Heidegger and Sartre follow Kant in saying that, properly speaking, there is no knowledge other than intuitive; and I agree. But what is intuition? From a *puthujjana*'s point of view, it can be described as immediate contact between subject and object, between "self" and the "world." This, however, is not yet knowledge, for which a reflexive reduplication is needed;

but when there is this reflexive reduplication we then have intuitive knowledge, which is (still for the *puthujjana*) immediate contact between *knowing* subject and *known* object. With the *arahat*, however, all question of subjectivity has subsided, and we are left simply with (the presence of) the *known thing.* (It is *present,* but no longer present "to somebody.") So much for judgement in general.

But now you say, "If all things are characterized by *dukkha* ..." This needs careful qualification. In the first place, the universal *dukkha* you refer to here is obviously not the *dukkha* of rheumatism or a toothache, which is by no means universal. It is, rather, the *saṅkhāra-dukkha* (the unpleasure or suffering connected with determinations) of this Sutta passage:

> There are, monks, three feelings stated by me: *sukha* feeling, *dukkha* feeling, *neither-dukkha-nor-sukha* feeling. These three feelings have been stated by me. But this, monk, has been stated by me: whatever is felt, that counts as *dukkha.* But that, monk, was said by me with reference just to the impermanence of determinations ...
>
> (SN 36:11/S IV 216)

But what is this *dukkha* that is bound up with impermanence? It is the *implicit* taking as pleasantly-permanent (perhaps "eternal" would be better) of what actually is impermanent. And things are implicitly taken as pleasantly-permanent (or eternal) when they are taken (in one way or another) as "I" or "mine" (since, as you rightly imply, ideas of subjectivity are associated with ideas of immortality). And the *puthujjana* takes *all* things in this way. So, for the *puthujjana,* all things are (*saṅkhāra-*) *dukkha.* How then—and this seems to be the crux of your argument—how then does the *puthujjana* see or know (or adjudge) that "all things are *dukkha*" unless there is some *background* (or criterion or norm) of *non-dukkha* (i.e. of *sukha*) *against which* all things stand out as *dukkha?* The answer is quite simple: he does *not* see or know (or adjudge) that "all things are *dukkha.*" The *puthujjana* has *no* criterion or norm for making any such judgement, and so he does not make it. The *puthujjana's* experience is (*saṅkhāra-*) *dukkha* from top to bottom, and the consequence is that he has no way of knowing *dukkha* for himself; for however much he "steps back" from himself in a reflexive effort he still takes *dukkha* with him. The whole point is that the *puthujjana*'s non-knowledge of *dukkha is* the *dukkha* that he has non-knowledge of;[30] and this *dukkha* that is at the same time non-knowledge of *dukkha* is the *puthujjana*'s (mistaken) acceptance of what seems to be a "self" or "subject" or "ego" at its face value (as *nicca/sukha/attā*, permanent/pleasant/self).

And how, then, does knowledge of *dukkha* come about? How it is with a Buddha I can't say (though it seems from the Suttas to be a matter of prodigiously intelligent trial-by-error over a long period); but in others it comes about by their hearing (as *puthujjanas*) the Buddha's Teaching, which goes *against* their whole way of thinking. They accept out of trust (*saddhā*) this teaching of *anicca/dukkha/anattā*; and it is *this* that, being accepted, becomes the criterion or norm with reference to which they eventually come to see for themselves that all things are *dukkha*—for the *puthujjana*. But in seeing this they cease to be *puthujjanas* and, to the extent that they cease to be *puthujjanas*,[31] to *that* extent *saṅkhāra-dukkha* ceases, and to *that* extent also they have in all their experience a "built-in" criterion or norm by reference to which they make further progress. (The *sekha*—no longer a *puthujjana* but not yet an *arahat*—has a kind of "double vision," one part unregenerate, the other regenerate.) As soon as one becomes a *sotāpanna* one is possessed of *apara-paccaya-ñāṇaṃ* or "knowledge that does not depend upon anyone else"; this knowledge is also said to be "not shared by *puthujjanas*," and the man who has it has (except for accelerating his progress) no further need to hear the Teaching—in a sense he *is* (in part) that Teaching.

30. In one Sutta (MN 44/M I 303) it is said that neither-*dukkha*-nor-*sukha* feeling (i.e. in itself neutral) is *dukkha* when not known and *sukha* when known.

31. Strictly, only those are *puthujjanas* who are wholly *puthujjanas*, who have nothing of the *arahat* at all in them. But on ceasing to be a *puthujjana* one is not at once an *arahat*; and we can perhaps describe the intermediate (three) stages as partly one and partly the other: thus the *sotāpanna* would be three-quarters *puthujjana* and one-quarter *arahat*.

Pali-English Glossary

anāgāmitā—non-returning
ānāpānasati—mindfulness of breathing
anattā—not-self
aññā—the *arahat*'s knowledge
arahat—one who is worthy (usually untranslated)
arahatta—worthiness
ariyapuggala—noble individual
ariyasāvaka—noble disciple
asmimāna—the conceit "I am"
attā—Self
avidyā (Sanskrit)—ignorance
avijjā—nescience; ignorance
bhavataṇhā—craving for being
bhikkhu—monk
bhikkhunī—nun
deva—deity
dibbacakkhu—divine eye
diṭṭhipatta—attained through view
dukkha—suffering, unpleasure
iddhi—accomplishment; power (usu. supernormal)
jhāna—meditation (more specifically, four levels of meditation attainable by an accomplished meditator)
kāmataṇhā—craving for sensuality
kamma—action
karuṇā—compassion
kāyasakkhi—body-witness
maithuna (Sanskrit)—sex
māna—conceit
māyā—(Sanskrit)—illusion
mettā—friendliness
mudhalali—(Sinhalese)—shopkeeper
nibbāna—extinction
nicca—permanent
nirodhasamāpatti—attainment of cessation (of perception and feeling); an attainment available to certain arahats and *anāgāmins*

paññā—understanding
parinibbāna—complete extinction
paritassanā—anxiety
prakriti—(Sanskrit)—nature
purusha—(Sanskrit)—the person
puthujjana—commoner; an unenlightened person
saddhā—faith; trust
saddhāvimutta—released through faith
sakadāgāmita—once-returning
sakkāyadiṭṭhi—personality-view (the view that there is a self to be found)
samādhi—concentration
samatha—calmness; mental concentration
samathabhāvanā—development of calmness
saṃsāra—running on (from existence to existence)
saṅkhāra—determination
sāsana—advice; usu. used today in the sense of "the Buddha's Dispensation"
sassatavādin—one who holds that self and the world are eternal; opposed to the *ucchedavādin*, who holds that both are non-eternal
sati—mindfulness
satisampajañña—mindfulness-and-awareness
sekha—trainee; one in training (to become an *arahat*)
shakti—(Sanskrit)—power
sotāpanna—stream-attainer
sotāpatti—attaining of the stream
sukha—pleasure
taṇhā—craving
upekkhā—indifference
yoni—(Sanskrit)—vagina

Gemstones of the Good Dhamma

(*Saddhamma-maniratana*)

An Anthology of Verses
from the Pali Scriptures

Compiled and translated by
Ven. S. Dhammika

WHEEL PUBLICATION NO. 342/343/344

Preface

The discourses of the Buddha and his direct disciples have been collected together into a huge body of literature known as the *Sutta Pitaka*. Made up of both prose and verse, much of this literature is little known to the average Buddhist because of its great size and also because in both style and content it is highly philosophical. One selection of this literature is, however, very well known. It is the *Dhammapada*, a collection of four hundred and twenty-three verses on various aspects of the Buddha's teachings. The Dhammapada's convenient size, pithy wisdom and, at times, great beauty has made it by far the most popular book in the *Sutta Pitaka*.

However, many other verses of equal relevance and appeal are to be found scattered throughout the *Sutta Pitaka*, which remain virtually unknown. I thought it useful, therefore, to collect some of these verses, arrange them according to subject, and present them in such a way that they may enrich the faith and deepen the understanding of those who read them. Most of the verses are the words of the Buddha himself; a lesser number is attributed to his enlightened disciples. But even these reflect the spirit of the Buddha's *Dhamma*, for it is said: "That which is well spoken is the word of the Buddha." (A IV 164).

This small work is dedicated to my good friend, Miss Constance Sandham. May this *Gemstones of the Good Dhamma* illuminate the path so that all beings may attain Nibbana!

Gemstones of the Good Dhamma

1. Āyācanā	**Request**
1. *Namo te purisājañña* *namo te purisuttama* *sadevakasmiṃ lokasmiṃ* *natthi te paṭipuggalo*	Homage to you so nobly bred. Homage to you amongst men supreme. Peerless are you in all the world. May all worship be given to you.
2. *Namo te buddha vīr'atthu* *vippamutto'si sabbadhi* *sambādhapaṭippanno 'smi* *tassa me saraṇaṃ bhava.*	Homage to you, Enlightened Hero, you who are completely free. I have fallen into great distress, be my refuge and my shelter.
3. *Passām'ahaṃ devamanussaloke* *akiñcanaṃ brāhmaṇaṃ iriyamānaṃ* *taṃ taṃ namassāmi samantacakkhu* *pamuñca maṃ Sakka kathaṃkathāhi.*	In the world of gods and men, I see this brahmin true, this simple man. You I worship, All-Seeing One, so free me, Sakka,[1] from my doubts.
4. *Anusāsa brahme karuṇāyamāno* *vivekadhammaṃ yaṃ ahaṃ vijaññaṃ* *yathāhaṃ ākāso va avyāpajjamāno* *idh'eva santo asito careyyaṃ.*	O Brahmā,[2] out of compassion teach me the lofty Dhamma so I may understand, and relying on nothing else, may live unclouded like the sky.
5. *Ye ca saṅkhātadhammāse* *ye ca sekhā puthū idha* *tesaṃ me nipako iriyaṃ* *puṭṭho pabrūhi mārisā.*	Those who have understood the Dhamma and those who train themselves in it: O wise and truly gracious one, tell me how they live their lives.

1. Sakka (Sakya): The Buddha's clan name.
2. Brahmā: he addresses the Buddha by the name of a deity.

2. Dhammavagga **Dhamma**

6. *Kittayissāmi te dhammaṃ*
diṭṭhe dhamme anītihaṃ
yaṃ viditvā sato caraṃ
tare loke visattikaṃ.

I will teach you a Dhamma,
not hearsay but to be directly seen.
Whoever discovers it and knows it
and lives by it with mindfulness,
will transcend craving for the world.

7. *Suvijāno bhavaṃ hoti*
suvijāno parābhavo
Dhammakāmo bhavaṃ hoti
dhammadessī parābhavo.

Prosperity in life is plain,
decline in life is also plain:
one who loves the Dhamma prospers,
one who hates the Dhamma declines.

8. *Yo ca dhammaṃ abhiññāya*
dhammaṃ aññāya paṇḍito
rahado va nivāto ca
anejo vūpasammati.

Thoroughly understanding the Dhamma
and freed from longing through insight,
the wise one rid of all desire
is calm as a pool unstirred by wind.

9. *Yesaṃ dhammā asammuṭṭhā*
paravādesu na nīyare
te sambuddhā sammadaññā
caranti visame samaṃ.

Those to whom the Dhamma is clear
are not led into other doctrines;
perfectly enlightened with perfect knowledge,
they walk evenly over the uneven.

10. *Na udakena sucī hoti*
bahv ettha nhāyatī jano
yamhi saccañ-ca dhammo ca
so sucī so ca brāhmaṇo.

Not by water is one made pure
though many people may here bathe,[3]
but one in whom there is truth and Dhamma,
he is pure, he is a brahmin.

11. *Ujuko nāma so maggo*
abhayā nāma sā disā
ratho akujano nāma
dhammacakkehi saṃyutto.

The path is called "straight,"
"without fear" is the destination;
the carriage is called "silent"
and its wheels are right effort.

---

3. The Buddha's contemporaries believed that people could be purified by bathing in sacred rivers.

12. *Hirī tassa apālambo* *saty-assa parivāraṇaṃ* *dhammāhaṃ sārathiṃ brūmi* *sammādiṭṭhipure javaṃ.*	Conscience is the rails and mindfulness the upholstery, Dhamma is the driver and right view runs ahead of it.
13. *Yassa etādisaṃ yānaṃ* *itthiyā purisassa vā* *sa ve etena yānena* *nibbānassa'eva santike.*	And whether it be a woman, or whether it be a man, whoever travels by this carriage shall draw close to Nibbāna.
14. *Ye keci osadhā loke* *vijjanti vividhā bahū* *dhammosadhasamaṃ natthi* *etaṃ pivatha bhikkhavo.*	Of all the medicines in the world, manifold and various, there is none like the medicine of Dhamma: therefore, O monks, drink of this.
15. *Dhammosadhaṃ pivitvāna* *ajarāmaraṇā siyuṃ* *bhāvayitvā ca passitvā* *nibbutā upadhikkhaye.*	Having drunk this Dhamma medicine, you will be ageless and beyond death; having developed and seen the truth, you will be quenched, free from craving.
3. Kilesavagga	**The Defilements**
16. *Kāmayogena saṃyuttā* *bhavayogena cūbhayaṃ* *diṭṭhiyogena saṃyuttā* *avijjāya purakkhatā* *sattā gacchanti saṃsāraṃ* *jātimaraṇagāmino.*	Bound by desire, tied to becoming, fettered tightly by false opinions, yoked to ignorance, whirled about: thus beings wander through saṃsāra, dying only to be born again.
17. *Na hiraññasuvaṇṇena* *parikkhīyanti āsavā* *amittā vadhakā kāmā* *sapattā sallabandhanā.*	Neither gold nor minted coins can make the defilements disappear. Sense desires are enemies and killers, hostile darts, rigid bonds.
18. *Ummādanā ullapanā* *kāmā cittapamathino* *sattānaṃ saṅkilesāya* *khippaṃ mārena oḍḍitaṃ.*	Desire is agitating and deceiving, a source of mental pain, a net cast out by Māra[4] to entangle and defile beings.

4. Mara: the Tempter, the Evil One.

19. *Pabbatassa suvaṇṇassa*
jātarūpassa kevalo
dvittā va nālaṃ ekassa
iti vidvā samañcare.

Were there a mountain all made of gold,
doubled that would not be enough
to satisfy a single man:
know this and live accordingly.

20. *Kodhano dubbaṇṇo hoti*
atho dukkhaṃ pi seti so
atho atthaṃ gahetvāna
anatthaṃ adhipajjati
tato kāyena vācāya.
vadhaṃ katvāna kodhano.

How ugly is the angry man!
His sleep is without comfort;
despite his wealth he is always poor.
Filled with anger as he is, he wounds
by acts of body and speech.

21. *Hantā labhati hantāraṃ*
jetāraṃ labhate jayaṃ
akkosako ca akkosaṃ
rosetārañ-ca rosako
atha kammavivaṭṭena
so vilutto vilumpati.

One who kills gets a killer,
one who conquers gets a conqueror,
one who reviles gets reviled.
Thus as a result of his own actions
the spoiler will in turn be spoiled.

22. *Natth'añño ekadhammo pi*
yeneva nivutā pajā
saṃsaranti ahorattaṃ
yathā mohena āvutā.

There is no other single thing
by which the human race is hindered,
by which it wanders day and night,
so much as by this: delusion.

23. *Imesu kira sajjanti*
eke samanabrāhmaṇā
viggayha naṃ vivadanti
janā ekaṅgadassino.

How they cling and how they wrangle,
yet claim to be recluses and brahmins.
Quarrelling and clinging to their opinions,
they see only one side of things.

24. *Ye ca rattiṃ divā yuttā*
sammāsambuddhasāsane
te nibbāpenti rāgaggiṃ
niccaṃ asubhasaññino.

Those who apply themselves day and night
to the teachings of the Buddha
will quench the burning fire of lust
by the perception of the impure.

25. *Dosaggiṃ pana mettāya* *nibbāpenti naruttamā* *mohaggiṃ pana paññāya* *yāyaṃ nibbedhagāminī.*	By love they will quench the fire of hate, by wisdom the fire of delusion. Those supreme men extinguish delusion with wisdom that breaks through to truth.
4. Dānavagga	**Giving**
26. *Na samaṇe na brāhmaṇe* *na kapaṇaddhikavaṇibbake* *laddhāna saṃvibhājeti* *annaṃ pānañca bhojanaṃ* *taṃ ve avuṭṭhikasamo'ti* *āhu naṃ purisādhamam.*	Not with recluses or brahmins, neither with the poor and needy does the base man share his food or give any drink or sustenance. People say that selfish man is like a drought, a rainless sky.
27. *Ekaccānaṃ na dadāti* *Ekaccānaṃ pavecchati* *taṃ ve padesavassīti* *āhu medhāvino janā.*	One who shares his wealth with some, but does not gladly give to others, is only like a local shower: in such a way the wise describe him.
28. *Subhikkhavāco puriso* *sabbabhūtānukampako* *āmodamāno pakireti* *detha dethā ti bhāsati.*	But one who rains down bountiful gifts, gladly giving here and there out of compassion for all beings, and who always says "Give, give, ..."
29. *Yathāpi megho thanayitvā* *gajjayitvā pavassati* *thalaṃ ninnañca pūreti* *abhisandanto va vārinā* *evaṃ eva idh'ekacco* *puggalo hoti tādiso.*	This type of person is like a giant cloud filled with rain, thundering and pouring down refreshing water everywhere, drenching the highlands and lowlands too, generous without distinctions.
30. *Dhammena saṃharitvāna* *utthānādhigataṃ dhanaṃ* *tappeti annapānena* *sammā satte vaṇibbake.*	With his wealth collected justly, won through his own efforts, he shares both food and drink with beings who are in need.

31. *Yathāpi kumbho sampuṇṇo* *yassa kassaci adhokato* *vamate udakaṃ nissesaṃ* *na tattha parirakkhati.*	Just as a pot filled with water if overturned by anyone, pours out all its water and does not hold any back,
32. *Tath'eva yācake disvā* *hīnamukkaṭṭhamajjhime* *dadāhi dānaṃ nissesaṃ* *kumbho viya adhokato.*	Even so, when you see those in need, whether low, middle or high, then give like the overturned pot, holding nothing back.
33. *Dānañ-ca peyyavajjañ-ca* *atthacariyā ca yā idhā* *samānattatā dhammesu* *tattha tattha yathārahaṃ* *ete kho saṅgahā loke* *rathass'āṇī va yāyato.*	Generosity, kind words, doing a good turn for others, and treating all people alike: these bonds of sympathy are to the world what the lynch-pin is to the chariot wheel.
34. *Annado balado hoti* *vatthado hoti vaṇṇado* *yānado sukhado hoti* *dīpado hoti cakkhudo.*	Giving food one gives strength, giving clothes one gives beauty, giving transport one gives delight, giving lamps one gives sight,
35. *So ca sabbadado hoti* *yo dadāti upassayaṃ* *amataṃ dado ca so hoti* *yo dhammaṃ anusāsati.*	Giving shelter one gives all; but one who instructs in the Dhamma, the excellent teaching of the Buddha, such a person gives ambrosia.
5. Sīlavagga	**Virtue**
36. *Sīlaṃ ev'idha sikkhetha* *asmiṃ loke susikkhitaṃ* *sīlaṃ hi sabbasampattiṃ* *upanāmeti sevitaṃ.*	Here in the world one should train carefully to purify virtue; for virtue when well cultivated brings all success to hand.
37. *Yo pāṇaṃ nātipāteti* *musāvādaṃ na bhāsati* *loke adinnaṃ nādiyati* *paradāraṃ na gacchati.*	Not harming living beings, not speaking lies, taking nothing in all the world unasked, nor going to the wives of other men,

38. *Surāmerayapānaṃ ca* *yo naro nānuyuñjati* *pahāya pañca verāni* *sīlavā iti vuccati.*	And never drinking intoxicants: One who gives up these five harmful acts and does not engage in them is truly called a virtuous man.
39. *Ādi sīlaṃ patiṭṭhā ca* *kalyāṇānañ-ca mātukaṃ* *pamukhaṃ sabbadhammānaṃ* *tasmā sīlaṃ visodhaye.*	Virtue is the foundation, the forerunner and origin of all that is good and beautiful; therefore one should purify virtue.
40. *Sīlaṃ balaṃ appaṭimaṃ* *sīlaṃ āvudham-uttamaṃ* *sīlaṃ ābharaṇaṃ seṭṭhaṃ* *sīlaṃ kavacam-abbhūtaṃ.*	Virtue is a mighty power, Virtue is a mighty weapon, Virtue is the supreme adornment, Virtue is a wonderful armour.
41. *Na jaccā vasalo hoti* *na jaccā hoti brāhmaṇo* *kammanā vasalo hoti* *kammanā hoti brahmaṇo.*	One is not low because of birth nor does birth make one holy. Deeds alone make one low, deeds alone make one holy.
42. *Anaṅgaṇassa posassa* *niccaṃ sucigavesino* *vālaggamattaṃ pāpassa* *abbhāmattaṃ va khāyati.*	To one who is without evil, always striving for purity, a wrong the size of a hair tip seems as big as a rain cloud.
43. *Puññaṃ eva so sikkheyya* *āyataggaṃ sukhudrayaṃ* *dānañca samacariyañca* *mettacittañ-ca bhāvaye.*	Train yourself in doing good that lasts and brings happiness. Cultivate generosity, the life of peace, and a mind of boundless love.
44. *Sīlaṃ ajarasā sādhu* *saddhā sādhu adhiṭṭhitā* *paññā narānaṃ ratanaṃ* *puññaṃ corehyahāriyaṃ.*	The good luck of virtue never fades, faith also brings great good. Wisdom is man's most precious gem, merit no thief can ever steal.
45. *Sabbadā sīlasampanno* *paññavā susamāhito* *ajjhattacintī satimā* *oghaṃ tarati duttaraṃ.*	In every virtue all-accomplished, with wisdom full and mind composed, looking within and ever mindful - thus one crosses the raging flood.

6. Vācāvagga	Speech
46. *Purisassa hi jātassa* *kuṭhārī jāyate mukhe* *yāya chindati attānaṃ* *bālo dubbhāsitaṃ bhaṇaṃ.*	Every fool who is born has an axe within his mouth with which he cuts himself when he uses wrong speech.
47. *Taṃ eva vācaṃ bhāseyya* *yay'attānaṃ na tāpaye* *pare ca na vihiṃseyya* *sā ve vācā subhāsitā.*	One should utter only words which do no harm to oneself and cause no harm for others: that is truly beautiful speech.
48. *Piyavācaṃ eva bhāseyya* *yā vācā paṭinanditā* *yaṃ anādāya pāpāni* *paresaṃ bhāsate piyaṃ.*	Speak kind words, words rejoiced at and welcomed, words that bear ill-will to none; always speak kindly to others.
49. *Tass'eva tena pāpiyo* *yo kuddhaṃ paṭikujjhati* *kuddhaṃ appaṭikujjhanto* *saṅgāmaṃ jeti dujjayaṃ.*	The worse of the two is he who, when abused, retaliates. One who does not retaliate wins a battle hard to win.
50. *Jayaṃ ve maññati bālo* *vācāya pharusaṃ bhaṇaṃ* *jayañc'ev'assa taṃ hoti* *ya titikkhā vijānato.*	The fool thinks he has won a battle when he bullies with harsh speech, but knowing how to be forbearing alone makes one victorious.
51. *Yaṃ samaṇo bahu bhāsati* *upetaṃ atthasaṃhitaṃ* *jānaṃ so dhammaṃ deseti* *jānaṃ so bahu bhāsati.*	When the recluse speaks much it is only to speak about the goal. Knowingly he teaches the Dhamma, knowingly he speaks much.
52. *Yo ve na byādhati patvā* *parisaṃ uggahavādinaṃ* *na ca hāpeti vacanaṃ* *na ca chādeti sāsanaṃ.*	If one addresses those who wish to learn, without wavering, imparting understanding, opening up and not obscuring the teaching,
53. *Asandiṭṭhañ-ca bhaṇati* *pucchito na ca kuppati* *sa ve tādisako bhikkhū* *dūteyyaṃ gantuṃ arahati.*	Speaking without hesitation nor getting angry when asked a question, a monk like this is worthy to proclaim the teachings.

54. *Nābhāsamānaṃ jānanti* *missaṃ bālehi paṇḍitaṃ* *bhāsamānañ-ca jānanti* *desentaṃ amataṃ padaṃ* *bhāsaye jotaye dhammaṃ* *paggaṇhe isinaṃ dhajaṃ.*	If he does not speak up, others know him not; he is just a wise man mixed up with fools. But if he speaks about and teaches the Deathless, others will know him. So let him light up the Dhamma, let him lift the sage's banner high.
55. *Yaṃ buddho bhāsatī vācaṃ* *khemaṃ nibbānapattiyā* *dukkhass 'antakiriyāya* *sā ve vācānam-uttamā.*	The Buddha speaks words that lead to the winning of security, the ending of sorrow and the attaining of Nibbāna. Truly, this is the speech supreme.
7. Bhogavagga	**Wealth**
56. *Jīvate vā pi sappañño* *api vittaparikkhayo* *paññāya ca alābhena* *vittavā pi na jīvati.*	The wise man continues to live even if he should lose his wealth. But the rich man without wisdom is not alive even now.
57. *Appakena pi medhāvi* *pābhatena vicakkhaṇo* *samuṭṭhāpeti attānaṃ* *aṇuṃ aggīva sandhamaṃ.*	Starting off with little wealth, the wise man skilfully increases it, just as a sudden draft of wind can make a spark of fire grow.
58. *Susaṃvihitakammantaṃ* *kāluṭṭhāyiṃ atanditaṃ* *sabbe bhogābhivaḍḍhanti* *gāvo sausabhā-m-iva.*	If he plans his project well, rises early and works untiringly, all his wealth will increase like cows penned in with a bull.
59. *Paṇḍito sīlasampanno* *jalaṃ aggīva bhāsati* *bhoge saṃhāramānassa* *bhamarass'eva iriyato.*	One who is virtuous and wise shines forth like a blazing fire; like a bee collecting nectar he acquires wealth by harming none.
60. *Catudhā vibhaje bhoge* *sa ve mittāni ganthati* *ekena bhoge bhuñjeyya* *dvīhi kammaṃ payojaye* *catutthañ-ca nidhāpeyya* *āpadāsu bhavissati.*	He divides his wealth in four and thus he wins friendship. One portion he uses for his needs, two portions for his business, the fourth portion he saves for times of emergency.

61. *Susaṃvihitakammantā saṅgahitaparijjanā bhattu manāpaṃ carati sambhataṃ anurakkhati.*	Deft and capable at her work, in harmony with other people, a wife is pleasing to her husband and carefully looks after his wealth.
62. *Saddhāsilena sampannā vadaññū vītamaccharā niccaṃ maggaṃ visodheti sotthānaṃ samparāyikaṃ.*	Endowed with faith and virtue, speaking gently, free from selfishness: such a woman purifies the pathway leading to future happiness.
63. *Saddhādhanaṃ sīladhanaṃ hiri ottappiyaṃ dhanaṃ sutadhanañ-ca cāgo ca paññā ve sattamaṃ dhanaṃ.*	The wealth of faith and virtue's wealth, the wealth of conscience and fear of blame, the wealth of learning and giving too, and as the seventh, wisdom's wealth:
64. *Yassa ete dhanā atthi itthiyā purisassa vā adaḷiddo 'ti taṃ āhu amoghaṃ tassa jīvitaṃ.*	Those who have these treasures true, be they women or be they men, are not poor or destitute, nor have their lives been lived in vain.
65. *Patirūpakārī dhuravā uṭṭhātā vindate dhanaṃ saccena kittiṃ pappoti dadaṃ mittāni ganthati.*	Whoever acts, strives and toils shall acquire wealth; by truthfulness one gains good repute, and by giving one binds friends.

8. Mittatāvagga — Friendship

66. *Asant'assa piyā honti sante na kurute piyaṃ asantaṃ dhammaṃ roceti taṃ parābhavato mukhaṃ.*	To be in communion with the bad, and choose the ways of the bad, to have no friends among the good, this is a source of suffering.
67. *Sabbhir-eva samāsetha sabbhi kubbetha santhavaṃ sataṃ saddhammaṃ aññāya paññā labbhati nāññato.*	Consort only with the good, come together with the good. To learn the teaching of the good gives wisdom like nothing else can.

68. *Pūtimacchaṃ kusaggena*
yo naro upanayhati
kusā pi pūti vāyanti
evaṃ bālūpasevanā.

If one strings a piece of putrid fish
on a blade of *kusa* grass,
the grass will soon smell putrid too:
the same with one who follows a fool.

69. *Tagarañ-ca palāsena*
yo naro upanayhati
pattā pi surabhi vāyanti
evaṃ dhīrūpasevanā.

If one wraps frankincense,
in any ordinary kind of leaf,
the leaf will soon smell sweet too:
the same with one who follows the wise.

70. *Tasma palāsapuṭass'eva*
natvā sampātaṃ attano
asante nūpaseveyya
sante seveyya paṇḍito.

Remembering the example of the leaf,
and understanding the results,
one should seek companionship
with the wise, never with the bad.

71. *Sattho pavasato mittaṃ*
mātā mittaṃ sake ghare
sahāyo atthajātassa
hoti mittaṃ punappunaṃ
sayaṃ katāni puññāni
taṃ mittaṃ samparāyikaṃ.

A companion is a traveller's friend,
a mother is a friend at home,
one who helps in time of need
is a good and steady friend.
And the good deeds done by oneself
are one's true friends in time to come.

72. *Upakāro ca yo mitto*
yo ca mitto sukhe dukkhe
atth'akkhāyī ca yo mitto
yo ca mittānukampako:

A friend who always lends a hand,
a friend in both sorrow and joy,
a friend who offers good counsel,
a friend who sympathises too:

73. *Ete pi mitte cattāro*
iti viññāya paṇḍito
sakkaccaṃ payirupāseyya
mātā puttaṃ va orasaṃ.

These are the four kinds of true friends:
one who is wise, having understood,
will always cherish and serve such friends
just as a mother tends her only child.

74. *Kalyāṇamitto yo bhikkhū*
sappatisso sagāravo
karaṃ mittānaṃ vācānaṃ
sampajāno patissato
pāpuṇe anupubbena
sabbasaṃyojanakkhayaṃ.

The monk who has a lovely friend,
who pays respect and deference to him,
and acts as his friend advises,
with mindfulness and comprehension clear,
will in time be freed from bonds;
all his fetters will be destroyed.

75. *Abbhatītasahāyassa*
atītagatasatthuno
n'atthi etādisaṃ mittaṃ
yathā kāyagatā sati.

For one whose friend has passed away,
for one whose teacher no more lives,
there is no other friend in this world
like mindfulness of the body.

9. Sutavagga — Learning

76. *Sussūsā sutavaḍḍhānī*
sutaṃ paññāya vaḍḍhanaṃ
paññāya atthaṃ jānāti
ñāto attho sukhāvaho.

Desire to learn increases learning;
learning makes wisdom increase.
By wisdom is the goal known;
knowing the goal brings happiness.

77. *Bahussutaṃ upāseyya*
sutañ-ca na vināsaye
taṃ mūlaṃ brahmacariyassa
tasmā dhammadharo siyā.

One should follow the learned man,
and should not neglect learning;
for that is the foundation of the holy life.
Therefore be well versed in Dhamma.

78. *Bahussutaṃ dhammadharaṃ*
sappaññaṃ buddhasāvakaṃ
nekkhaṃ jambonadass'eva
ko taṃ ninditum arahati
devāpi naṃ pasaṃsanti
brahmuṇā pi pasaṃsito.

Learned, knowing the Dhamma,
truly wise, the Buddha's disciple
is like the finest gold of Jambu.
Who can find any blame in him?
Even the gods sing his praise;
Brahmā himself sings his praise.[5]

79. *Appassuto pi ce hoti*
sīlesu susamāhito
sīlato naṃ pasaṃsanti
nāssa sampajjate sutaṃ.

If one who has little learning
is strong in virtue, others
will praise his virtue only,
because his learning is incomplete.

5. Brahmā: A high divinity in the ancient Indian pantheon.

80. *Bahussuto pi ce hoti* *sīlesu samāhito* *sīlato naṃ garahanti* *tassa sampajjate sutaṃ.*	If one who has much learning is weak in virtue, others will blame him for his conduct though his learning is complete.
81. *Bahussuto pe ce hoti* *sīlesu susamāhito* *ubhayena naṃ pasaṃsanti* *sīlato ca sutena ca.*	But if one has much learning and is also strong in virtue, he will be praised for both his virtue and his learning.
82. *Bahussuto appasutaṃ* *yo sute nātimaññatī* *andho padīpadhāro va* *tath'eva paṭibhāti maṃ.*	A learned man who, because of his learning, despises one with little learning, seems to me like a stone-blind man walking around with a lamp in hand.
83. *Tasmā hi attakāmena* *mahantaṃ abhikaṅkhatā* *saddhammo garukātabbo* *saraṃ buddhāna-sāsanaṃ.*	One who loves his own true welfare, who is concerned with his own good, should pay homage to the Dhamma and always remember the Buddha's words.
84. *Sammā manaṃ panidhāya* *sammā vācaṃ abhāsiya* *sammā kammāni katvāna* *kāyena idha puggalo.*	Having a rightly directed mind, speaking rightly spoken speech, doing here with the body only deeds that are right and good.
85. *Bahussuto puññakaro* *appasmiṃ idha jīvite* *kāyassa bhedā sappañño* *saggaṃ so upapajjati.*	Learned, doing much that is worthy even in a life that is short— a wise person such as this will be reborn in a happy place.

10. Sāvakavagga — **The Disciple**

86. *Mātari pitari cāpi* *yo sammā paṭipajjati* *tathāgate vā sambuddhe* *athavā tassa sāvake* *bahuñ-ca so pasavati* *puññaṃ etādiso naro.*	If one behaves rightly toward his mother and his father, towards the Buddha well-attained, and the disciples of the Buddha, such a person generates an abundant store of good.

87. *Bhikkhū ca sīlasampanno*
bhikkhunī ca bahussutā
upāsako ca yo saddho
yā ca saddhā upāsikā
ete kho saṅghaṃ sobhenti
ete hi saṅghasobhanā.

The monk well-possessed of virtue,
the nun who is widely learned,
male and female lay disciples
who are fully endowed with faith—
it is they who illuminate the Saṅgha,
"lights of the Saṅgha" they are called.

88. *Yassa sabrahmacārīsu*
gāravo nūpalabbhati
ārakā hoti saddhammā
nabhaṃ puthuviyā yathā.

One who has no respect for those
who live the holy life with him,
is as far from this good Dhamma
as the sky is from the earth.

89. *Yassa sabrahmacārīsu*
gāravo upalabbhati
so virūhati saddhamme
khette bījaṃ va bhaddakaṃ.

One who has respect for those
who live the holy life with him,
comes to growth in this good Dhamma
like a healthy seed in the field.

90. *Itthibhāvo kiṃ kayirā*
cittamhi susamāhite
ñāṇamhi vattamānamhi
sammā dhammaṃ vipassato.

A woman's nature is unimportant
when the mind is still and firm,
when knowledge grows day by day,
and she has insight into Dhamma.

91. *Yassa nūna siyā evaṃ*
itthāhaṃ puriso'ti vā
kiñci vā pana asmīti
taṃ māro vattum-arahati.

One who thinks such thoughts
as "I am a woman" or "I am a man"
or any other thought "I am ..."
Māra is able to address that one.

92. *Dummedhehi pasaṃsā ca*
viññūhi garahā ca yā
garahā va seyyo viññūhi
yañ-ce bālappasaṃsanā.

The fools offer praise and the wise
offer blame. Truly the blame
of the wise is much better
than the praise of the fool.

93. *Sāgārā anagārā ca*
ubho aññoññanissitā
ārādhayanti saddhammaṃ
yogakkhemaṃ anuttaraṃ.

Home dwellers and the homeless both,
by depending upon one another
come to realize the good Dhamma,
the utter freedom from bondage.

94. *Anubandho pi ce assa* *mahiccho va vighātavā* *ejānugo anejassa* *nibbutassa anibbuto* *giddho so vītagedhassa* *passa yāvañ-ca ārakā.*	Though physically close behind, if one is acquisitive and restless, how far is that turbulent one from one freed from turbulence, that burning one from one cooled, that hankering one from the greedless!
95. *Sukhā saṅghassa sāmaggī* *samaggānañ-c'anuggaho* *samaggarato dhammaṭṭho* *yogakkhemā na dhaṃsati.*	A happy thing is concord in the Saṅgha! One who assists in making harmony, loving concord and righteousness, does not fall away from freedom.
11. Cittavagga	**Mind**
96. *Cittena nīyati loko* *cittena parikissati* *cittassa ekadhammassa* *sabb'eva vasaṃ anvagū.*	The world is led around by mind, by mind the world is plagued. Mind is itself the single thing, which brings all else beneath its sway.
97. *Mano pubbaṅgamā dhammā* *mano seṭṭhā manomayā* *Manasā ce pasannena* *bhāsati vā karoti vā* *tato naṃ sukhamanveti* *chāyā va anapāyinī.*	Mind precedes all things; mind is their chief, mind is their maker. If one speaks or does a deed with a mind that is pure within, happiness then follows along like a never departing shadow.
98. *Sududdasaṃ sunipuṇaṃ* *yatthakāmanipātinaṃ* *cittaṃ rakkhetha medhāvi* *cittaṃ guttaṃ sukhāvahaṃ.*	Difficult to detect and very subtle, the mind seizes whatever it wants; so let a wise man guard his mind, for, a guarded mind brings happiness.
99. *Dunniggahassa lahuno* *yatthakāmanipātino* *cittassa damatho sādhu* *cittaṃ dantaṃ sukhāvahaṃ.*	Wonderful it is to train the mind so swiftly moving, seizing whatever it wants. Good is it to have a well-trained mind, for a well-trained mind brings happiness.

100. *Phandanaṃ capalaṃ cittaṃ* *durakkhaṃ dunnivārayaṃ* *ujum karoti medhāvī* *usukāro va tejanaṃ.*	As a fletcher straightens an arrow, even so one who is wise will straighten out the fickle mind, so unsteady and hard to control.
101. *Na taṃ mātā pitā kayirā* *aññe vāpi ca ñātakā* *sammāpaṇihitaṃ cittaṃ* *seyyaso naṃ tato kare*	No mother nor father nor any other kin can do greater good for oneself than a mind directed well.
102. *Anabhijjhālu vihareyya* *avyāpannena cetasā* *sato ekaggacittassa* *ajjhattaṃ susamāhito.*	Live without covetous greed, fill your mind with benevolence. Be mindful and one-pointed, inwardly stable and concentrated.
103. *Pañca kāmaguṇā loke* *manochaṭṭhā paveditā* *ettha chandaṃ virājetvā* *evaṃ dukkhā pamuccati.*	There are five strands of sensual pleasure with the mind as the sixth; by overcoming desire for these one will be freed from suffering.
104. *Mama selūpamaṃ cittaṃ* *ṭhitaṃ nānupakampati* *virattaṃ rajanīyesu* *kuppanīye na kuppati* *mam'evaṃ bhāvitaṃ cittaṃ* *kuto maṃ dukkhaṃ essati.*	My mind is firm like a rock, unattached to sensual things, no shaking in the midst of a world where all is shaking. My mind has thus been well-developed. So how can suffering come to me?
105. *Yo caraṃ vā yo titthaṃ vā* *nisinno udavā sayaṃ* *vitakkaṃ samayitvāna* *vitakkopasame rato* *bhabbo so tādiso bhikkhū* *phuṭṭhuṃ sambodhimuttamaṃ.*	Whether he walks or stands or sits or lies, a monk should take delight in controlling all thoughts. Such a monk is qualified to reach supreme enlightenment.

12. Sikkhāvagga — The Training

106. *Atisītaṃ atiuṇhaṃ* *atisāyaṃ idaṃ ahu* *iti vissaṭṭhakammante* *atthā accenti mānave.*	"It's too cold, it's too hot, it's too late." With such excuses one who gives up the practice lets his opportunities slip.

107. *Yo ca sītañ-ca uṇhañ-ca*
tiṇā bhiyyo na maññati
karaṃ purisakiccāni
so sukhā na vihāyati.

But one who looks on cold and heat
as no more obstructive than straw
and continues with the practice
does not fall short of happiness.

108. *Alīnacitto ca siyā*
na cāpi bahu cintaye
nirāmagandho asito
brahmacariyaparāyaṇo.

So rid the mind of sloth and dullness.
Give up thinking of many things.
Be healthy and unattached to pleasure.
Be devoted to the holy life.

109. *Unūdaro mitāhāro*
appich'assa alolupo
sa ve icchāya nicchāto
aniccho hoti nibbuto.

Lean in body, frugal in food,
content with little and undisturbed,
vain wishes gone and craving stilled,
thus the wantless attain Nibbāna.

110. *Sa jhānapasuto dhīro*
vanante ramito siyā
jhāyetha rukkhamūlasmiṃ
attānam-abhitosayaṃ.

One who is stable in meditation
will delight at the woodland's edge,
meditating at the foot of a tree
until joy and contentment are won.

111. *Kāmacchando ca vyāpādo*
thīnamiddhañ-ca bhikkhuno
uddhaccaṃ vicikicchā ca
sabbaso va na vijjati.

Sense desire, ill will,
sloth, laziness, agitation,
and doubt are not found
in a true and worthy monk.

112. *Na sabbato mano nivāraye*
na mano sayatattaṃ āgataṃ
yato yato ca pāpakaṃ
tato tato mano nivāraye.

Do not hold back the mind from all,
for it is not yet put to sleep.
But whenever evil things arise,
then should the mind be held in check.

113. *Viriyasātaccasampanno*
yuttayogo sadā siyā
na ca appatvā dukkhantaṃ
vissāsaṃ eyya paṇḍito.

Possessed of energy and perseverance,
be always earnest in applying yourself.
The wise one should not be confident
until the end of suffering is reached.

114. Samādhiratanamālassa kuvitakkā na jāyare na ca vikkhipate cittaṃ etaṃ tumhe piḷandhathā.	With the jewelled necklace of concentration, wrong thoughts cannot arise nor can the mind be distracted. So let this be your adornment.
115. Ānāpānasati yassa paripuṇṇā subhāvitā anupubbaṃ paricitā yathā buddhena desitā so'maṃ lokaṃ pabhāseti abbhā mutto va candimā.	One who has gradually practised, developed and brought to perfection mindfulness of the in-and-out breath, as taught by the Enlightened One, illuminates the entire world like the moon when freed from clouds.
13. Vāyāmavagga	**Effort**
116. Pamādo rajo pamādā pamādānupatito rajo appamādena vijjāya abbūḷhe sallaṃ attano.	Indolence is dust; dust comes in the wake of indolence. With knowledge and vigilance, draw out the arrow from yourself.
117. Niddāsīlī sabhāsīlī anuṭṭhātā ca yo naro alaso kodhapaññāṇo taṃ parābhavato mukhaṃ.	When one loves company and sleep, when one is lax and slack, when one is often given to anger— this is a source of suffering.
118. Saṃvaro ca pahānañ-ca bhāvanā anurakkhanā ete padhānā cattāro desitādiccabandhuno.	The effort to restrain, to abandon, to develop and to maintain: these are the four exertions taught by the Kinsman of the Sun.
119. Uṭṭhahatha nisīdatha ko attho supitena vo? āturānaṃ hi kā niddā sallaviddhāna-ruppataṃ?	Arise! Sit up! Of what use are your dreams? How can you continue to sleep when you are sick, pierced with the arrow of grief?
120. Amoghaṃ divasaṃ kayirā appena bahukena vā yaṃ yaṃ vijahate rattiṃ tadūnaṃ tassa jīvitaṃ.	Make your day productive whether by little or by much. Every day and night that passes, your life is that much less.

121. *Yo dandhakāle dandheti*
taranīye ca tāraye
yoniso saṃvidhānena
sukhaṃ pappoti paṇḍito.

The wise one who hurries when
hurrying is needed and who slows down
when slowness is needed, is happy
because his priorities are right.

122. *Āraddhaviriye pahitatte*
niccaṃ daḷhaparakkame
samagge sāvake passa
esā buddhāna-vandanā.

See the disciples in perfect harmony,
resolute and making effort,
always firm in their progress—
this is the best worship of the Buddha.

123. *Niddaṃ tandiṃ*
vijambhikaṃ
aratiṃ bhattasammadaṃ
viriyena naṃ panāmetvā
ariyamaggo visujjhati.

Sloth, torpor and drowsiness,
boredom and heaviness after meals—
by expelling these with energy
the noble path is purified.

124. *Saddhāya tarati oghaṃ*
appamādena aṇṇavaṃ
viriyena dukkhaṃ acceti
paññāya parisujjhati.

The flood is crossed by faith,
by vigilance the sea is crossed,
pain is overcome with vigour
by wisdom one is purified.

125. *Ujumaggamhi akkhāte*
gacchatha mā nivattatha
attanā coday'attānaṃ
nibbānaṃ abhihāraye.

The straight path has been clearly shown:
walk forward and don't turn back.
Urge yourself onwards by yourself;
in that way attain Nibbāna.

14. Sativagga — Mindfulness

126. *Sambādhe vāpi vindanti*
dhammaṃ nibbānāpattiyā
ye satiṃ paccalatthaṃsu
sammā te susamāhitā.

Even when obstacles crowd in,
the path to Nibbāna can be won
by those who establish mindfulness
and bring to perfection equipoise.

127. *Sace dhāvati te cittaṃ*
kāmesu ca bhavesu ca
khippaṃ niggaṇha satiyā
kiṭṭhādaṃ viya duppasuṃ.

If your mind runs wild among
sensual pleasures and things that arise,
quickly restrain it with mindfulness
as one pulls the cow from the corn.

128. *Ubhinnaṃ atthaṃ carati attano ca parassa ca paraṃ saṅkupitaṃ ñatvā yo sato upasammati.*	Knowing that the other person is angry, one who remains mindful and calm acts for his own best interest and for the other's interest, too.
129. *Ubhinnaṃ tikicchantānaṃ attano ca parassa ca janā maññanti bālo'ti ye dhammassa akovidā.*	He is a healer of both himself and the other person; only those think him a fool who do not understand the Dhamma.
130. *Yataṃ care yataṃ tiṭṭhe yataṃ acche yataṃ saye yataṃ sammiñjaye bhikkhu yatamenaṃ pasāraye.*	Whether he walks, stands, sits or lies, stretches out his limbs or draws them in again, let a monk do so with composure.
131. *Uddhaṃ tiriyaṃ apācinaṃ yāvatā jagato gatī samavekkhitā va dhammānaṃ khandhānaṃ udayabbayam.*	Above, across or back again, wherever he goes in the world let him carefully scrutinise the rise and fall of compounded things.
132. *Evaṃ vihāriṃ ātāpiṃ santavuttiṃ anuddhataṃ cetosamathasāmīciṃ sikkhamānaṃ sadā sataṃ satataṃ pahitatto'ti āhu bhikkhuṃ tathāvidham.*	Living thus ardently, at peace within, not restless or mentally agitated, training himself, always mindful: people call such a monk "one constantly resolute."
133. *Na so rajjati dhammesu dhammaṃ ñatvā patissato virattacitto vedeti tañ-ca n'ajjhosāya tiṭṭhati.*	Not excited by mental phenomena, one knows them through mindfulness; thus with a mind well detached one understands and does not cling.

134. *Satipaṭṭhānakusalā* *bojjhaṅga bhāvanā ratā* *vipassakā dhammadharā* *dhamma nagare vasantite.*	Those skilled in the foundations of mindfulness, delighting in the enlightenment factors, with knowledge of Dhamma and keen insight, live in the city of Dhamma.
135. *Sammappadhāna* *sampanno* *satipaṭṭhāna gocaro* *vimuttikusumasañchanno* *parinibbissaty-anāsavo ti.*	Possessed of persevering energy, practicing the foundations of mindfulness, bedecked with the blossoms of freedom, you will be cooled and undefiled.
15. Attaparavagga	**Oneself and Others**
136. *Sabbe tasanti daṇḍassa* *sabbesaṃ jīvitaṃ piyaṃ* *attānaṃ upamaṃ katvā* *na haneyya na ghātaye.*	All tremble at punishment. Life is dear to all. Put yourself in the place of others; kill none nor have another killed.
137. *Attanā va kataṃ pāpaṃ* *attanā saṅkilissati* *attanā akataṃ pāpaṃ* *attanā va visujjhati* *suddhi asuddhi paccattaṃ* *nañño aññaṃ visodhaye.*	By doing evil, one defiles oneself; by avoiding evil, one purifies oneself. Purity and impurity depend on oneself: no one can purify another.
138. *Attadatthaṃ paratthena* *bahunā 'pi na hāpaye* *attadatthaṃ abhiññāya* *sadattha pasuto siyā.*	Let no one neglect one's own welfare for the welfare of others however much. Clearly understanding one's own welfare strive always for one's own true good.
139. *Attānameva paṭhamaṃ* *patirūpe nivesaye* *ath'aññaṃ anusāseyya* *na kilisseyya paṇḍito.*	One should first establish oneself in what is proper and only then try to instruct others. Doing this, the wise one will not be criticized.

140. Attānaṃ ce tathā kayirā *yath'aññaṃ anusāsati* *sudanto vata dametha* *attā hi kira duddamo.*	If only you would do what you teach others then being yourself controlled you could control others well. Truly self-control is difficult.
141. Yo c'attānaṃ samukkaṃse *parañ-ca-m-avajānāti* *nihīno senamānena* *taṃ jaññā vasalo iti.*	One who exalts himself and disparages others because of smugness and conceit; know him as an outcaste man.
142. Na paresaṃ vilomāni *na paresaṃ katākataṃ* *attano va avekkheyya* *katāni akatāni ca.*	Look not to the faults of others, nor to their omissions and commissions. But rather look to your own acts, to what you have done and left undone.
143. Paravajjānupassissa *niccaṃ ujjhānasaññino* *āsavā tassa vaḍḍhanti* *ārā so āsavakkhayā.*	When one looks down at others' faults and is always full of envy, one's defilements continually grow; far is one from their destruction.
144. Sudassaṃ vajjaṃ aññesaṃ *attano pana duddasaṃ* *paresaṃ hi so vajjāni* *opunāti yathābhūsaṃ* *attano pana chādeti* *kaliṃ va kitavā saṭho.*	Easily seen are the faults of others, one's own are difficult to see. By winnowing the chaff of others' faults, one's own are obscured, like a crafty fowler hidden behind the branches.
145. Attanā coday' attānaṃ *paṭimāse attaṃ attanā* *so attagutto satimā* *sukhaṃ bhikkhu vihāhisi.*	You yourself must watch yourself, you yourself must examine yourself, and so self-guarded and mindful, O monk, you will live in happiness.
16. (I) Mettāvagga	**Love (I)**
146. Anatthajanano doso *doso cittappakopano* *bhayaṃ antarato jātaṃ* *taṃ jano nāvabujjhati.*	Hate brings great misfortune, hate churns up and harms the mind; this fearful danger deep within most people do not understand.

147. *Duṭṭho atthaṃ na jānāti. duṭṭho dhammaṃ na passati andhaṃ tamaṃ tadā hoti yaṃ doso sahate naraṃ.*	Thus spoilt one cannot know the good, cannot see things as they are. Only blindness and gloom prevail when one is overwhelmed by hate.
148. *Yo na hanti na ghāteti na jināti na jāpaye mettaṃ so sabbabhūtesu veraṃ tassa na kenaci.*	He who does not strike nor makes others strike, who robs not nor makes others rob, sharing love with all that live, finds enmity with none.
149. *Satimato sadā bhaddaṃ satimā sukhaṃ edhati satimato su ve seyyo verā na parimuccati.*	For the mindful one there is always good; for the mindful one happiness increases; for the mindful one things go better yet he is not freed from enemies.
150. *Yassa sabbaṃ ahorattaṃ ahiṃsāya rato mano mettaṃ so sabbabhūtesu veraṃ tassa na kenaci.*	But he who both day and night takes delight in harmlessness sharing love with all that live, finds enmity with none.
151. *Yo ve mettena cittena sabbalok'ānukampati uddhaṃ adho ca tiriyañ-ca appamāṇena sabbaso.*	When one with a mind of love feels compassion for all the world— above, below and across, unlimited everywhere.
152. *Appamāṇaṃ hitaṃ cittaṃ paripuṇṇaṃ subhāvitaṃ yaṃ pamāṇakataṃ kammaṃ na taṃ tatrāvasissati.*	Filled with infinite kindness, complete and well-developed— any limited actions one may have done do not remain lingering in one's mind.
153. *Mettacittā kāruṇikā hotha sīlesu saṃvutā āraddhaviriyā pahitattā niccaṃ daḷhaparakkamā.*	Develop a mind full of love; be compassionate and restrained in virtue; arouse your energy, be resolute, always firm in making progress.

154. *Yathāpi ekaputtasmiṃ*
piyasmiṃ kusalī siyā
evaṃ sabbesu pāṇesu
sabbattha kusalo siyā.

Just as a loving mother would guard
her only dearly beloved child,
so towards creatures everywhere
one should always wish for their good.

155. *Cittaṃ ca susamāhitaṃ*
vippasannaṃ anāvilaṃ
akhilaṃ sabbabhūtesu
so maggo brahmapattiyā.

A mind composed, well-concentrated,
purified and undefiled,
full of kindness towards all beings—
this is the way that leads to Brahmā.

17. (II) Mettāvagga — **Love (II)**

156. *Yathāpi udakaṃ nāma*
kalyāṇe pāpake jane
samaṃ pharati sītena
pavāheti rajomalaṃ.

Just as water cools
both good and bad
and washes away all
impurity and dust,

157. *Tath'eva tvaṃ pi hitāhite*
samaṃ mettāya bhāvaya
mettāpāramitaṃ gantvā
sambodhiṃ pāpuṇissasi.

In the same way you should
develop thoughts
of love to friend and foe alike,
and having reached perfection in love,
you will attain enlightenment.

158. *"Yathā ahaṃ tathā ete*
yathā ete tathā ahaṃ."
attānaṃ upamaṃ katvā
na haneyya na ghātaye.

"As I am, so are others;
as others are, so am I."
Having thus identified self and others,
harm no one nor have them harmed.

159. *Apādakehi me mettaṃ*
mettaṃ dīpādakehi me,
catuppādehi me mettāṃ
mettaṃ bahuppādehi me.

I have love for the footless,
for the bipeds too I have love;
I have love for those with four feet,
for the many-footed I have love.

160. *Mā maṃ apādako hiṃsi*
mā maṃ hiṃsi dīpādako
mā maṃ catuppādo hiṃsi
mā maṃ hiṃsi bahuppādo.

May the footless harm me not,
may the bipeds harm me not,
may those with four feet harm me not,
may those with many feet harm me not.

161. *Sabbe sattā sabbe pāṇā*
sabbe bhūtā ca kevalā
sabbe bhadrāni passantu
mā kañci pāpamāgamā.

May all creatures, all living things,
all beings one and all,
experience good fortune only.
May they not fall into harm.

162. *Sabbamitto sabbasakho*
sabbabhūtānukampako
mettaṃ cittañ-ca bhāvemi
abyāpajjharato sadā.

I am a friend and helper to all,
I am sympathetic to all living
beings.
I develop a mind full of love
and always delight in harmlessness.

163. *Asaṃhīraṃ asaṅkuppaṃ*
cittaṃ āmodayām'ahaṃ
brahmavihāraṃ bhāvemi
akāpurisasevitaṃ.

I gladden my mind, fill it with joy,
make it immovable and unshakable.
I develop the divine states of mind
not cultivated by evil men.

164. *Tasmā sakaṃ paresaṃ pi*
kātabbā mettābhāvanā
mettacittena pharitabbaṃ
etaṃ buddhāna sāsanaṃ.

Therefore the meditation on love
should be done for oneself and
others.
All should be suffused with love:
this is the teaching of the Buddha.

165. *Yo ca mettaṃ bhāvayati*
appamāṇaṃ patissato
tanū saṃyojanā honti
passato upadhikkhayaṃ.

Whoever makes love grow
boundless, and sets his mind
for seeing the end of birth:
his fetters are worn thin.

18. Sukhavagga

Happiness

166. *Yo pubbe karaṇīyāni*
pacchā so kātuṃ icchati
sukhā so dhaṃsate ṭhānā
pacchā ca m-anutappati.

One who later wishes to do
the things he should have done
before
falls away from happiness
and long afterwards repents.

167. *Kodhaṃ chetvā sukhaṃ seti*
kodhaṃ chetvā na socati
kodhassa visamūlassa
madhuraggassa brāhmaṇa
vadhaṃ ariyā pasaṃsanti
taṃ hi chetvā na socati.

Slay anger and you will be happy,
slay anger and you will not sorrow.
For the slaying of anger in all its
forms
with its poisoned root and sweet
sting—
that is the slaying the nobles praise;
with anger slain one weeps no more.

168. *Yaṃ pare sukhato āhu*
tad ariyā āhu dukkhato
yaṃ pare dukkhato āhu
tad ariyā sukhato vidū
passa dhammaṃ durājānaṃ
sammuḷh'ettha aviddasu.

What others call happiness,
the noble call pain;
what others call pain,
the noble call happiness.
Behold this Dhamma hard to comprehend
by which the dull are utterly baffled.

169. *Sabbadā va sukhaṃ seti*
brāhmaṇo parinibbuto
yo na limpati kāmesu
sītibhūto nirūpadhi.

Always happy is the holy man
who is wholly free within,
who is not stained by sense desires—
cooled is he and free from clinging.

170. *Yaṃ ca kāmasukhaṃ loke*
yaṃ c'idaṃ diviyaṃ sukhaṃ
taṇhakkhayasukhassa te
kalaṃ n'āgghanti soḷasiṃ.

The happiness of sensual lust
and the happiness of heavenly bliss
are not equal to a sixteenth part
of the happiness of craving's end.

171. *Sabbā āsattiyo chetvā*
vineyya hadaye daraṃ
upasanto sukhaṃ seti
santiṃ pappuyya cetasā.

With all his attachments cut,
with the heart's pinings subdued,
calm and serene and happy is he,
for he has attained peace of mind.

172. *Pāmujjabahulo bhikkhu*
dhamme buddhappavedite
adhigacche padaṃ santaṃ
saṅkhārūpasamaṃ sukhaṃ.

A monk who has abundant joy
in the Dhamma taught by the Buddha,
will attain peace and happiness,
with the calming of the constructs.

173. *Sukho viveko tuṭṭhassa*
sutadhammassa passato
avyāpajjhaṃ sukhaṃ loke
pāṇabhūtesu saṃyamo.

Solitude is happiness for one who is content,
who has heard the Dhamma and clearly sees.
Non-affliction is happiness in the world—
harmlessness towards all living beings.

174. *Sukhā virāgatā loke*
kāmānaṃ samatikkamo
asmimānassa yo vinayo
etaṃ ve paramaṃ sukhaṃ.

Freedom from lust is happiness in the world,
the going beyond all sensual desires.
But the crushing out of the conceit "I am"—
this is the highest happiness.

175. *Susukhaṃ vata nibbānaṃ* *sammāsambuddhadesitaṃ* *asokaṃ virajaṃ khemaṃ* *yattha dukkhaṃ* *nirujjhatī.*	The fully perfected Buddha has taught Nibbāna as the highest happiness— without grief, immaculate, secure, the state where all suffering ceases.
19. Tuṇhīvagga	**Silence**
176. *Samānabhāvaṃ kubbetha* *gāme akuṭṭhavanditaṃ* *manopadosaṃ rakkheyya* *santo anuṇṇato care.*	Develop the quiet even state of mind, when praised by some, condemned by others, free the mind from hate and pride and gently go your way in peace.
177. *Tan nadīhi vijānātha* *sobbhesu padaresu ca* *saṇantā yanti kussubbhā* *tuṇhīyanti mahodadhī.*	Learn this from the waters: in mountain clefts and chasms, loud gush the streamlets, but great rivers flow silently.
178. *Yad-ūnakaṃ taṃ saṇati* *yaṃ pūraṃ santaṃ eva taṃ* *aḍḍhakumbhūpamo bālo* *rahado pūro va paṇḍito*	Things that are empty make a noise, the full is always quiet. The fool is like a half-filled pot, the wise man like a deep still pool.
179. *Kāyamuniṃ vācāmuniṃ* *manomunim-anāsavaṃ* *muni moneyyasampannaṃ* *āhu nihātapāpakaṃ.*	Silent in body, silent in speech, silent in mind, without defilement, blessed with silence is the sage. He is truly washed of evil.
180. *Upasanto uparato* *mantabhāṇī anuddhato* *dhunāti pāpake dhamme* *dumapattaṃ va māluto.*	Peaceful, quiet and restrained, speaking little, without conceit— such a one shakes off all evil as wind shakes leaves off a tree.
181. *Cakkhumāssa yathā andho,* *sotavā badhiro yathā* *paññāv'assa yathā mūgo* *balavā dubbaloriva.*	Let one with sight be as though blind, and one who hears be as though deaf, let one with tongue be as though dumb, let one who is strong be as though weak.

182. *Avitakkaṃ samāpanno* *sammāsambuddhasāvako* *ariyena tuṇhībhāvena* *upeto hoti tāvade.*	Having attained the meditative state where all thoughts come to a stop, the disciple of the perfected Buddha thereby possesses the noble silence.
183. *Yathā jaḷo ca mūgo ca* *attānaṃ dassaye tathā* *nātivelaṃ pabhāseyya* *saṅghamajjhamhi paṇḍito.*	The wise one in the midst of an assembly should not speak excessively long. He should let himself appear like a simpleton or a dullard.
184. *Etaṃ nāgassa nāgena* *īsādantassa hatthino* *sameti cittaṃ cittena* *yaṃ eko ramatī vane.*	In this both mighty beings agree, the enlightened sage and the elephant with tusks resembling the poles of ploughs: both love the solitude of the forest.
185. *Vihavihābhinadite* *sippikābhirutehi ca* *na me taṃ phandati cittaṃ* *ekattanirataṃ hi me*	Amidst the chirping and twittering of the birds in the woods this mind of mine does not waver for I am devoted to solitude.

20. Vipassanāvagga — Insight

186. *Pañcaṅgikena turiyena* *na rati hoti tādisī* *yathā ekaggacittassa* *sammā dhammaṃ vipassato.*	Music from a five-piece ensemble cannot produce as much delight as that of a one-pointed mind with perfect insight into things.
187. *Ye ca santacittā nipakā* *satimanto ca jhāyino* *sammā dhammaṃ vipassanti* *kāmesu anapekkhino.*	Those peaceful in mind, discerning, mindful and meditative, having perfect insight into things, unconcerned with sense desires,
188. *Appamādaratā santā* *pamāde bhayadassino* *abhabbā parihānāya* *nibbānass'eva santike.*	calm, delighting in diligence, seeing fear in negligence, can never fall away or fail, for they are close to Nibbāna.
189. *Atītaṃ nānusocanti* *nappajappanti nāgataṃ* *paccuppannena yāpenti* *tena vaṇṇo pasīdati.*	They do not lament over the past, they yearn not for what is to come, they maintain themselves in the present, thus their complexion is serene.

190. *Atītaṃ nānvāgameyya*
nappaṭikaṅkhe anāgataṃ
yad-atītaṃ pahīnaṃ taṃ
appattañ-ca anāgataṃ.

The past should not be followed after
and the future not desired;
what is past is dead and gone
and the future is yet to come.

191. *Paccuppannañ-ca yo dhammaṃ*
tattha tattha vipassati
asaṃhīraṃ asaṅkuppaṃ
taṃ vidvā m-anubrūhaye.

But whoever gains insight into things
presently arisen in the here and now,
knowing them, unmoved, unshaken,
let him cultivate that insight.

192. *Cittaṃ upaṭṭhapetvāna*
ekaggaṃ susamāhitaṃ
paccavekkhatha saṅkhāre
parato no ca attato.

Establish the mind, set it up
in one-pointed stability;
look upon all formations
as alien and as not self.

193. *Pheṇapiṇḍūpamaṃ rūpaṃ*
vedanā bubbulūpamā
marīcikūpamā saññā
saṅkhārā kadalūpamā
māyupamañca viññānaṃ.

The body is like a ball of foam,
feelings are like bubbles,
perception is like a mirage,
mental constituents like a pithy tree,
and consciousness like a magic trick.

194. *Sabbalokaṃ abhiññāya*
sabbaloke yathātathaṃ
sabbalokavisaṃyutto
sabbaloke anūpayo.

Knowing the world in full directly,
the whole world just as it is,
from the whole world he is freed;
he clings to naught in all the world.

195. *Sabbe sabbābhibhū dhīro*
sabbaganthappamocano
phuṭṭhassa paramā santi
nibbānaṃ akutobhayaṃ.

This sage all-victorious
with all bonds loosened,
has reached perfect peace:
Nibbāna that is void of fear.

21. Buddhavagga — The Buddha

196. *Yathāpi udake jātaṃ*
puṇḍarīkaṃ pavaḍḍhati
nopalippati toyena
sucigandhaṃ manoramaṃ,

As the lotus is born in the water
and grows up beneath the water,
yet remains undefiled by the water,
fragrant and beautiful,

197. *Tath'eva ca loke jāto* *buddho loke viharati* *nopalippati lokena* *toyena padumaṃ yathā.*	Just so the Buddha is born in the world, grows up and dwells in the world, but like the lotus unstained by water he is not defiled by the world.
198. *Mahāsamuddo paṭhavī* *pabbato anilo pi ca* *upamāya na yujjanti* *satthu varavimuttiyā.*	The mighty ocean, the earth so broad, the mountain peak or the wind are not adequate similes to describe the awesome freedom of the Teacher.
199. *Appameyyaṃ paminanto* *ko'dha vidvā vikappaye* *appameyyaṃ pamāyinaṃ* *nivutaṃ maññe akissavaṃ.*	Who can measure the immeasurable one? Who can fathom and determine him? To try to measure the immeasurable one betrays a mind devoid of wisdom.
200. *Arañño rukkhamūle vā* *suññāgāre va bhikkhavo* *anussaretha sambuddhaṃ* *bhayaṃ tumhākaṃ no siyā.*	When in the forest, amongst the roots of trees, or when retired to an empty place, just call to mind the Buddha and no fear or trembling will arise.
201. *Hitānukampī sambuddho* *yad-aññaṃ anusāsati* *anurodhavirodhehi* *vippamutto tathāgato.*	When the Buddha teaches others he does so out of compassion, because the Tathāgata is wholly freed from both favour and aversion.
202. *Yathā rattikkhaye patte* *suriyass'uggamanaṃ dhuvaṃ* *tath'eva buddhaseṭṭhānaṃ* *vacanaṃ dhuvasassataṃ.*	It is certain that the sun will rise when the darkness of night fades away; so too the words of the supreme Buddha are always certain and reliable.

203. *Satthugaru dhammagaru saṅghe ca tibbagāravo appamādagaru bhikkhu paṭisanthāragāravo abhabbo parihānāya nibbānass'eva santike.*	Deeply reverent towards the Teacher, reverent towards the Dhamma and Saṅgha, reverent towards vigilance, having kindness and good will: a monk like this cannot fail, for he is close to Nibbāna.
204. *Tena h'ātappaṃ karohi idh'eva nipako sato ito sutvāna nigghosaṃ sikkhe nibbānaṃ attano.*	So stir up your energy now, be skilful and be ever mindful. When you have heard my voice train yourself to attain Nibbāna.
205. *Ye pavutte satthipade anusikkhanti jhāyino kāle te appamajjantā na maccuvasagā siyuṃ.*	Those who do their best and train in all the teachings that I have taught, alert and meditative, shall in time go beyond the power of death.
22. Kittisadda	**Praise**
206. *Esa sutvā pasīdāmi vaco te isisattama amoghaṃ kira me puṭṭhaṃ na maṃ vañcesi brāhmaṇo.*	Hearing your voice, O sage supreme, my heart is filled with joy. My questions truly were not in vain, the brahmin did not deceive me.
207. *Anusāsi maṃ ariyavatā anukampī anuggahi amogho tuyhaṃ ovādo antevāsī'hi sikkhito.*	You have taught me the noble practice, you were compassionate and helpful to me. Your exhortation was not in vain for I am now your trained disciple.
208. *Upemi buddhaṃ saraṇaṃ dhammaṃ saṅghañ-ca tādinaṃ samādiyāmi sīlāni taṃ me atthāya hehiti.*	I go for refuge to the Buddha, to the Dhamma and to the Saṅgha. I undertake the rules of conduct which will be for my true welfare.

209. *Asokaṃ virajaṃ khemaṃ* *ariyaṭṭhaṅgikaṃ ujuṃ* *taṃ maggaṃ anugacchāmi* *yena tiṇṇā mahesino.*	I shall follow that eightfold path, griefless, immaculate, secure, the straight way by following which the great sages have crossed the flood.
210. *So ahaṃ vicarissāmi* *gāmā gāmaṃ purā puraṃ* *namassamāno* *sambuddhaṃ* *dhammassa ca* *sudhammataṃ.*	I will now go from town to town, I will go from city to city, praising the Buddha and the Dhamma so excellently taught by him.

References

References to Dhammapada, Jātaka, Suttanipāta, Theragāthā and Therīgāthā are to verse number; references to other works are to the volume and page number of the Pāli Text Society editions. An asterisk indicates the Buddha's own words

1. Sn 544
2. S I 50
3. Sn 1063
4. Sn 1065
5. Sn 1038
6. Sn 1053*
7. Sn 92*
8. It 91*
9. S I 4*
10. Ud 6*
11. S I 33*
12. S I 33*
13. S I 33*
14. Mil 335
15. Mil 335
16. A II 10*
17. Thī 347
18. Thī 357
19. S I 117*
20. A IV 96*
21. S I 85*
22. It 8*
23. Ud 69*
24. It 93*
25. It 93*
26. It 66*
27. It 66*
28. It 66*
29. It 66*
30. It 66*
31. J 128
32. J 129
33. A II 32*
34. S I 32*
35. S I 32*
36. Th 608
37. A III 205*
38. A III 206*
39. Th 612
40. Th 614
41. Sn 1 36*
42. Th 1001
43. It 16*
44. S I 37*
45. Sn 174*
46. Sn 657*
47. Sn 451
48. Sn 452
49. S I 162*
50. S I 163*
51. Sn 722*
52. A IV 196*
53. A IV 196*
54. A II 51*
55. Sn 454
56. Th 499
57. J 4*
58. J 341*
59. D III 188*
60. D. III 188*
61. A IV 271*
62. A IV 271*
63. A IV 6*
64. A IV 6*
65. Sn 187*
66. Sn 94*
67. S I 17*
68. It 68*
69. It 68*
70. It 68*
71. S I 37*
72. D III 188*
73. D III 188*
74. It 10*
75. Th 1035
76. Th 141
77. Th 1027
78. A II 8*
79. A II 8*
80. A II 8*
81. A II 8*
82. Th 1026
83. A II 21
84. It 60*
85. It 60*
86. A II 4*
87. A II 8*
88. Th 278
89. Th 391
90. S I 129
91. S I 129
92. Th 668
93. It 111*
94. It 91*
95. It 12*
96. S I 39*
97. Dhp 1*
98. Dhp 36*
99. Dhp 35*
100. Dhp 33*
101. Dhp 43*
102. A II 29*
103. Sn 171*
104. Th 194
105. It 117*
106. D III 185*
107. D III 185*
108. Sn 717*
109. Sn 707*
110. Sn 709*
111. A V 16*
112. S I 14*
113. Th 585
114. Mil 337
115. Th 548
116. Sn 334*
117. Sn 96*
118. A II 17*
119. Sn 331*
120. Th 451
121. Th 293
122. Thī 161
123. S I 7*
124. Sn 184*
125. Th 637
126. S I 48*
127. Th 446
128. S I 162*

129. S I 162*
130. It 120*
131. It 120*
132. It 121*
133. Th 816
134. Mil 342
135. Th 100
136. Dhp 130*
137. Dhp 165*
138. Dhp 166*
139. Dhp 158*
140. Dhp 159*
141. Sn 132*
142. Dhp 50*
143. Dhp 253*
144. Dhp 252*
145. Dhp 379*
146. It 84*
147. It 84*
148. It 22*
149. S I 208*
150. S I 208*
151. J 37
152. J 38
153. Th 979
154. Th 33
155. S IV 118
156. J 168
157. J. 169
158. Sn 705*
159. A II 72*
160. A II 72*
161. A II 72*
162. Th 648
163. Th 649
164. Mil 394
165. It 21*
166. Th 225
167. S I 161*
168. S IV 127*
169. S I 212*
170. Ud 11*
171. S I 212*
172. Th 11
173. Ud 10*
174. Ud 10*
175. Th 227
176. Sn 702*
177. Sn 720*
178. Sn 721*
179. It 56*
180. Th 2
181. Th 501
182. Th 650
183. Th 582
184. Ud 42*
185. Th 49
186. Th 398
187. It 40*
188. It 40*
189. S I 5*
190. M III 131*
191. M III 131*
192. Thī 177
193. S III 142*
194. It 122*
195. It 122*
196. Th 700
197. Th 701
198. Th 1013
199. S I 149
200. S I 220*
201. S I 111*
202. J 122
203. A III 331*
204. Sn 1062*
205. S I 52*
206. Th 1276
207. Th 334
208. Thī 250
209. Thī 361
210. Sn 192

ABOUT PARIYATTI

Pariyatti is dedicated to providing affordable access to authentic teachings of the Buddha about the Dhamma theory (*pariyatti*) and practice (*paṭipatti*) of Vipassana meditation. A 501(c)(3) nonprofit charitable organization since 2002, Pariyatti is sustained by contributions from individuals who appreciate and want to share the incalculable value of the Dhamma teachings. We invite you to visit www.pariyatti.org to learn about our programs, services, and ways to support publishing and other undertakings.

Pariyatti Publishing Imprints

Vipassana Research Publications (focus on Vipassana as taught by S.N. Goenka in the tradition of Sayagyi U Ba Khin)

BPS Pariyatti Editions (selected titles from the Buddhist Publication Society, copublished by Pariyatti)

MPA Pariyatti Editions (selected titles from the Myanmar Pitaka Association, copublished by Pariyatti)

Pariyatti Digital Editions (audio and video titles, including discourses)

Pariyatti Press (classic titles returned to print and inspirational writing by contemporary authors)

Pariyatti enriches the world by

- disseminating the words of the Buddha,
- providing sustenance for the seeker's journey,
- illuminating the meditator's path.

www.ingramcontent.com/pod-product-compliance
Lightning Source LLC
Chambersburg PA
CBHW020349170426
43200CB00005B/105
9781681722085